MW00528797

THE
Healthy
Marriage

DEVOTIONAL

365 Daily Inspirations
to Bring You Closer Together

JIM DALY

PRESIDENT OF FOCUS ON THE FAMILY
with Kenny Chapman

FOCUS
ON THE FAMILY.

A Focus on the Family resource
published by Tyndale House Publishers

The Healthy Marriage Devotional: 365 Daily Inspirations to Bring You Closer Together
Copyright © 2022, 2024 by Focus on the Family. All rights reserved.

A Focus on the Family book published by Tyndale House Publishers, Carol Stream, Illinois 60188

Previously published as *Thriving Together: Perspective to Help Strengthen Your Marriage* under
ISBN 978-1-64607-100-5

Focus on the Family and the accompanying logo and design are federally registered trademarks of Focus on the Family, 8605 Explorer Drive, Colorado Springs, CO 80920.

Tyndale and Tyndale's quill logo are registered trademarks of Tyndale House Ministries.

Cover design by Ron C. Kaufmann

Cover and interior illustrations of striped leaves pattern copyright © Oleksandra Martiukova/Depositphotos. All rights reserved.

Cover photograph of couple on swing copyright © Ajda Gorjanc/Depositphotos. All rights reserved.

Author photo copyright © 2022 by Sally Dunn. All rights reserved.

Scripture quotations are from The ESV® Bible (The Holy Bible, English Standard Version®), copyright © 2001 by Crossway, a publishing ministry of Good News Publishers. Used by permission. All rights reserved.

All stories in this book are true. Some people's names and certain details of their stories have been changed to protect the privacy of the individuals involved. However, the facts of what happened and the underlying principles have been conveyed as accurately as possible.

For information about special discounts for bulk purchases, please contact Tyndale House Publishers at csresponse@tyndale.com, or call 1-855-277-9400.

ISBN 978-1-64607-158-6

Printed in China

30 29 28 27 26 25 24
7   6   5   4   3   2   1

Contents

Foreword

My wife may be one of the world's healthiest eaters, so when I was invited to participate in an Alaskan fishing trip for halibut and salmon, she practically pushed me out the door. Fresh, wild-caught salmon that's flash frozen as soon as your boat returns to shore? She couldn't wait.

I'm not a big fisherman myself (though I was looking forward to the fellowship), so I honestly think Lisa was more excited about the trip than I was.

If you were to look in our freezer today, you'd see the Alaskan fish labeled with *H* for halibut, *S* for salmon, and *R* for some rockfish. Lisa is spacing out the fillets, hoping she can make them last until next summer.

In the book you're holding, Jim Daly has fished the pure, healthy Alaskan waters to bring us nourishing spiritual meals for our marriages. He's dipped his line deep into Scripture and pulled up life-changing truths for us to apply. Even better than fish that are flash frozen, these meals come fully prepared: They are seasoned with life experience, the insightful words of so many Focus on the Family guests, and Jim's own wisdom. It's as delicious and delightful a meal as it is nourishing.

I marvel at the quality of these devotions. Day by day, Jim offers up another tasty morsel, giving you plenty to talk about, pray about, and think about. Prepare yourself for a feast-filled year of marital nourishment.

Gary Thomas
Pastor, international speaker, and author of Sacred Marriage,
Cherish, *and* A Lifelong Love

Introduction

Something powerful happens when a couple sits together sharing their hearts with each other and seeking the Lord together as husband and wife: God creates a masterpiece.

Consider a work of art like Rembrandt's *The Return of the Prodigal Son*. Is it merely splotches of color and well-placed brushstrokes? Or a classic novel like Charles Dickens's *A Tale of Two Cities*. Can his eloquence be reduced to letters on a page? A masterpiece isn't something we look *at*, but something we look *through*. It's a window to something richer and more meaningful than the mechanics of the work itself.

It's the same with your marriage.

The picture of marriage in Scripture is of a man and a woman "becoming one flesh" (see Genesis 2:24; Matthew 19:5; Mark 10:8; Ephesians 5:31). *Becoming* requires a willingness to rediscover each other every day. The intimacy you desire might be hidden beneath past wounds, fears, or disappointments. To uncover it, you need to become an engaged spouse who digs beneath the surface of your relationship to find something deeper and life-giving.

The Healthy Marriage Devotional comprises 365 daily thoughts, all designed to help you along the journey of *becoming*. These devotions originated as radio commentary segments and have been enhanced with additional Scripture references and other insights. We've focused on helping you and your spouse get beneath the surface of your relationship and spark meaningful conversation.

Great marriages aren't *found*; they're *formed*. As you and your spouse journey across the years together, I pray you will discover one another anew, deepen your intimacy and commitment, and create a marriage masterpiece.

Let's begin.

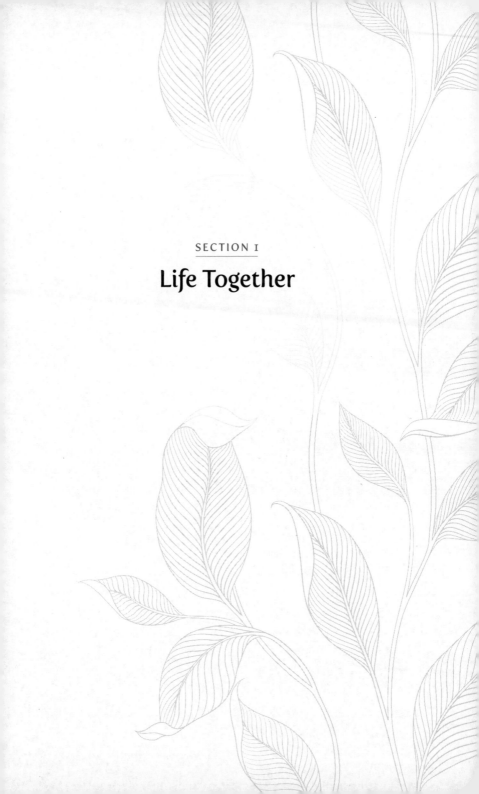

SECTION I

Life Together

Seeds into Flowers

Well-known author Dr. Gary Smalley officiated a lot of weddings. He used an effective illustration to help couples understand the nature of their relationship.

Midway through the ceremony, he'd gesture to the beautiful flowers adorning the venue and say to the couple, "You probably believe the garland, the boutonnieres, and the bridal bouquet represent your love—vibrant and in full bloom." Then he'd reach into his pocket and hand the bride and groom a packet of seeds.

"It's actually more like this," he'd continue. "A seed is filled with potential that can only be discovered if it's given the right elements—sun, water, good soil, and time. Likewise, your relationship is filled with the potential to be more than it already is, but it's hidden within mysteries that only reveal themselves over time as you nurture your love."

No matter how long you and your spouse have been together, your marriage is a garden rich with untapped potential. But it must be nurtured and allowed to unfold day by day. Each new circumstance, each shift in seasons, is an opportunity to love each other in new, life-giving ways.

Love isn't a commitment you make just once, on your wedding day. It's a journey you take together—each moment a step forward into the unknown, yet rooted in a daily rededication to knit your hearts together as one.

> For everything there is a season, and a time for every matter under heaven: a time to be born, and a time to die; a time to plant, and a time to pluck up what is planted.
>
> ECCLESIASTES 3:1-2

Nurture our marriage relationship into full bloom, Lord. Thank You for the gift of planting and growing a lifetime of love and beauty.

Don't Ignore Trouble

It doesn't take a rocket scientist to have a happy marriage. Or does it?

Getting to the moon is no easy task. The rockets NASA built for the space program took years to design and consisted of nearly two million parts. The engineers had to factor in thousands of calculations, including the rocket's speed, the earth's orbit through space, and the path of the moon around the earth. Every detail was subjected to exacting standards. There was no room for ignoring trouble. Doing so invited disaster.

In marriage, ignoring problems can escalate conflict, breed uncertainty, and fuel disunity. The willingness to embrace the truth of your relationship, on the other hand, can open the door to wisdom, which is essential if you and your spouse hope to find common ground, resolve disagreements, and lift your marriage to another level.

Seek truth together. When there's a problem, commit to finding solutions. And above all, learn new ways of communicating, connecting, and fostering deeper intimacy. With time, the engines of your relationship will ignite, and you'll soon be soaring to the stars.

> O Lord, who shall sojourn in your tent? Who shall dwell on your holy hill? He who walks blamelessly and does what is right and speaks truth in his heart.
> PSALM 15:1-2

Jesus, thank You for being the Way and the Truth and the Life. Pour out Your Spirit on my marriage to help my spouse and me deal with the realities of our relationship and stay steady in our love and respect for each other.

Does Your Marriage Need Help?

It's important for couples facing difficulty to ask for help. Unfortunately, some couples don't realize their marriage is on the rocks until it's too late.

What are some indications that it might be time to seek help? Friends and family members can sometimes spot trouble that you might miss. They may be the first to observe unusual attitudes or behaviors. Listen to those who know you best.

Your children are also a good measure of your marital health. Kids have a special ability to sense tension. If they begin acting out, it might be time to look at your home life.

Compare your relationship now with what it once was. Remember how you used to love spending time together and serving each other? If that's no longer true, it should be a warning sign. All marriages need basic nurturing to survive.

More serious indicators of trouble include physical abuse, sexual problems, extramarital affairs, substance abuse, and destructive patterns such as criticism and nagging. Any of these struggles is cause for seeking immediate help.

If you suspect that you and your spouse need counseling, find a professional in your area or look into the Marriage Intensive through Focus on the Family's Hope Restored program.

God is our refuge and strength, a very present help in trouble.
PSALM 46:1

All-powerful God, nothing is too difficult for You to restore and mend. My marriage could use some revival and a return to solid communication. Thank You for already working on our behalf.

Love with Style

Theresa had a stroke eighteen years ago. She has a hard time doing simple things in life, like styling her own hair.

Andrew, Theresa's husband of nearly forty-five years, knows how much joy a new hairstyle brings her. So he went to his wife's salon and bought the hair products that he needed to re-create his wife's look at home. Then Theresa's hairstylist gave him lessons, and Andrew spent hours practicing with a brush, curling iron, and hair spray. He's not ready to declare mastery over hairstyling, but he sure enjoys seeing the smile on Theresa's face.

Expressions of love like Andrew's are inspiring. You don't hear about them often, since the media prefer to expose the latest gossip on marriages that *don't* work out. But we need to hear stories like Theresa and Andrew's. They remind us that every marriage has obstacles to overcome, and most couples hang in there when things get tough. Not only do they find a way to stay together, but they also turn their challenges into the very thing that deepens their love even more.

Endurance produces character, and character produces hope.
ROMANS 5:4

Father, Your Word makes it clear that good things can come from the challenges we face in life, and the same is true for the challenges we face in marriage. Please show us how to navigate tough times so that You are glorified and our love for each other grows stronger in the process.

Formed, Not Found

Ninety-three percent of Americans say that a happy marriage is one of their most important goals. So how does a couple's dream of a happy life together become a nightmare that ends in divorce?

Marriages break up for a lot of reasons, but a common one is the false idea that lasting marriages are the result of finding your "soulmate"—that one person who "gets you." You love each other so naturally that your relationship is effortless. Every day is like a romantic, carefree walk in the park. And why wouldn't it be? You're soulmates. You're meant for each other.

Soulmates are an entertaining plot device for a movie, but real life rarely works that way. A relationship as intimate as marriage can't be created without some work. The illusion of an effortless marriage shatters at the first sign of conflict. That's when doubt creeps in, and you'll wonder, *What if this isn't my soulmate after all?*

Here's the good news: Soulmates aren't found, they're formed. You don't magically stumble into a happy, healthy marriage. You build one across time by committing to love your spouse through thick and thin, for better or worse.

> Do not be conformed to this world, but be transformed by the renewal of your mind, that by testing you may discern what is the will of God, what is good and acceptable and perfect.
> ROMANS 12:2

Father, help me not to buy into the world's view of romantic love but to embrace Your thoughts on what it means to build a strong, lasting marriage that honors You.

Roles and Chores

When you and your spouse fell in love and spent hours gazing into each other's eyes, did you discuss how the two of you would divide up household chores after marriage? Probably not.

Mandy and Tom settled the chores issue like this: Everything *inside* the house would be her responsibility; everything *outside* would be his. This worked until Mandy decided taking the garbage all the way to the curb wasn't "inside" work. Needless to say, Tom wasn't happy to come home from work and find a trash bag sitting by the front door!

Fortunately, there's a better way to organize chores. Mandy and Tom could have avoided a lot of unnecessary grief if they'd simply discussed their assumptions beforehand. In particular, it's a good idea to have open, honest conversations that detail your expectations. Give serious thought to who each of you is and how you want your household to operate. Concentrate on giftedness rather than gender. So instead of emphasizing "male" and "female" roles, talk about which jobs each of you enjoys.

And the best part? If you tackle the work as a team, not only will you conquer household chores, but you'll also strengthen your relationship along the way.

A fool takes no pleasure in understanding, but only in expressing his opinion.

PROVERBS 18:2

Strengthen our relationship even through what seems insignificant. Let us refine each other daily and encourage each other toward You and toward our marriage.

Five Secrets of a Happy Marriage

Who knows the secrets of a happy marriage better than couples who have been together many decades?

I asked one of my colleagues to survey a group of these couples and learn their secrets. Here are five key tips they shared:

1. Don't keep secrets. Be open and honest. Share the deeper parts of your hearts with each other.
2. Don't hold grudges. Learn to forgive. Grudges lead to bitterness and invite couples to start pulling away from each other and looking for an exit door.
3. Address your conflicts and work through them, but don't dwell on your disagreements. Put your past behind you and focus on the positive parts of your marriage.
4. Understand that your love will change over the years because *you* will change. You can only create a happy marriage if you stay committed to each other across the seasons of life.
5. Support your spouse in his or her interests. Learn what activities your spouse is passionate about, and join in on the fun.

The secrets to a happy marriage really aren't secrets at all. The magic comes from your willingness to jump in and do the work.

I perceived that there is nothing better for them than to be joyful and to do good as long as they live.
ECCLESIASTES 3:12

Lord, a happy, joyful marriage is such a rich treasure.
Thank You for all the incredible couples out there
who have been married fifty years or more and
still model the secrets of a fulfilling marriage.
May my marriage be one of them someday.

More Than a Piece of Paper

The phrase *till death do us part* has been a popular element of wedding vows for generations—and with good reason. Marriage is a sacred commitment to be as dedicated to your spouse in the bad times as you are in the good times. Devotion that deep is a couple's only hope if they want to build a marriage that lasts a lifetime.

But here's the catch: Commitment doesn't naturally bubble to the surface in a moment of crisis. It's cultivated over time as husbands and wives live out their love for one another each and every day. Commitment is what makes marriage more than just a piece of paper or a box to check on a tax form. Marriage is a sacred union that bestows countless benefits on the couple, their children, and society—benefits that cannot be replicated by any other relationship.

Neither your individual household nor society at large will flourish without the foundation of stable marriages. That's because healthy cultures and healthy marriages require the same thing: selfless people who seek each other's happiness, not just their own.

Marriage is a commitment so deep and meaningful that it can only be described with a vow as profound as "till death do us part."

Let marriage be held in honor among all.
HEBREWS 13:4

Lord, help us live out our vows to each other daily. Bless our union with the strength to face challenges hand in hand. Help us center our hearts on You as the cornerstone of our marriage.

SECTION 2

Communication

Women Are Women; Men Are Men

One of the biggest challenges of creating a successful marriage is that men communicate like men and women communicate like women. This is something a lot of couples overlook.

In recent years, voices within the culture have argued that men and women and boys and girls are essentially the same. One toy company decided to capitalize on that idea. They designed a dollhouse to be used by either gender. The results weren't what the company expected. In tests, girls acted like girls, and boys acted like boys. The girls had tea parties, pretend marriages, and kids playing outside. But the boys created war scenes or drove the baby carriage off the roof in a fiery crash.

The differences remain into adulthood. Men often connect by doing things. Guys go hunting or play golf together. They work on their cars together. Communication happens along the way.

Women, in turn, tend to connect by talking. They stop, look at each other, and talk.

Neither style of communication is right or wrong . . . just different. Both are important. Couples have to make room for each spouse's unique personality. Communication and connection shouldn't be one-sided. Someone will wind up not feeling heard or having his or her needs met.

God created man in his own image, in the image of God he created him; male and female he created them.
GENESIS 1:27

Creator God, thank You that You designed men and women differently and that Your design includes our unique personalities and communication styles. Help me joyfully make room for my spouse's differences in how we connect.

Oceans of Intimacy

In Israel, the Jordan River flows into the Dead Sea. It's called the Dead Sea because water flows *in*, but nothing flows *out*. Dr. Gary Chapman says some spouses communicate like that—they interact with the world around them, but they're perfectly happy not to talk about it.

Babbling brooks, on the other hand, are a constant flow of water. These spouses interact with the world as well, but they *love* to talk about it.

Those differences can pose quite a problem for a marriage. The babbling brooks complain that their Dead Sea spouse doesn't talk much. And the Dead Sea spouses complain that their babbling brook talks all the time.

One answer to this dilemma is to recognize that the goal isn't for one spouse's communication style to win out over the other. Instead, grow toward each other. That means Dead Sea spouses can learn to speak more than they normally do, and babbling brooks can talk less, ask more questions, and become better listeners.

Seek common ground and find ways to meet each other's needs. The goal isn't for couples to be Dead Seas *or* babbling brooks but to swim together in an ocean of intimacy.

> Whatever you wish that others would do to you, do also to them,
> for this is the Law and the Prophets.
> MATTHEW 7:12

God, thank You for how You uniquely designed
me and my spouse. Help us unite as one.

Waffles and Spaghetti

Opposites attract. For the most part, with a little communication, those differences can be navigated. But sometimes differences in communication itself are the problem.

Authors Bill and Pam Farrel offer a simple word picture that illustrates the distinction between how men and women typically communicate: Men are like waffles; women are like spaghetti.

Imagine a plate of spaghetti. The noodles run in random directions, and they all seem to touch each other. It's a visual for the way many women easily jump from one subject to another within a conversation.

Now picture a waffle. It's essentially a collection of boxes, which represents how most men process life. Their thinking is divided into boxes that have room for one issue and one issue only.

So how should a husband track with his wife when she's jumping from one issue to another? First, don't immediately propose a solution. Guys are usually looking for an answer and think finding it is the goal. Not so for many women. Their goal is to talk something through. Like spaghetti noodles that all run together, women are often thinking about the next thing, and the next thing after that, and it's all connected emotionally.

Second, be willing to set aside whatever you're doing—whether that's work or watching the game on television—and listen. Focus on what she's saying and let her talk it through, wherever it may lead.

If the whole body were an eye, where would be the sense of hearing? If the whole body were an ear, where would be the sense of smell? But as it is, God arranged the members in the body, each one of them, as he chose.
1 CORINTHIANS 12:17-18

Loving Creator, You have wired men and women differently, and we need each other's individual giftings. Help me embrace my spouse's unique personality and communication style as a true gift from You.

Simplicity and Clarity

"**M**ayday! Mayday!"

Perhaps you recognize that distress call. The fact that even children have a rough idea of what it means demonstrates the importance of good communication.

The Mayday distress code was created by London airport radio officer Frederick Mockford in 1923. His boss challenged him to think up an emergency distress code that would be easily understood. Much of the air traffic at the time was between London and Paris, so Mockford proposed the expression *Mayday*. It was easy to say, and it sounded like the French term for "Help me." *Mayday* is still used today all over the world.

Simplicity and clarity. Those two elements are essential to good communication. A lot of couples forget that when they're arguing. A disagreement about dinner plans can easily morph into an argument about the car, the kids, or money. Simplify. Narrow your focus to one problem, and don't allow other irritations to sidetrack you.

And don't forget this: Good communication is as much about how you listen and respond as it is about what you say. Find ways to communicate your point of view as clearly as possible.

When conflict hits your marriage, remember "Mayday!" It's your cue to communicate simply and clearly.

He who loves purity of heart, and whose speech is gracious,
will have the king as his friend.
PROVERBS 22:11

*Father God, send me a Mayday signal when my
speech is out of line. Help me speak gracious, kind
words to my spouse throughout each day.*

Little White Lies

Do you tell "little white lies" to your spouse? It's common behavior for many couples, and most excuse it as no big deal.

So-called little white lies look something like this: A husband tells his wife that he did run an errand she asked him to—when in reality, he didn't. Or a wife buys new shoes but fibs about the price, so her husband believes they were cheaper than they really were.

Why do husbands and wives lie to each other about such trivial matters? The answer for many couples often ranges from "to avoid conflict" to "it's just easier." They put a positive spin on what is actually a deeper issue.

Spouses often lie when they feel there's not enough safety in the relationship to be honest. Rather than handling situations with understanding, maybe a spouse reacts with anger. Or instead of compassion, he or she offers insults. It's a breakdown in the relationship's trust and intimacy. In some cases, it may mean those traits were never there in the first place.

So the next time you feel compelled to lie to your spouse, give some thought to why. It could be an indication your relationship needs a little work.

Do not lie to one another, seeing that you have put off the old self with its practices.
COLOSSIANS 3:9

You always speak truth, Lord. I want that to be true of my life. Nudge my spirit the next time I'm tempted to tell a white lie. Lying does not reflect my new life in You.

Unmet Expectations

What would you say is the most significant issue facing marriages today? The phrase *unmet expectations* probably wouldn't cross your mind.

When you get married, you might think your relationship is a blank slate. In reality, we all bring a long list of expectations with us into the marriage. It could be anything from hoping your spouse will be romantic to how clean he or she will keep the house. These expectations define what we want from our spouse and from our marriage.

The problem is that many couples don't realize they have certain expectations. So when a need goes unmet, they feel hurt and blame the other spouse for being so rude and uncaring. The spouse then feels attacked because he or she had no idea there was a line to be crossed. That's when conflict ensues.

So how does a couple deal with this problem? The first step is to recognize your expectations. After that, you need to discuss them openly with your spouse so your mate understands your needs. You may discover some of your hopes aren't reasonable and should be adjusted. Through dialogue and compromise, a husband and wife can agree on how to meet each other's needs so they both feel loved and cherished.

The simple inherit folly, but the prudent are crowned with knowledge.
PROVERBS 14:18

God, grant me a greater understanding of myself and of my spouse. Guide us in deeper intimacy and knowledge of each other.

Little Slips, Big Mistakes

When it comes to space flight, precision matters. The slightest miscalculation in space can take a rocket light-years from where you want it to go. The same can be said for little mistakes we make with our families.

On September 4, 1962, the *Mariner 2* spacecraft had been hurtling through space for nine days. That's when NASA engineers discovered the craft was off course and would miss its target—the planet Venus—by more than two hundred thousand miles.

The solution? Mission Control fired the spacecraft's boosters for just a few seconds, altering its trajectory by only a fraction of a degree. But that one small correction, over the course of the next three months, put the craft right on target. The moral of the story? Given time, even a tiny adjustment can make a big difference.

The same principle holds true in our relationships as well. A tiny slip-up today—a harsh word, an insensitive comment, ill-timed sarcasm—can produce a broken marriage if the wound is allowed to fester. On the other hand, a tiny adjustment—especially those two little words *I'm sorry*—can often get a relationship that's off course back on track.

[Bear] with one another and, if one has a complaint against
another, [forgive] each other; as the Lord has forgiven you,
so you also must forgive.
COLOSSIANS 3:13

*Jesus, thank You for making the ultimate sacrifice in
forgiving us. Teach us again and again how to bear
with one another and forgive as You have forgiven us.*

A Trip to the ICU

For a marriage to thrive, a husband and wife have to connect at a heart level. One of the best ways to do that is with something called a "Heart Talk"—communication designed to foster connection and bonding rather than sharing information or solving problems.

A lot of well-meaning couples focus their energy on problem-solving. Those are important discussions because they deal with the practical nuts and bolts of the relationship. The most fulfilling marriages, though, are those where the couple gets beyond logistical matters and connects at a heart level. Heart Talks help unify a couple and connect spouses emotionally.

But heart-to-heart communication doesn't come naturally for every couple. If you and your spouse could use some help getting beneath the surface, remember this acronym: *ICU*.

Identify each other's feelings. Are you angry? Do you feel lonely? What is each of you feeling?

Care about each other's feelings. Don't dismiss or minimize your spouse's feelings.

Understand each other's feelings. Don't assume anything.

It's wise to talk about and solve problems in your marriage, but to connect with each other's heart, you need the ICU: identify, care, and understand.

My mouth shall speak wisdom; the meditation of my heart shall be understanding.
PSALM 49:3

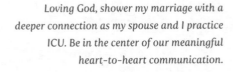

Loving God, shower my marriage with a deeper connection as my spouse and I practice ICU. Be in the center of our meaningful heart-to-heart communication.

When Your Spouse Won't Talk

One partner feeling that the other won't open up and talk is one of the most common marriage problems. If that sounds like your relationship, here are a few ideas that might help.

For starters, recognize that your spouse is probably just quieter than you. If you're a caring spouse who understands that perspective, the next step will be easier: Make sure you're safe to talk to. Don't criticize, roll your eyes, or disregard what your spouse says.

Another idea is to plan a time when you're both rested from your day and ready to talk. If conversation doesn't flow easily at first, start simple. Take five minutes to talk about something of common interest. Talk about something light—maybe a book or a television show.

Even with these ideas, developing conversation may not be as easy as it sounds. Long-held patterns are often hard to break. But if you persevere, your efforts can become a turning point in your marriage and change a good relationship into a great one.

So give it a try. If you find yourselves struggling, seek out some professional help. A wise counselor can help you overcome the obstacles that hinder healthy and vibrant conversation.

Let the words of my mouth and the meditation of my heart be acceptable in your sight, O LORD, my rock and my redeemer.
PSALM 19:14

May my thoughts and words be pleasing to You, Lord, and help my spouse feel loved and safe with me. Draw us closer together through deeper, more meaningful conversations.

Ten Minutes to Intimacy

Ten minutes is all it takes to completely transform your marriage. Multiple studies show that couples who spend just ten minutes a day talking about meaningful things are happier together and experience deeper intimacy.

The key is to get below the surface. Weekly date nights are ideal for connection, but life is moving fast, and it's not easy to stop for an entire evening.

So I encourage you to commit to just ten minutes a day. A short time of focused energy is a great way to reconnect. If making an appointment with your spouse feels too calculated, don't worry. After a while, you may not need any structure.

Open your hearts and share about something deeper than the weather or your schedules. Get to some deeper feelings. Discuss your relationship. Ask each other questions like "What's going on in your life?" or "How are you doing with the kids?" You can talk about anything as long as you both feel you're making a heart-to-heart connection.

Building intimacy doesn't have to be a major undertaking or cost a lot of money. But it does require some commitment. Carve out ten minutes daily for you and your spouse to reconnect about what really matters—each other.

The purpose in a man's heart is like deep water, but a man of understanding will draw it out.
PROVERBS 20:5

Setting aside just ten minutes a day for deeper conversation with my spouse brings joy to my heart. Lord, help us both richly enjoy and look forward to our daily reconnection times.

Tell Your Spouse First

Relationship expert Dr. Greg Smalley talks to a lot of couples who want an intimate, romantic marriage. What they have instead more closely resembles a business relationship. Sometime after the honeymoon, they stopped connecting at a heart level. Conversations became about bills, household responsibilities, and the kids.

Practical matters are a part of life, but when your priorities drift away from your relationship, your partner will get your leftover emotion and time. Your leftover energy and commitment. Leftovers are lousy for marriage.

To correct this trend, turn to your spouse first. If something exciting happens at work, who's the first person you tell? A coworker? A friend? Try telling your spouse first.

There's something important about the first telling—particularly for men. The first telling of a story naturally carries more emotion. Whomever you share a story with first will get most of your emotion and, therefore, most of your heart. If you share the story with your spouse last, she'll get your leftover emotion.

If your marriage has grown dull, reignite your passion by connecting with each other at a heart level. Don't settle for leftovers. Give your marriage your best. Turn to your spouse first.

The wise of heart is called discerning, and sweetness of speech increases persuasiveness.
PROVERBS 16:21

God, bless our marriage with sweetness of speech. Rekindle our passion for connecting at a heart level today and always.

Quick to Listen

There's no such thing as a formula in marriage, but there's a particular way of arguing that comes close. This pattern of communication is almost guaranteed to make your conflict worse and your marriage weaker.

Frank and Barb fell into this trap. They would get into a disagreement and lose their cool. They'd spend the next thirty minutes shouting over each other to get their points across. They *had* to yell because neither one of them was listening to the other.

Notice the progression: Anger first. Lots of talking. And no listening. It's a pattern of conflict that's repeated in thousands of marriages every day. The results are just as predictable. Once somebody gets angry, the conflict will escalate quickly. And nothing good happens when couples start shouting and stop listening.

If you get stuck in unhealthy patterns of conflict that lead nowhere, there's another formula that works in exactly the reverse order. Biblical wisdom advises, "Be quick to hear, slow to speak, slow to anger" (James 1:19).

You can't avoid all conflict, and you shouldn't, but your marriage won't suffer if you know how to disagree effectively. Listen first, speak second, and don't be in such a hurry to get angry.

Know this, my beloved brothers: let every person be quick to hear, slow to speak, slow to anger.
JAMES 1:19

I confess that I sometimes struggle with anger and increasing my volume to talk over my spouse. Lord, help me be fervent in hearing and slow in my speech and anger.

Love like Computer Code

Nothing says "I love you" like a text message. My guess is that you don't believe that. Neither do I.

Texts and emails are incredibly practical for staying in touch with family and friends . . . or for short messages to your spouse to pick up a gallon of milk. Sure, telling someone "I love you" is always a great sentiment, no matter how it's transmitted. But studies show that the most meaningful expressions of love hinge on four elements: spoken words, body language, facial expressions, and tone of voice. Those are all human characteristics that no electronic device can fully reproduce.

We all instinctively know that digital communication doesn't make us come alive like the warmth and intimacy of human interaction.

If you want your relationships to be deeply connected, don't simply rely on your smartphone. Spend time together. Talk over dinner, enjoy a shared weekend activity, or walk through your neighborhood together. Talk. Laugh. Look into each other's eyes. And if your special someone is away from home, skip the texting and emails at times and make a call. Hear each other's voice.

Relationships have life, which is why love isn't best expressed through sterile computer code. Love flourishes in the presence of intimacy, warmth, and human interaction.

O my Strength, I will sing praises to you, for you, O God,
are my fortress, the God who shows me steadfast love.
PSALM 59:17

Thank You, God, for showing me steadfast love—the kind of steady love that I can share authentically with my spouse. Remind me to rely less on texts and emails to say "I love you" and to be more fully present with my partner.

First Impressions

It's been said that you never get a second chance to make a first impression. But you can make a positive first impression with your spouse every day.

Some mornings are hectic. The alarm clock blares, then it's a mad dash to get your family dressed, fed, and out the door. In the midst of all the commotion, connecting meaningfully with your spouse is probably the last thing on your mind.

But there's a first impression you can make each morning that'll set a positive tone for the day—and it only takes a few seconds. When you wake up beside your spouse, don't mumble an anemic "Good morning" and then rush off to get everyone moving. Instead, look each other in the eye and say something meaningful like "I love you, and I'm glad to be waking up with you by my side."

Give it a try. The words you speak to each other are powerful. They'll build up your spouse and reassure him or her of your love and commitment. Kind words probably won't get everyone out the door on time. But a few seconds of meaningful interaction first thing in the morning will definitely set a positive tone for the rest of your day.

Be kind to one another.
EPHESIANS 4:32

Lord, as each new day begins, help us greet each other with kindness, love, and the encouragement we need to face the day united in purpose. May Your blessings fill our mornings with joy and a positive tone.

Common Courtesy at Home

When was the last time you said thank you to your spouse for all the small things he or she does, like folding the laundry, cooking dinner, or mowing the lawn?

Yet expressing appreciation is one of the simplest ways to create an atmosphere of gratitude in your family.

My wife, Jean, is a competent and capable woman, but it still matters to her when I show appreciation for even the routine things she does every day. A simple comment like "That was such a great meal tonight. Thanks for putting that all together" means a lot to her. And these were great things for me to say in front of our boys. Such remarks built their respect for their mother and helped them understand just how much she does in our lives.

Listen, I'm not saying a couple has to follow each other around the house saying thank you for every mundane thing. But even an occasional compliment can have a big impact. It's a great way to show your husband or wife gratitude when it's least expected.

> To make an apt answer is a joy to a man, and a word in season, how good it is!
> PROVERBS 15:23

Lord, show me the right times to bless my spouse with words of appreciation and gratitude.

Douse Your Fake Emotions

I once appeared on a cable-news talk show that I expected to be a political debate. It was more like entertainment.

Before my segment, I watched the television host attack his first guest. I don't remember what they were talking about, but I do remember how intensely they disagreed with each other. The host was ruthless—he even called her an idiot live on air.

What surprised me most, however, was what happened at the commercial breaks. The host's attitude and demeanor changed entirely. At one break, he turned to the guest and, like one friend to another, said, "What time do you want me to pick you up for dinner? You like Italian food, don't you?" The two chatted casually until the show went live again, and then—wham!—they went right back at each other.

Fake emotion like that doesn't happen just on television. You see the same thing on social media—and even in relationships. People like to sweep the rest of us into their faux hysteria.

Instead of adding fuel to the fire, we can deprive it of oxygen. Answer hysteria and discord with calm and civility. Speak the truth, but do it in love.

[Cast] all your anxieties on him, because he cares for you.
I PETER 5:7

God, let me not be caught up in hysteria, discord, and
unnecessary drama. Instead, help me have a calm mind
and a civil temperament in my marriage and life.

Talk about Your Relationship

One of the greatest steps a couple can take to build a strong, healthy marriage is to talk openly with each other about the state of their relationship.

Think of it like a business undergoing a quarterly review. To make good choices about its future, a company must understand what is working well and what isn't, and then find solutions.

The same is true for married couples. To make good choices about their future, a husband and wife ought to have honest conversations about their relationship. Healthy dialogue will highlight what's working well, what isn't, and solutions to those issues that arise.

Thinking of your marriage like a business may sound like a sterile approach that will kill the intimacy in your relationship. But just the opposite is true. Talking about your relationship removes the obstacles that keep your intimacy from flourishing.

It's been said that a relationship is only as strong as its secrets. It's only as strong as the issues you never talk about as well.

To help your marriage thrive, discuss your relationship. Talk about what's working well and what isn't, and then work together to create solutions.

> Nothing is hidden that will not be made manifest, nor is anything secret that will not be known and come to light.
> LUKE 8:17

Mighty God, we need help to remove the obstacles that keep our intimacy from flourishing. Please bring to light the issues in our lives that need to be resolved, and help us address them in a godly way.

Two Things to Improve Your Marriage

Ask your spouse to share two things you do in your marriage that he or she appreciates . . . and two things you can do to make your marriage better.

The first part—hearing what you do well—is easy. We all love pats on the back and being told the ways we shine. It's the second part—what you can do better—that'll take some courage to hear.

I once asked my wife if there was something that I could do better in our relationship. I thought she might take some time to think about it. Instead, she had an immediate answer for me. "I can think of two things," Jean said. Such a quick response was tough to hear, just like constructive feedback might be tough for you to hear too.

But that's why marriage is for grown-ups. Strong relationships don't happen by accident. They're built by husbands and wives who can hear feedback without getting defensive or lashing out. Most of the suggestions your spouse makes will probably be improvements you ought to want for yourself anyway. If you're growing as a person, you'll grow in your marriage.

> Walk in a manner worthy of the calling to which you have been called, with all humility and gentleness, with patience, bearing with one another in love.
> EPHESIANS 4:1-2

Heavenly Father, please help us give and receive healthy critiques of each other humbly, gently, and patiently. We desperately want this so that we can improve our marriage.

Learn a New Language

L earning a new language can change your life.

No one understood that better than Helen Keller. At nineteen months old, an unknown illness left her both deaf and blind. She was cut off from humanity with no way to communicate.

Then Anne Sullivan, a teacher, taught Helen how to communicate by spelling words into Helen's hand. The breakthrough moment came when Anne poured cool water over Helen's left hand while spelling *water* into her right. Helen later said, "Somehow the mystery of language was revealed to me in that moment. I knew that W-A-T-E-R meant the wonderful, cool something that was flowing over my hand." Helen had discovered the world of language, and it opened a whole *new* world of relationship to her.

You can make the same wonderful discovery in your marriage. You got married thinking that you and your spouse speak the same language. But you don't. You see life one way. Your spouse sees it another.

The solution is to learn a *new* language—your partner's. When you communicate love to your spouse in ways that he or she understands, it will open a whole new world of intimacy and connection in your relationship.

Walk in wisdom toward outsiders, making the best use of the time. Let your speech always be gracious, seasoned with salt, so that you may know how you ought to answer each person.
COLOSSIANS 4:5-6

Father, if I am to use wisdom in knowing how to speak to strangers, how much more should I use wisdom in speaking to my own spouse! Show me what words to choose that will communicate love in the way my spouse will resonate with best.

More Together Than Apart

Sometimes what couples think is a parenting problem is actually a marriage issue.

Let me illustrate what I mean with a common disagreement between many husbands and wives. One spouse might insist that it's important for children to maintain high standards at school—that is, homework and good grades should be a top priority at all times. The other spouse is a free spirit who doesn't believe good grades are the end-all and be-all of childhood. As long as children put their best foot forward, that's what really matters.

These differing perspectives could easily result in conflict when report card time comes around. One parent insists that the child is putting in plenty of effort at school, while the other says more can and should be done. What many couples don't understand is this: Although their conflict is *about* their child's grades, the root of their disagreement is their own disunity.

In every area of life, do your best to find common ground and agree to acceptable compromises. You and your spouse are distinct individuals, so you won't see eye to eye on everything—and that's okay. You're not meant to. Each of you brings a unique perspective to bear on your relationship.

Even in your differences, find ways to be more together than apart. Talk it out. Compromise. Sacrifice for each other. Figure out standards you can both live with, and come together in unity.

In Christ Jesus you are all sons of God, through faith.
GALATIANS 3:26

Lord, unify our relationship. Channel our differences in positive directions, and help us find common ground that binds us together. May Your divine love guide our hearts and foster a harmonious and resilient connection.

What We Say and Hear

What comes to mind if I say, "Green right X-shift to viper right three eighty-four X-stick lookie"? Or "Trips left, sloopy nine fifty fade. Go on two"?

Those aren't random phrases. They're not military jargon or air traffic control lingo, either. They're football plays. To you and me, they might sound like gibberish. But to veteran football players, they make perfect sense—because they understand the language.

When most couples get married, they assume they speak the same language. Over time, however, they discover that the words they use and the meanings they ascribe to them are not always the same. For example, have you ever had a disagreement that reaches a point where you forget what started the argument in the first place? That happens because you think you're communicating effectively when you're really not.

What you *say* and what your spouse *hears* can be two different things. Effective communication requires you to pay attention to your spouse's tone, emotion, and body language as much as you do to their words.

The happiest couples learn how to get past the language barrier. Don't just listen to what your spouse *says*; learn what he or she *means*.

At this sound the multitude came together, and they were bewildered, because each one was hearing them speak in his own language.

ACTS 2:6

God, give us wisdom and understanding with each other. May we open our hearts and learn our spouse's language so our love for one another thrives.

SECTION 3

Appreciating Differences

A Losing Strategy

Do you remember when you were dating? You probably overlooked the quirky things your partner did. But after you walked down the aisle, those innocent quirks suddenly became annoying habits that now drive you crazy.

If that's you, here's a suggestion for what not to do: Don't try to change your spouse into somebody else. If your spouse is an introvert, for example, don't expect your mate to become an extrovert. People who try to change their spouse usually wind up frustrated. Many resort to criticism and manipulation to get the job done. That's always a losing strategy.

Instead, focus on specific behaviors, and voice your feelings to your spouse honestly and respectfully. Successful couples are those that pursue growth together—changing habits that can be changed and learning to accept those that can't.

So be proactive about putting your relationship on a stronger footing. It's always worthwhile to address behavior that's complicating your relationship. But remember, it was likely those differences that brought you together in the first place. So don't try to eliminate them. Learn how to use them to bring character and richness to your relationship.

Love is . . . not arrogant or rude. It does not insist on its own way; it is not irritable or resentful.

I CORINTHIANS 13:4-5

Holy Spirit, guide me in how to flex with my spouse's quirky habits, realizing that I have some too. Rekindle the richness of our relationship as we both put aside being arrogant, rude, and irritable.

The Paradox

Marriage is a paradox. For a relationship to be successful, spouses have to limit their independence. But at the same time, they have to thrive as individuals. Confused yet?

A good marriage truly takes two people. On your own, you may be a roaring success in your career. But in marriage, unless you work together with your spouse, your relationship will flounder. When two people each let go of some of their personal ambitions for the sake of the relationship, the bond between them will strengthen.

But that's just one side of the coin. The other is this: The more connected you and your spouse become, the more important it is that you grow as individuals. Why? Because a healthy marriage consists of two unique people who can stand on their own. Entering marriage doesn't mean you suddenly stop being who you are. It's just the opposite. You bring yourself into your marriage, so it's important to become the best "you" you can be. It's those differences that help make a good marriage truly great.

So should your marriage bring you and your spouse together as one? Or should the two of you be strong individuals? The answer is yes! That's the paradox of marriage.

> Two are better than one, because they have a good reward for their toil. For if they fall, one will lift up his fellow. But woe to him who is alone when he falls and has not another to lift him up!
>
> ECCLESIASTES 4:9-10

Thank You, Lord, that my spouse and I can bring our best selves into our marriage and remain united, yet individuals. May we put aside our own selfish ambitions to work together as unified partners.

Embracing Your Differences

If you're married, you are learning that your mate sees the world through different eyes. You fall asleep to noise, but your spouse needs quiet. You're a night owl, but your spouse enjoys mornings. For the most part, these differences are easy to navigate. But others can be more challenging.

Throughout my adult life, for example, I've been a positive person. When adversity comes, I tend to push forward with the help of my faith. But I learned the hard way that I can't expect everyone to share a similar outlook.

Some years ago, my wife, Jean, was going through an especially challenging time, and with my usual optimism, I encouraged her to move on. She knew I meant well, but her response surprised me. "Jim," she said, "some of us can't pull ourselves up by our bootstraps and just get going." That day I understood for the first time that, in many ways, Jean's whole approach to life was different from mine.

Our differences don't need to be obstacles to a healthy relationship. Our spouse's strengths are meant to complement our weaknesses. With patience, we can learn to embrace our spouse's unique viewpoint, and as we do, we'll find our marriage enriched.

Every way of a man is right in his own eyes, but the LORD weighs the heart.
PROVERBS 21:2

Lord, we each have our own giftings and approach to life. May my way not be the only way to view situations in my marriage. Grant me the insight and patience to draw out and be sensitive to my spouse's differences.

Valuing Social Intimacy

Many couples think building marital intimacy is about candlelit dinners and deep conversation. Opening your hearts to each other is powerful, but there's another kind of intimacy that can be just as beneficial to a couple: social intimacy.

Social intimacy means you share activities together. Maybe you both enjoy riding bikes, exercising, or gardening together. The two of you probably already share a lot of common interests.

But there's another angle to social intimacy that's tricky to navigate. More than likely you'll both have to go beyond your individual comfort zones and agree to do activities that don't matter to you but are important to your spouse.

Maybe your spouse loves going to the symphony, but you don't care for it. Go to the symphony anyway. In some marriages, the wife likes to watch cooking shows and the husband enjoys football. Watch a little of both together. Make a concerted effort to engage in each other's interests, and your intimacy has a good chance of deepening.

That's the heart and soul of social intimacy. It's about more than just "doing stuff together." It's about showing your spouse how much you value him or her by honoring what's important to your beloved.

Encourage one another and build one another up, just as you are doing.
I THESSALONIANS 5:11

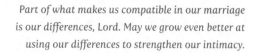

Part of what makes us compatible in our marriage is our differences, Lord. May we grow even better at using our differences to strengthen our intimacy.

Look-Alike Couples

I'm not sure whether it's true that if couples are married long enough, they start to look like each other. But I think couples do often look like the *other couples* they hang out with.

It may feel more comfortable to be friends with someone who's just like you, but you're depriving your marriage of growth. Relating to someone in the same place in life as you or who has common interests is easy. You can empathize about career challenges, share parenting highs and lows, or compare favorite music, movies, and hobbies.

But there's also tremendous value in spending time with a couple who is different from you. An older couple can share years of wisdom with a younger couple and help them develop some long-term stability in their marriage. Younger couples can bring a sense of energy to the friendship or help an older couple feel younger and more revived in their own relationship.

To add deeper richness to your marriage, build a friendship with another couple who doesn't see life the same way as you. Their different perspective can challenge you to grow, and it just might create the spark you need to strengthen your marriage for years to come.

There are varieties of gifts, but the same Spirit.
I CORINTHIANS 12:4

Differences are a gift, God. Thank You that we can stretch and grow our marriage by connecting with others who are not exactly like us.

Together though Separate

I know couples who got married thinking the secret to happiness was having the exact same interests. It didn't take long for them to find out that we're rarely just like our spouse. The good news is that we don't have to be. Successful marriages aren't the result of perfect chemistry. They're built—in part—by learning how to bring our separateness together.

Ted and Cindy are a good example of this. Ted likes to fish. Cindy doesn't really care for it, but she loves to read and loves the Colorado outdoors. So nearly every Saturday in the summer, they drive into the Rocky Mountains together, and he fly-fishes while she sits on the bank and enjoys a book. They have a picnic together. They laugh. They talk. They enrich their marriage. But that deeper connection doesn't come about by forcing their individual interests onto each other. It comes from bringing their separateness together.

It just goes to show that differences can strengthen a couple's bond rather than weakening it. It takes patience and a willingness to embrace our spouse's unique view of life. But if we do that, we'll discover a deeper intimacy with our spouse than we ever thought possible.

Let each of you look not only to his own interests, but also to the interests of others.
PHILIPPIANS 2:4

Lord, I love knowing that my spouse and I do not need to share the exact same interests. Help us both look out for more fun and enriching opportunities to share our separateness together.

Empty Yourself

If you don't appreciate the small things about your spouse, even a salad will cause a fight.

That's what marriage experts Drs. Les and Leslie Parrott discovered early in their marriage. They were making a salad together when he noticed how incorrectly she held the knife as she chopped carrots. His way, he suggested, was much safer and more efficient.

Thinking he was being helpful, Les demonstrated to Leslie his "proper" way to cut carrots. Leslie didn't lash out or get offended. She accepted his advice with poise and even tried a couple of his suggestions, but then returned to what was most comfortable for her.

Les and Leslie are both psychologists, and they later agreed that his behavior that night valued "being right" more than his relationship with Leslie. While she was able to defuse the problem, it didn't change the fact that instead of criticizing his wife, Les should have tried *connecting* with her by emptying himself . . . of himself.

Move toward deeper intimacy by appreciating the small things about your spouse. When Les did that, he discovered that he loved the way Leslie cut carrots. Her method was quirky, but it was *her*. He wouldn't change it now for the world.

When you empty yourself of yourself, the things that once drove you apart can bring you together.

When pride comes, then comes disgrace, but with the humble is wisdom.
PROVERBS 11:2

Jesus, You emptied Yourself and took on the form of a human. I am grateful for how You model humility and servanthood. May I empty myself in my relationships so those I love truly sense my love.

Flames of Individuality

The unity candle is one of the most beautiful yet most misunderstood symbols in a wedding.

In a unity candle ceremony, two candles are used to light a larger one, symbolizing that the bride and groom are becoming one in marriage. Typically, the couple then extinguishes the smaller candles.

To some observers, this might imply that the husband and wife are no longer individuals. Their identity exists only within the context of their marriage.

However, I contend that a thriving marriage doesn't erase each person's individuality. Instead, it puts each person's uniqueness to work in service of the relationship. Individuality and unity can absolutely coexist. Becoming one still allows the man's and the woman's individual flames to burn bright.

> As in one body we have many members, and the members do not all have the same function, so we, though many, are one body in Christ, and individually members one of another.
>
> ROMANS 12:4-5

Father God, we are grateful for being both individuals and a couple in our marriage. Help us embrace each other's unique personality, skills, and talents while at the same time recognizing that we are a united team.

The Need for Space

Marital intimacy is all about closeness. At least, that's what a lot of married couples believe. The truth is that intimacy has to do with separateness as well.

I'm reminded of a friend who desperately wanted a border collie when he was a kid. His parents told him no but suggested he do some research to understand why. He discovered that border collies need room to roam. They're much happier on a farm with open fields.

The need for space is wired into their natures. If border collies aren't given adequate room to move about, they become easily aggravated and will nip at your heels.

A lot of marriages are like that. Spouses who have a hard time getting along often think the problem is that they aren't close enough. But sometimes they're too close. Too much of anything—even togetherness in marriage—can be a bad thing. When a husband and wife don't have any separation in their relationship, they can get on each other's nerves.

I'm a talker and thrive on lively conversation. My wife is just the opposite. She often needs more space. For our marriage—and *your* marriage—to be healthy, we need to find the right balance between space and closeness.

> When you pray, go into your room and shut the door and pray to your Father who is in secret. And your Father who sees in secret will reward you.
> MATTHEW 6:6

God, help us understand the difference between space and closeness. We know that we may need space to draw closer together, and we trust You with our marital health.

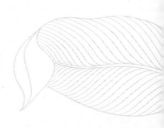

Your Spouse's Friends

When two people marry, they inherit each other's network of friends. So what do you do if you don't get along with your spouse's friends?

The first question to ask is this: *Why* do you not like your spouse's friends? Are they engaging in irresponsible or immoral conduct? Worse yet, does your spouse get pulled into that behavior? If so, then you have a legitimate concern, and you and your spouse need to work through the situation carefully. It might require your mate to decide whether those friendships are really worth maintaining. (This is the kind of issue that can easily erupt into marital conflict, so if you find that happening, be sure to speak to a counselor.)

But what if you simply have different tastes and interests from your spouse's friends? In that case, it's up to you to work at getting to know these folks and finding some common ground. At first, you may find it a struggle. But if you think of your efforts as a way to strengthen your relationship with your spouse, you'll find it easier to be patient with his or her friends. Who knows? Maybe you'll even learn to enjoy and embrace them one day.

Complete my joy by being of the same mind, having the same love, being in full accord and of one mind.
PHILIPPIANS 2:2

I truly value relationships, Lord, so help me be open to accepting my spouse's friendships. Guard our own closeness as we seek to be of one mind on the people we include in our marital circle of friends.

Take Joy in Each Other

Clay and Julie are happily married. But they'll be the first to tell you that their happiness doesn't come easy.

Their taste in music is just one example of how far apart their lives can be. Julie likes pop music. Clay likes to crank up the volume and headbang to heavy metal bands. When Julie plays a pop song on the radio, Clay dismisses it with a funny expression.

Instead of letting their differences come between them, Clay and Julie turn them into opportunities to connect with each other. Like the summer her favorite pop star came to town. Clay bought two tickets—one for Julie, and one for himself. Julie loved the concert, and Clay loved watching Julie have a great time.

That's how you build a great marriage—channeling your differences in a positive direction. Common interests may bolster your marriage, but the way you handle your differences is the key to a marriage that thrives.

Successful relationships aren't about so-called chemistry, good luck, or wishful thinking. They're about two people who sacrifice their own interests for the sake of each other.

These things I have spoken to you, that my joy may be in you,
and that your joy may be full.
JOHN 15:11

God, help me be observant of how different
my spouse and I are. I want to rejoice in those
differences! Also, please help me see those differences
as opportunities to sacrifice my own interests
for the one I love so that my joy may be full.

The Hot and Cold of Marriage

Antarctica is one of the coldest places on earth, in some areas averaging seventy degrees below zero. One of its most prominent features is Mount Erebus, an active volcano pocked with dozens of hydrothermal vents. When hot gas is released from those vents into the frigid surrounding air, it can form massive ice structures nearly forty feet tall. They're an oddly beautiful sight in such a barren and unforgiving environment. That beauty exists because opposing forces come together in spectacular form.

Which brings me to marriage. Differences between you and your spouse can push you apart and make a thriving marriage seem impossible. But take heart. When you approach these issues thoughtfully and intentionally, your opposing traits can come together in a way that transforms your marriage into something spectacular.

With an open heart and a willingness to learn, you can transform your differences into sources of strength. Instead of battling each other when you don't see eye to eye, figure out what it takes to come together. Cold plus cold and hot plus hot equal nothing out of the ordinary. But when hot and cold meet in marriage, incredible things can happen!

Finally, all of you, have unity of mind, sympathy, brotherly love, a tender heart, and a humble mind.

I PETER 3:8

God, help us have the patience to understand each other's unique perspectives and the humility to embrace our differences. May our love reflect Your unifying power.

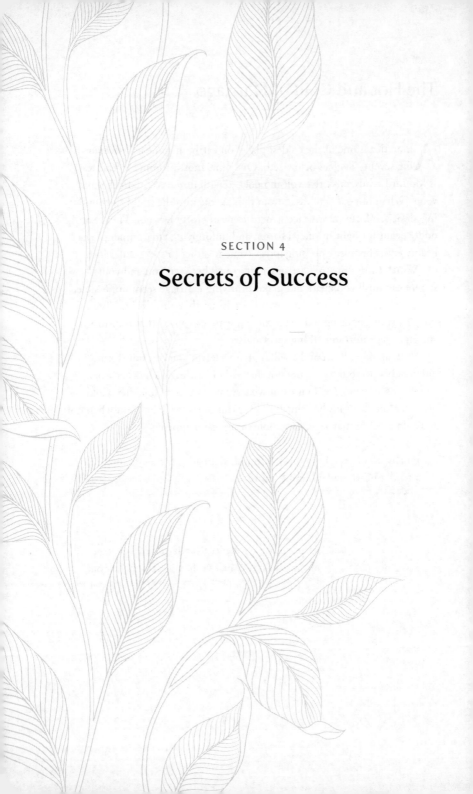

SECTION 4

Secrets of Success

Disorder in the Home

You don't have to be a rocket scientist to have a strong marriage, but a little scientific understanding *can* help you have a better relationship.

The second law of thermodynamics says that things become *disordered* over time. In other words, leave anything to itself, and it will eventually deteriorate. Think of an old, weathered barn crumbling after years in the rain and the sun; or consider the effect on your car if you stopped maintenance. Without proper care and attention, *everything* eventually rusts, breaks, or stops functioning.

That principle also applies to marriages. Relationships aren't self-sustaining. Even good marriages will drift over time if they're not properly cared for, and—sooner or later—they'll crumble entirely.

The way to keep your relationship alive and strong is to invest in it. Give it the nourishment it needs to grow and flourish. How? Talk more. Touch more. Find activities that you and your spouse enjoy doing together. Go to dinner. Take walks. Go fishing.

However you do it, be intentional every day about infusing your relationship with new life. Give your marriage the same care and attention that you'd give to anything else you want to last.

> Let us not grow weary of doing good, for in due season we will reap, if we do not give up.
> GALATIANS 6:9

God, prepare space for me and my spouse to intentionally connect. Point out the places where our relationship is crumbling, and restore our romance and friendship.

Change Yourself

There's a story told about a psychiatrist who thought he could transform his fiancée into the perfect wife. His plan was to lead her through a series of counseling sessions. Not long into the marriage it became apparent that his strategy wasn't working so well. The problem? He'd forgotten that the only person you have the power to change is yourself.

Relationships break down when a partner is consumed by what his spouse should change to better love *him*, rather than what *he* can do to better love his spouse. Even struggling relationships can be turned around in a hurry if each person will pay less attention to his or her spouse's shortcomings and more to how he or she can improve themselves.

Does that mean it's wrong to want your spouse to make some personal improvements? Not at all. But instead of trying to reshape your spouse into what you want, encourage her to grow into the person she was meant to become. Your role is to support your spouse along her journey, not force her to walk your path.

So if your relationship seems stuck, start changing your focus. Consider what you can do to make things better.

I have been crucified with Christ. It is no longer I who live, but Christ who lives in me. And the life I now live in the flesh I live by faith in the Son of God, who loved me and gave himself for me.
GALATIANS 2:20

God, point out the things that I can do to love my spouse better. Help me die to self daily, and empower me to love in the way You love.

Take the High View

Navigating life can be difficult, but flight technology may offer some helpful insights.

For decades, airplane navigation relied solely on ground-based beacons. Now, satellite-driven procedures give pilots three-dimensional views, leading to more precise routes. One airport reported that the new system cut down on time, fuel, and noise from what used to be a "spaghetti-like tangle of flight paths."

Too often, we only work from a ground-level view. We address family problems as they come up—trying to dodge the mountains, so to speak, and just make it to the next layover in one piece.

But what if we used satellite imagery? Taking a high-level view lets us see how the multiple dimensions of our lives intersect, and it can help us gain a more precise perspective about how to strengthen our family.

For example, providing discipline for our children isn't about getting them to behave at a restaurant. It's about helping them establish a lifelong pattern of self-control. And being loving and respectful to our spouse isn't about hoping he or she will do something for us. It's about building authentic, lasting intimacy.

If we view our circumstances with the final destination in mind—a deeply committed marriage that fosters confident, connected kids—we'll stay steadier when turbulence comes.

My thoughts are not your thoughts, neither are your ways my ways, declares the LORD. For as the heavens are higher than the earth, so are my ways higher than your ways and my thoughts than your thoughts.
ISAIAH 55:8-9

Lord, Your thoughts and Your ways are perfect and much higher than mine. Lead my marriage into greater authenticity and intimacy as we both view our circumstances from a heavenly perspective.

A Nation Built through Marriage

History shows that without women and marriage, European settlements in America might have never gotten off the ground.

Jamestown was settled in 1607 by just over a hundred rugged individuals. But women were missing from that initial group. According to *New York Times* columnist Gail Collins, without women present, the men struggled in the New World and achieved only limited success. They spent most of their time "goofing off" and had no motivation to provide beyond what they needed for themselves.

When women finally arrived a year later, Collins says they landed in a "rowdy fraternity party, minus food." But something changed as soon as the men and women began to marry. The men became productive. They now had something beyond themselves to work for. Thanks to the influence of women and the impact of marriage, the colonies flourished within a few decades.

Marriage inspired a ragtag group of men to lay the foundation for an entire nation. Marriage provided the majority of the men with the incentive to work and to build a new country. Society cannot thrive without the influence of women *or* without healthy marriages. Strong marriages are critical for our economy and entire culture to thrive into the future.

> Charm is deceitful, and beauty is vain, but a woman who fears the Lord is to be praised.
>
> PROVERBS 31:30

Lord, You created women to be strong influencers in our world. Thank You! Remind me of the divine worth of every woman and her impact on marriages, families, and society as a whole.

Let Love Win

Some couples have one goal in mind when they get into an argument: to win. Instead of listening respectfully and understanding each other's point of view, they go on the offensive and fight to get their own way.

There's a much better approach. In every disagreement, ask yourself, *Do I want to win? Or do I want my marriage to win?* Winning an argument is a hollow victory if your relationship becomes adversarial in the process. Do you want your spouse to be your opponent or your ally? After all, you don't compromise with opponents. You defeat them. Wounding or manipulating your spouse to get your way is like sawing through the tree branch you're sitting on. Even when you win, you lose.

Only a handful of issues are important enough to warrant a stubborn refusal to give in. There's no room for compromise when it comes to infidelity or domestic violence, for example. Yet for most disagreements, finding solutions that are agreeable to both of you is the objective. You can resolve almost any problem if your ultimate goal is to protect the health and well-being of your relationship.

Healthy couples protect their marriage by treating each other with dignity and respect, even in the midst of conflict. They attack the problem, not each other. To help your relationship thrive, keep what's most important in focus. Instead of trying to defeat your spouse and win an argument, let love win.

Has God forgotten to be gracious? Has he in anger shut up his compassion?
PSALM 77:9

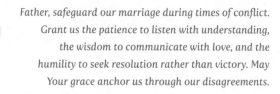

Father, safeguard our marriage during times of conflict.
Grant us the patience to listen with understanding,
the wisdom to communicate with love, and the
humility to seek resolution rather than victory. May
Your grace anchor us through our disagreements.

Gears That Work Together

I once asked Jean, "What's one thing I could do differently in our marriage to make our relationship stronger and your life easier?" She told me, "You're spontaneous, and I'm not. Sometimes you have to give me time to prepare for things."

She was right. I have a tendency to say something out of the blue like "Hey, let's all go to Disney World!" To me, a surprise like that means fun and excitement. But it puts my wife in a bind. She wants to talk about it first. There are reservations to make and schedules to organize. My spontaneity can create a mess that Jean has to manage.

Jean and I are like two gears in a machine. Our relationship operates well when we're sensitive to each other's needs and work together. The best scenario for us is when I am free to have fun and brainstorm ideas, but also when her need for structure and order is taken into account.

Parts of your relationship work the same way. You see life one way, and your spouse sees it another. You're like two gears that have to work *together* to make your marriage run like a well-oiled machine.

Iron sharpens iron, and one man sharpens another.
PROVERBS 27:17

Lord God, You are such a divine craftsman,
engineering how our relationships allow for
uniqueness and unity. Anoint my marriage with
oil to help our relationship operate smoothly.

Wifestyles

Ten percent of married women say they don't have a close female friend. That means a lot of wives have no support *outside* the home when times are tough *inside* the home. For a happier, healthier marriage, author Jen Weaver suggests that wives identify their "wifestyle": either frayed or braided.

A frayed wife is worn out because she's trying to hold everything together herself. She believes she has to have all the answers as a mom and a wife. She gives to others but doesn't make time for herself. She feels lonely and unappreciated.

The solution for the frayed wife is to become a braided wife who has female friends she can rely on for support and wisdom. Just as "a threefold cord is not quickly broken" (Ecclesiastes 4:12), the braided wife has friendship strands woven through her life.

There are no true days off from motherhood, and moms may rarely hear "Thank you." Who could understand the stress you're under better than another wife and mom?

Women have an opportunity to be a force for good in one another's lives. Braided wives can celebrate each other when times are good and support each other when times are tough.

Though a man might prevail against one who is alone, two will withstand him—a threefold cord is not quickly broken.
ECCLESIASTES 4:12

Gracious Lord, You weave together my female friendships, and I am beyond grateful. May I be compassionate and understanding of other wives and moms. Keep us all steady and strong in You.

You've Gotta Keep Going

A bare spot in my lawn reminded me that you've got to keep doing what's right even when what's right doesn't seem to be working.

To repair a bare spot in my yard, I prepared the soil, planted seed, and watered. A couple of weeks went by. All the time I spent watering with a hose appeared to be wasted. And then one day—success! Little green sprouts of grass broke through the surface.

Chinese bamboo is another example. The plants grow sometimes several feet in one day. But getting them to *start* growing is tough. Chinese bamboo can take more than a year to germinate. Which means day after day you could be looking at a bare spot on the ground, wondering if you've done something wrong.

Life works like that for you and me as well. We strive to do what's right for our marriages, our children, and our careers, yet it often seems like nothing good is happening. But keep at it. Hard work, consistency, and diligence are necessary parts of life. Success takes all three. Even when you think nothing is happening, a vast root system is developing. Once there's a breakthrough, there'll be no stopping it.

> Neither he who plants nor he who waters is anything, but only God who gives the growth.
> I CORINTHIANS 3:7

God, I'm grateful that You are the Master Gardener and know just when I will experience breakthrough and growth in my life. May I stay hardworking, consistent, and diligent as I wait for Your perfect timing to come to fruition.

Don't Try This at Home

Men, if you want to see angry sparks fly from your wife, there's one sure way to do it. But don't try this at home.

If you knew Kevin, you'd probably agree that he's a smart guy. Which is what made his blunder with his new bride, Terri, so laughable.

One day, with complete innocence, he asked, "Terri, why aren't you more like my mother?"

Ouch! Well, what he *meant* to ask was how Terri felt she was different from his mother. He wanted to better understand his wife's needs so they could grow as a couple. But between the bolted bedroom door and Terri's convulsive sobs, Kevin never got the opportunity to explain.

A wife doesn't like to be compared with her mother-in-law or feel like her husband needs to be cared for or babied. A woman wants a man with character and inner strength, someone who will love her for who she is.

Instead of comparing your bride with someone else, consider listing some of her wonderful qualities in a way that will leave her feeling cherished and valued. Build up and affirm your wife every chance you get. That's the best way to avoid an unplanned explosion, and it'll enrich your relationship along the way!

Gracious words are like a honeycomb, sweetness to the soul and health to the body.
PROVERBS 16:24

Lord, teach me to share gracious, uplifting words with my spouse to build her up and encourage her. Enrich our relationship through positive speech and kind actions.

It Doesn't Take Much

In research for a book he was writing, Dr. Greg Smalley discovered something alarming about marriage. He found that most people don't feel prepared to commit their lives to another person.

The reasons for that shouldn't come as a surprise. Consider that a medical license requires some twenty thousand hours of training. A counselor's license requires as many as three to four thousand hours. Even a driver's license might require one hundred hours of experience behind the wheel.

But a marriage license? Zero. No classes, no preparation, no training. Nothing. You sign on the dotted line, and you're committed to another person—for the rest of your life.

The truth is that most couples invest more in their wedding ceremony than they do in the marriage itself. Their only strategy for a happy life together is hoping that their feelings for each other last. Is it any wonder that so many marriages fail?

The good news? Any marriage can thrive if couples will invest *something* into their relationship, no matter how small. Be proactive and learn how to be married. Read some marriage books. Have a regular date night. See a counselor. Build a marriage that's deep enough and wide enough to help your family thrive.

A man's ways are before the eyes of the LORD, and he ponders all his paths.
PROVERBS 5:21

Lord, teach me to ponder my paths and consider how to invest more deeply in my marriage. I truly long to build a marriage that is both deep and wide.

The Lost Art of Commitment

These days, the most popular commitment seems to be *not* to commit to anything—a career, a marriage, becoming a parent.

Choosing not to commit can be both good and bad. On the positive side, we have more opportunities available in our modern world. A hundred years ago, people couldn't travel the globe as easily. They couldn't choose among dozens of jobs. And with no social media, they couldn't connect with people all over the world. Committing to things back then was easier because there were fewer options.

By contrast, we're overwhelmed with choices today, so why commit to just one thing? After all, the more choices we have, the happier we'll be, right? Except that's not how life usually works.

Commitment is ultimately what creates good things in life. Instead of waiting for the "right thing" to come along, committed people dig in and get to work making something happen. Renowned business consultant Peter Drucker reputedly once said, "Without commitment, there are only hopes and dreams, but no plans."

Instead of searching the world for the perfect spouse, the perfect job, or the perfect cause to support, focus on what's right in front of you. Options can be beneficial, but success comes from commitment.

> Whoever works his land will have plenty of bread, but he who follows worthless pursuits lacks sense.
>
> PROVERBS 12:11

Rather than chasing the wind, help me commit to the things before me. Meet me in that commitment and shape me to look more like You.

Maximizing Everyday Moments

Most couples know they need to spend alone time together. But life can get busy. So instead of waiting for the perfect circumstances to come along, take advantage of key moments that already happen every day.

The first is when you say goodbye in the morning. On a typical day, one or both of you will leave the house. How you say goodbye can strengthen your marriage. The key is to give your spouse a kiss. But not just a quick peck on the cheek. Make it a meaningful one.

In the same way, think about how you greet your spouse at the end of the day. Maximize this moment with attention and affection. Meet your spouse at the door. Or at least greet each other soon after and let your spouse know you're glad he or she is home.

Finally, instead of saying good night and immediately falling asleep, offer some positive affirmation or express gratitude for something your spouse did that day. Thank him for dinner or tell her how grateful you are for all she does for the family.

You're not adding anything new to your already full plate. You're simply taking advantage of everyday moments that are already there.

> Encourage one another and build one another up, just as you are doing.
> I THESSALONIANS 5:11

Don't let me miss small chances to be an encouragement,
Father. Remind me of things that I love about
my spouse all throughout the day today.

What Makes a Couple Resilient?

John and Ann Betar weren't typical marriage experts. They didn't have college degrees in the subject, and they didn't conduct seminars or write books. So what made them so qualified to offer marriage advice? They were married for more than *eighty years*.

The Betars were officially recognized as America's longest-married couple at the time, and a national newspaper sponsored a social media campaign featuring John and Ann responding to marriage questions. An overwhelming number of people wanted to know how to overcome relationship challenges.

The Betars' answer shouldn't be too surprising: If you hope to have a marriage that not only goes the distance but also thrives, you need to be resilient.

What makes a couple resilient?

They devote their energy to solving problems instead of blaming each other. Criticism and accusations never unite two people.

Resilient couples also understand that even if they can't choose their circumstances, they can choose their attitude. A positive attitude is always the best way to work through a problem and resolve it.

If you want a relationship that will endure, you're going to need some stick-to-it-iveness. Resilient couples may fall down, but they help each other get up and keep moving forward . . . *together*.

> Since we are surrounded by so great a cloud of witnesses, let us also lay aside every weight, and sin which clings so closely, and let us run with endurance the race that is set before us.
> HEBREWS 12:1

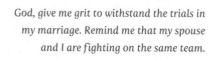

God, give me grit to withstand the trials in my marriage. Remind me that my spouse and I are fighting on the same team.

The Antibiotic of Forgiveness

The assassination of our twentieth president, James Garfield, teaches an important lesson that can save your marriage.

Let's start with *when* he was assassinated. It's hard to say exactly. He was shot on July 2, 1881, but he didn't die until seventy-nine days later on September 19.

It's also difficult to say exactly who killed him, because Garfield didn't die from his gunshot wound. He died from an infection caused by his doctors.

In those days, the medical community knew almost nothing about microbiology. So when doctors probed Garfield's wound for the assassin's bullet, they thought nothing of using dirty instruments and fingers. Within days, Garfield became ill. Within weeks, infection had spread throughout his body, and he died.

Your marriage can survive a bullet. Adultery, financial disaster, and other problems are tough to get through, but they won't deal the fatal blow to your relationship. *That* comes from deadly relationship germs that overtake you, like resentment, bitterness, and jealousy.

There's only one antibiotic for those kinds of infections: forgiveness. Only forgiveness will heal your wounds and bring you—and your marriage—back to life.

> Judge not, and you will not be judged; condemn not, and you will not be condemned; forgive, and you will be forgiven.
> LUKE 6:37

Father, You can bring us through so much together, but if we refuse to forgive each other, it is all for naught. Help us forgive each other today and every day.

"Good Enough"

Nobody wants a bad marriage . . . and nobody can have a perfect one. So how can you find your relationship sweet spot?

World-renowned therapist and researcher Dr. John Gottman says the marriage sweet spot is what he calls "good enough" marriages. That may not inspire visions of love and romance—in fact, a "good enough" marriage kind of sounds like you're waving a white flag, like you're only happy because you've lowered your expectations so far that misery doesn't feel so bad anymore.

But it's not like that at all, according to Dr. Gottman. He says "good enough" marriages don't settle for anything. They're strong in three important areas: respect, love, and affection. Happy couples don't always agree. But if they're affectionate, and if they love and respect each other, they almost always report feeling good about their marriage.

There's something quietly special about ordinary couples who love each other—however imperfectly—and cherish their lives together. That kind of meaningful commitment may not set off fire alarms in your romance, but it's the backbone of any healthy marriage.

Don't ever stop pursuing all that your marriage *can* be, but recognize that, in the meantime, "good enough" really is good enough.

As you wish that others would do to you, do so to them.
LUKE 6:31

Father, despite all the imperfections in me, in my spouse, and in our marriage, help me treat my beloved with respect, love, and affection. Help me focus on cherishing the gift You have given me in my partner rather than nurture unrealistic expectations.

Contempt for Contempt

Y ou can learn a lot about what to do in marriage by observing other married couples. You can also learn what *not* to do.

Like the couple author Gary Thomas met for dinner one night. When Gary asked the man about his profession (he was a chef), the wife criticized him before he even had a chance to answer. "He's not a chef," she said. "He's just a cook. A chef prepares full meals. He just heats things up."

In truth, the man ran a fully staffed kitchen at a retirement home that fed nearly two hundred residents every day. However, a tight operating budget prevented him from making every meal from scratch, so he and his staff filled out their menu with side items that were repurposed and heated up.

You can't help but wonder what that wife thought she was accomplishing. Did she really think that treating her husband with contempt was going to benefit their relationship?

Contempt has never produced a more fulfilling or happy marriage. Instead, have *contempt* for contempt. Cherish your husband. It'll open his heart to you.

When you pass through the waters, I will be with you; and through the rivers, they shall not overwhelm you; when you walk through fire you shall not be burned, and the flame shall not consume you.
ISAIAH 43:2

Lord God in heaven, I do not hold contempt for You.
I appreciate what You have done for me in my life.
Let me not hold my spouse in contempt. Rather, help
me treat my spouse with utmost appreciation.

Laughing Together

With so much bad news bombarding us every day, the old saying "Laughter is good for the soul" is more important than ever.

Drs. Les and Leslie Parrott, who are authors and marriage experts, have identified some ways husbands and wives can inject a little bit of humor into their marriage. For example, they encourage spouses not to take themselves so seriously all the time. A heated discussion or argument can easily be defused if the participants are willing to look at the big picture and laugh at themselves a little.

The Parrotts also advise couples to laugh even when they don't feel like laughing. If you've had a long and tough day at work, that's the best time to laugh. Spouses need to help each other find something to laugh about.

It's also important to know what makes your spouse laugh. Some people appreciate dry humor. Others enjoy goofy jokes. Or maybe you get the giggles when you're watching an old TV show like *I Love Lucy* or *Andy Griffith*. Pay attention to the kinds of things that make your spouse laugh, and then try to incorporate those into your day.

> Sarah said, "God has made laughter for me; everyone who hears will laugh over me."
> GENESIS 21:6

Lord, please help my spouse and me laugh even when we do not feel like laughing. Please remind us of Sarah, who felt joy and laughter even at an elderly age. Prompt in our minds the moments we shared that we can laugh about together.

Don't Try to Go It Alone!

Are you looking for ways to keep your relationship vibrant? Consider allowing another couple to mentor you.

Authors Bill and Pam Farrel decided early in their relationship to be intentional about building a healthy marriage. Key to their strategy was seeking out older couples who had been married for years, had a stable relationship, and were genuinely happy together. When they came across folks who fit that description, Bill would ask, "You two look like you are in love. How did you do it?" The usual response was, "There's no simple answer to that. Let's get together and talk about it."

Although the Farrels didn't realize it at the time, these older couples were mentoring them in their marriage. The immediate impact was that Bill and Pam were taught how to prepare the groundwork for a lasting relationship. But it also planted seeds that eventually blossomed into books and seminars the Farrels have since used to strengthen marriages all over the world.

If you're newly married, seek out the wisdom of those with years of gratifying experience. And if you possess that kind of relationship, take a young couple under your wing. You never know what your investment might produce.

> Where there is no guidance, a people falls, but in an abundance
> of counselors there is safety.
> PROVERBS 11:14

*Father, lead us to other couples who can share
with us their marriage wisdom—as well as, in
time, couples we can mentor and encourage.*

Three Tips for a Better Marriage

To make a good marriage great—or to infuse a struggling marriage with new life—give the following three ideas a try.

First, work to limit sarcasm. The word *sarcasm* comes from a Greek verb that is sometimes translated as "to tear flesh." Sarcasm strips a joke of its humor and replaces it with anger, resentment, and jealousy. There's often a thorn beneath the laugh that jabs people. Instead of sarcasm, season your words with love and respect.

Second, make a daily habit of expressing gratitude and appreciation. Try this: Place five coins in your right pocket. Every time you tell your spouse "Thank you" or "I appreciate you," move one coin to the left pocket. Every time you correct, criticize, or complain, move a coin from left to right. Then challenge yourself: How many days in a row can you move all five coins from the right pocket to the left?

Third, control your conflict by scheduling your disagreements. Work to avoid regular conflicts about things that are emotionally distressing by structuring when those conversations take place. Discuss such problems on odd days, or even days, or on Wednesday nights. Control your conflict instead of allowing your conflict to control your relationship.

Let all bitterness and wrath and anger and clamor and slander be put away from you, along with all malice.
EPHESIANS 4:31

Lord, empower us to communicate with love and respect. Infuse our daily interactions with gratitude. May Your divine presence enrich us with a marriage that reflects the beauty of Your enduring love.

Learn Your Tools

If I do say so myself, I have an outstanding set of tools in my garage. I have hammers, chisels, a circular saw, a miter saw, a router—almost every tool a guy could want.

The trouble is that I'm not much of a handyman. I've never learned how to use most of my tools. That circular saw? I've never operated it. The router? I'm not entirely sure what it's for. As a result, this collection of tools is not particularly useful to me.

A lot of men face the same problem in marriage. They have all the necessary tools for building a good relationship, but they don't know how to use them. Like the tool of communication. In many marriages, women talk to share feelings, not to share facts. There's what your wife *says*, and then there's what your wife *means*.

Romance is another tool men should learn about. Know your wife's love language. Understand what makes her feel valued. Discover her likes and dislikes. Celebrate the little quirks that make her uniquely her.

Conflict resolution is also important. Marriage isn't about *me*, it's about *we*. Resolving conflict isn't about winning an argument; it's about two people tackling a problem instead of each other.

I encourage men to become experts in their wives—to learn as much as possible about how to craft a positive relationship. After all, our tools are only useful when we know how to use them.

All things should be done decently and in order.
I CORINTHIANS 14:40

*Lord, grant me the wisdom to become an
expert in my wife in ways that foster love,
understanding, and unity in my marriage.*

Untangle the Knot

Almost every couple has what's known as a Gordian knot—a problem in their marriage they can't seem to untangle.

My wife and I had a hard time figuring out which of us should be responsible for our boys when I got home from work. Jean was exhausted after chasing a five- and a three-year-old all day. When I stepped inside the door at night, she was usually right there waiting for me.

"Take them," she said. That was her hello. I knew she was tired, but I'd often had a long, grueling day of my own. We were both desperate for time to recharge, but we couldn't seem to figure out how to solve the problem and help each other.

Your marriage's knot might be a financial problem, a sexual issue, or wounds from your past. Whatever the disagreements that seem impossible to overcome in your relationship, remember this: The Gordian knot is a myth. In ancient literature the Gordian knot was unsolvable, but that doesn't have to be true for your marriage. Problems often have more solutions than you might think. In our case, Jean suggested that I take fifteen minutes after I got home to decompress from my day. Then the kids were all mine for a while.

Some problems are more complicated, and so are the solutions. But if you're willing to get creative, seek wise counsel, and stay open to compromise, I'm guessing you can figure out how to unravel your knot together.

> I appeal to you, brothers, by the name of our Lord Jesus Christ,
> that all of you agree, and that there be no divisions among you,
> but that you be united in the same mind and the same judgment.
> I CORINTHIANS 1:10

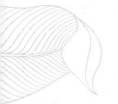

God, may Your love anchor us through turbulent times
and empower us to overcome conflicts together, hand
in hand. Loosen the knots that tangle our relationship
so we can untie them and our marriage can be free.

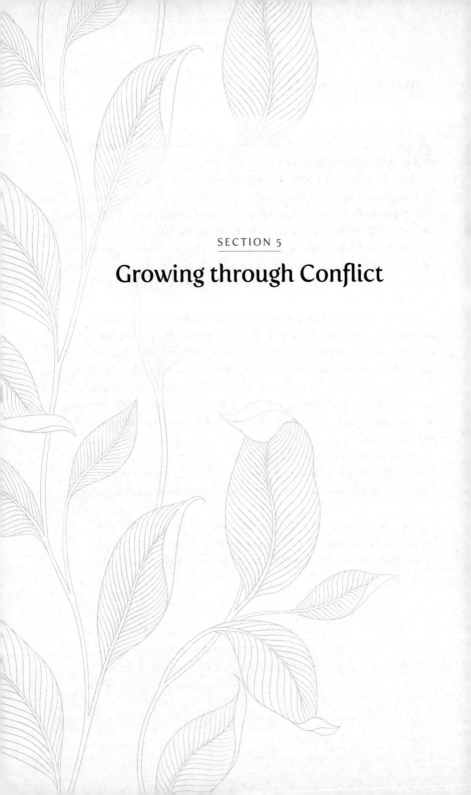

SECTION 5

Growing through Conflict

Your Spouse Is Not the Enemy

Do you ever feel as if you're enemies with your spouse? As though you're pitted against each other when you should be working together? It starts with a disagreement and ends with the couple bitterly locked in a me-versus-you mentality. But it doesn't have to be that way.

Remember that you're on the same team. When I played football, my teammates and I may have had our differences, but our "enemy" was the opposing team, not each other. My wife and I have sought to approach our marriage in the same way. We don't agree on everything, but we direct our energy toward solving the problems we need to work through.

To achieve unity in your marriage, talk about the conflict that has driven a wedge between you. It can take some time to work through those matters, and maybe even the help of a counselor. But it's an important step. Unresolved conflict leads to resentment and bitterness, and it's why couples can't get on the same page.

So learn how to embrace the differences in your relationship and work together as a couple. Make your spouse your teammate, not your adversary.

Better is a dinner of herbs where love is than a fattened ox and hatred with it.

PROVERBS 15:17

> Dear Lord, please help my spouse and me direct
> our energy toward solving the conflict wedged
> between us. Help us remember that we are not
> bitter enemies, but loving teammates.

How You Fight Is Important

Both of you see the world through different eyes, so it's inevitable that you'll disagree on some things. But remember this: What you argue about is far less important than *how* you argue.

Some couples fight with one goal in mind: winning the argument at all costs. Instead of trying to understand each other's point of view, they fight to get their own way. That's when things can get ugly with name calling, criticism, or even verbal abuse or physical threats. These are destructive behaviors that will scar your marriage long after your disagreement has been resolved or abandoned.

A better idea is to pursue a solution that works for both of you. You can work through almost anything if your ultimate goal is the health and well-being of your relationship. The more complicated the issue, the more important healthy choices become.

You can be defensive, or you can be open to your spouse's feelings. You can be self-righteous, or you can be humble. You can be stubborn, or you can be understanding.

Winning an argument is a hollow victory if you're wrecking your marriage in the process. Make a strong relationship your goal. Attack the problem, not each other.

Let all that you do be done in love.
1 CORINTHIANS 16:14

*Father, attacking my spouse to win an argument
is the antithesis of love. As disagreements arise
in my marriage—and they inevitably will—
guide me in my motives, words, and deeds.
Let all that I do and say be done in love.*

He Said, She Said

Sometimes, instead of dealing with an actual problem, couples fight over each other's *perception* of the problem.

I once returned home from a trip and saw a note my wife, Jean, had taped to our refrigerator door regarding one of our boys. It read: *Trent owes six dollars for a toy he bought at the store.* Jean then came downstairs and said, "Trent already spent his money. Don't give him any more!"

And so began one of the oddest disagreements Jean and I have ever had. We didn't argue about an actual mistake I had made but about something she perceived that I did too often and might have done again!

Sometimes perception is everything. How many husbands and wives argue over who does more around the house? Who spends money less wisely? Who takes a greater role with the kids? A healthy conversation will uncover the true problem. But arguing about perception simply throws more dirt on top of it.

Instead, get on the same page about where your issues really lie. The more understanding you share, the more effectively you both can identify what the true problem is and resolve it.

Whoever keeps his mouth and his tongue keeps himself out of trouble.
PROVERBS 21:23

Father, it's so easy to assume the worst of each other, arguing over generalities or things we fear our spouse may do. Rather than spinning our wheels arguing about what-ifs, give us the wisdom and courage to address what needs to be addressed in ways that are fruitful and honoring.

Selfish Demands vs. Selflessness

You know what they say: It's a dog-eat-dog world. To make it in life, you have to be aggressive and forceful, never taking no for an answer. But whether you're building a business or building a marriage, demanding your own way only creates problems.

There's a business phenomenon known as the "winner's curse" when two companies enter a bidding war. Negotiations eventually drive a contract's price beyond what is reasonable for one of the companies to pay. At that point, otherwise savvy business leaders may do something strange: They'll refuse to allow their competitor to win the contract. The outbidden company will stubbornly push ahead to secure the deal anyway. This is usually the case when people are so determined to get their way that they lose sight of what's most important.

There's something akin to a "winner's curse" in marriage as well. Spouses often demand their own way without considering what's best for their marriage. It's a selfish attitude that weakens the relationship. A healthy marriage, on the other hand, is based on mutual respect and treating both spouses' interests equally.

Decisions in marriage can no longer be about what's best for me; they have to be about what's best for us.

Let each of you look not only to his own interests, but also to the interests of others.

PHILIPPIANS 2:4

God, please nudge me when a selfish attitude
begins to weaken my marriage. Help me keep my
self-interest from overwhelming my thinking.

Assume the Best of Your Spouse

A common mistake in marriage is to assume the worst about each other. It's like a cartoon strip that features a husband who's clearly in trouble with his wife. There's a thought bubble over his head with a list of what happened and why. His wife is reaching into his thought bubble with a Sharpie and replacing his view of things with her own.

According to brain studies, that cartoon isn't so far off. Just like that illustration, our minds love narrative arcs with a beginning, a middle, and an end. So when our spouse's actions don't immediately make sense to us, we seek closure by filling in the gaps. We make up stories about what happened. And why.

But our brains don't always get the details right. Our minds tolerate inaccuracy as long as the narrative we're feeding them feels complete. You'll believe your spouse is late or overspending for all kinds of bad reasons . . . as long as the story connects the dots in your mind.

Negative assumptions stir up conflict. Instead, stir up a little trust and respect. Assume the *best* about your spouse. Get out of your mate's thought bubble, and fill up your own with truth, grace, and love.

Lead me in your truth and teach me, for you are the God of my salvation; for you I wait all the day long.

PSALM 25:5

Lord, lead me in Your truth in all aspects of my life and marriage. Teach me not to assume or think the worst about my spouse, especially when we face a disagreement.

Tips for Fighting Well

Do you and your spouse fight well? Every couple disagrees, but healthy couples resolve problems while protecting the relationship.

First, when healthy couples disagree, they listen respectfully to each other. Many couples are so determined to win that they don't listen to each other or focus on actually resolving the problem.

Second, healthy couples stay calm and constructive. No matter how passionate they feel about their disagreement, they avoid yelling and calling each other names. Not only will destructive behavior not solve anything, but it'll drive a wedge between a husband and wife as well.

And third, healthy couples never threaten divorce. Emotions can run high in an argument. If a spouse needs to, he or she can walk out of the room to calm down, but threats to end the marriage should never be made. At best, that's a way to manipulate the situation so that one spouse gets his or her own way. At worst, it'll damage the relationship well beyond the issue the couple is arguing about.

So remember: Even healthy couples disagree. They *remain* healthy by treating each other with respect even in the midst of conflict. Toxic fighting is about winning the argument. Healthy fighting is about resolving the problem while preserving the relationship.

A man of wrath stirs up strife, and one given to anger causes much transgression.
PROVERBS 29:22

God, I long to honor and serve my spouse even in conflict. Use our conflict to help us grow in intimacy together.

It's My Spouse's Fault

Almost every marriage in crisis shares an identical problem: At least one spouse has a habit of blaming his or her own poor behavior on the other. A husband blames his wife for his affair. Or a wife blames her husband for her unhappiness. Or they blame each other for angry outbursts, critical attitudes, pornography, alcohol addictions, and so on.

Blaming avoids responsibility and keeps a marriage stuck in conflict and at high risk for divorce. After all, if a problem is your fault, then you're the one who needs to change, not me. That attitude prevents couples from getting to the source of their issues and resolving them.

If you're stuck in the blame game, there's only one way to turn things around: recognizing that your behavior is your own responsibility.

Your spouse may have a knack for getting under your skin and provoking you. Still, how you respond is up to you. You can choose to meet your spouse's poor choices head-on with a healthy response of your own.

It takes some humility. But when each partner acknowledges his or her own shortcomings and refuses to shift blame, even the most difficult conflict has a chance of resolution.

Those of crooked heart are an abomination to the LORD, but those of blameless ways are his delight.
PROVERBS 11:20

God, steer our marriage clear of blaming each other. It's easy to point fingers and attack when we're hurt or upset. Help us choose life-giving words today and always.

Attack Your Conflict

Simple misunderstandings in marriage can easily escalate. Author Jen Weaver and her husband traveled together while she was on business, and they returned home on her birthday, upon which she was hoping to be treated to dinner. She even dropped hints about her expectations a few days before. But he hadn't planned a thing.

That situation didn't escalate into conflict because Jen took her own advice. She tells her readers to ATTACK the conflict, not each other:

Acknowledge your role in the disagreement.

Tell your spouse how you wish *you* had handled the situation differently.

Talk about how you can approach conflict the next time.

Ask what your spouse wants.

Compliment your spouse for what he or she did right.

Kiss each other and move on.

Marriage won't always go the way you expect it to. But how you and your spouse manage conflict will significantly impact the quality of your relationship.

So the next time you're standing at the crossroads of conflict together, remember to attack your conflict. Not each other.

Good sense makes one slow to anger, and it is his glory to overlook an offense.
PROVERBS 19:11

Jesus, You are the Prince of Peace. Allow us to love each other well and overlook offenses by helping us attack our conflict and not each other.

Take a Time-Out

Time-outs are a great way to help kids cool off when their emotional pot is about to boil over. But did you know that time-outs can be good for husbands and wives too?

Some of the ugliest marital conflicts are when spouses react instead of respond to each other. She says or does something, and he fires right back with a thoughtless word of anger. A simple disagreement quickly escalates into all-out conflict. Ignoring this common problem can do serious damage to a marriage. One of the best solutions for taming marital conflict comes right out of parenting handbooks: Take a time-out.

The primary rule of time-outs is to call one as soon as you feel you're getting upset. Tell your spouse, "I'm upset, and I need a break before I can discuss this. Can we talk about this in an hour or so?" Be sure to negotiate a time to come back together so you're not simply avoiding the issue. Then find a quiet place to collect your thoughts, honestly assess your reactions, and decide how best to respond. It's a great way to navigate through emotional issues and to resolve disagreements instead of making them worse.

The heart of the righteous ponders how to answer, but the mouth of the wicked pours out evil things.
PROVERBS 15:28

I am grateful that time-outs can defuse conflict with my spouse. Lord, help me lean into these cooling-off periods as a way to hear Your voice and respond to my spouse with openness and love.

Win Any Argument

There are simple ways to win every argument you have with your spouse—but there *is* a catch.

1. Yell and scream. If you shout over your spouse, you'll never hear your spouse. If you can't hear your partner, you can claim the win.
2. If that doesn't work, give your spouse the silent treatment. It dismisses your partner's arguments and dismisses your partner.
3. When everything else fails, drag your friends and family into the argument. Your spouse will use up so much energy in self-defense, there will be nothing left to fight you.

You'll win any argument against your spouse with these three guaranteed tactics, but there's just one catch: You'll lose your marriage.

Making victory your goal in an argument is a dead end. Your marriage will turn adversarial. Your spouse will become your opponent to defeat. So if you're wounding or manipulating your spouse to get your way, you lose even when you win.

The goal isn't to win an argument for yourself, it's to win it *together*. Treat each other with love and respect. Find solutions that benefit both of you. Make your goal victory, for sure. But not just for *you*—for your marriage.

A soft answer turns away wrath, but a harsh word stirs up anger.
PROVERBS 15:1

Help me not use harsh words against my spouse to prove my points. I am grateful Your Spirit lives inside me to guide my tongue with gentleness and peace.

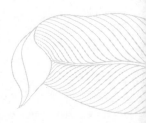

Humor: A Bridge to Reconciliation

Sometimes it is best to ease marital tension with laughter.

In his book *Ragman and Other Cries of Faith*, Walter Wangerin Jr. describes how he and his wife lived in a small apartment when they were first married. When they had disagreements, Walter would often storm out the front door and walk until he cooled down.

On one occasion, he grabbed his coat and huffed out but shut his coat in the door. It was pouring rain. He stood there getting soaked and thinking of what he should do. He could slip off his coat and walk in the rain without it, or he could ring the bell and wait for his wife to open the door, facing certain embarrassment.

Walter chose to ring the bell. The door immediately opened, and his wife laughed uncontrollably. She could see that Walter's coat was stuck in the door, but she'd waited to see what he would do. Reflecting back on that moment, Walter admits that he could have laughed along with her and allowed humor to become a bridge to reconciliation. But he refused. Instead he gathered up his coat and walked off into the rainy evening— a prisoner of his own refusal to laugh.

Let's all learn from Walter's experience. Don't miss opportunities to connect with your spouse through humor, even amid conflict. By humbling yourself, you can strengthen your bond as a couple.

A time to weep, and a time to laugh; a time to mourn, and a time to dance.

ECCLESIASTES 3:4

Jesus, You are such a heartwarming role model of when to weep and when to be glad. May laughter be a winsome characteristic of my marriage. Teach us both to laugh freely, especially at our silly mistakes.

The Positive Side of Conflict

The presence of conflict doesn't necessarily mean a relationship is in trouble. In fact, certain kinds of conflict can actually be an indicator that a relationship is strong.

There's a positive side to why spouses are at odds. Conflict can easily occur when two people are close. Husbands and wives know each other inside and out, so it's easier for them to rub each other the wrong way. Although that dynamic has the potential to create problems, it also shows there's an intimate bond.

Spouses can also argue because they're both thinking, opinionated adults. They know what they like, what they want, and what they believe. Again, that can create challenges, but on its own, it's one of the characteristics that can make a marriage truly great.

And believe it or not, spouses often have conflict because they really love each other. Each partner genuinely cares about what the other says and does. This can lead to some heated exchanges, but it's usually for a good cause.

Every relationship is susceptible to conflict, especially one as close as marriage. That's why it's important to handle conflict in a healthy way so you build up your relationship rather than tearing it down.

For the moment all discipline seems painful rather than pleasant, but later it yields the peaceful fruit of righteousness to those who have been trained by it.
HEBREWS 12:11

Remind me that conflict can bring about greater intimacy. Use the conflict in my marriage to transform me into Your likeness.

Through Your Spouse's Eyes

I remember an awkward moment for me and my wife while we were at a friend's house for dinner. Everything was fine until the host couple got into a brief argument at the table.

When we got into the car later that night, I turned to Jean and said, "Can you believe he started a fight with her right there at the dinner table?" Jean responded, "What do you mean? She's the one who started it."

We talked about our friends' argument all the way home. We were amazed that we had each noticed entirely different behavior from the wife and from the husband. Looking back, it's no surprise. Jean and I are different—in a lot of ways. In fact, the list of differences is remarkable. It's why we each see the world through unique eyes.

I'm sure you know what I mean. You're probably as different from your spouse as I am from Jean. It's why you see relationships differently—including your own. It's also why you may have a hard time settling your disagreements.

My suggestion? Change your viewpoint. The solution you're looking for might lie somewhere in the overlap of your and your spouse's perspectives.

Have nothing to do with foolish, ignorant controversies; you know that they breed quarrels.
2 TIMOTHY 2:23

God, I am desperate to see through my spouse's eyes and, more importantly, Yours. Take off my prideful blinders and guide me into humility.

The Fire of Conflict

Persistent conflict in a relationship can be just as destructive to a home as a fire. It can leave a marriage and a family decimated. The solution is to remember that, just like a fire, conflict can't burn without three key elements: combustion, fuel, and oxygen.

The *combustion* of conflict is whatever ignites the disagreement a couple is fighting about. Until the issue is resolved, it'll continue to cause problems in the marriage.

The *fuel* is the unhealthy way the couple communicates about their issue. If there's yelling or harsh words, it'll keep the conflict going.

The *oxygen* is unresolved anger or negative feelings toward a spouse. It's impossible to solve conflict when spouses assume the worst about each other.

Remove any one of those three elements, and a flame can't burn. But with a fire of conflict, you need to remove them all. Ultimately, you must resolve the disagreement. To do that, you and your spouse have to be able to talk things through respectfully. And to do *that*, you need to get beneath the surface and heal the negative emotions you feel for your spouse.

> Refrain from anger, and forsake wrath! Fret not yourself; it tends only to evil.
> PSALM 37:8

Father, life will always hand us things to disagree about. Help me remember that while I can't always control what comes our way, I do have control over how I respond. Don't let me add fuel to the fire with harsh words or hidden anger!

Fight It Out

The foundation of marriage is actually weakened when we avoid healthy conflict in the interest of keeping the peace. Even the most emotionally stable and well-rounded of couples need to hash things out from time to time.

With that in mind, family counselor Matthew Turvey has developed a list of three principles to help couples embrace healthy conflict:

1. Remember that emotions are nothing to avoid or be afraid of. Emotions just *are*. Husbands and wives need to learn to celebrate them in all their messiness, complexity, joy, and pain.
2. The more you can understand your spouse's emotions, the better you can understand the message behind his or her words. Learn from these emotions.
3. Marriage simply works better when spouses work through conflict and honestly confront emotions. Men, it may not sound manly, but your ability to cry with your wife and to better understand her pain will lead to increased intimacy in other areas of your relationship.

The bottom line is that avoiding conflict will hurt your marriage rather than help it. Don't be afraid to bring things out into the open and address them head-on.

If your brother sins against you, go and tell him his fault, between you and him alone. If he listens to you, you have gained your brother.
MATTHEW 18:15

Lord God, we need Your help to emotionally understand each other. Help us properly navigate conflict in our lives so that we honor each other in a godly way.

Is Your Marriage in Trouble?

E very marriage has conflict. Yet some couples thrive, some get by, and some are in deep trouble. Which category does your marriage fall into?

When the lawn mower broke down, Toby's wife asked him repeatedly to take care of it. He meant to, but he was always too busy. One day, to embarrass him into fixing the mower, she sat down in the lawn and began clipping it with a pair of scissors. Toby watched for a few minutes, and then he came out of the house with a toothbrush. "When you finish cutting the grass," he said, "you might as well sweep the driveway."

Well, if Toby's marriage isn't in trouble yet, it soon will be. But it won't be because he and his wife experienced conflict. It'll be because they don't have the skills to resolve their disagreements. A key indicator of what separates a marriage that thrives from one that's in trouble is the ability to ease the sarcasm and work through issues.

That may come as a surprise to couples who've been taught that a successful relationship has no conflict. No, a healthy marriage is where spouses learn to work together and find common ground in areas where they don't see eye to eye.

When the cares of my heart are many, your consolations cheer
my soul.
PSALM 94:19

---

*Father, it's easy to console and cheer my spouse
when outside circumstances are creating stress.
It's not so easy when the thing that is stressing
my spouse is me. Help us both learn how to
navigate conflict in a way that draws us closer
rather than creates distance between us.*

Fight for the Right Things

A malaria epidemic more than a hundred years ago illustrated what happens when we fail to recognize the true source of a problem. In the early years of the Panama Canal's construction, more than twenty-five thousand men got sick and died—almost two hundred a month at one point. And for a time, no one understood why it was happening.

It was not widely known at the time that mosquitoes transmitted infectious diseases like yellow fever and malaria, so nothing was done to control them. So when Panama's rainy season came, pools of standing water—where mosquitoes breed—were everywhere. They were in the streets, in drainage ditches, and even in hospitals, where pans of water were placed beneath the beds to keep ants away from patients. Once the main cause of the deaths among construction workers was identified, the mosquito problem was brought under control and thousands of lives were saved.

Married couples often struggle with a similar problem. They might blame their troubles on a certain thing when the real problem lies somewhere else. For example, have you ever argued with your spouse about what's for dinner when you're actually irritated about a completely different issue? We sometimes focus on the wrong thing while the true problem goes unresolved.

Building a marriage that lasts a lifetime isn't easy. You have to fight for it. The key is to fight for the right things.

You will know the truth, and the truth will set you free.
JOHN 8:32

Heavenly Father, help us seek truth in our marriage.
Focus our attention on the right things so minor
issues won't overshadow our true problems.

Jump First

Like many kids, I was pretty adventurous growing up. One day a buddy and I were out exploring the woods when we stumbled upon a small ravine. We quickly calculated the distance across and the drop to the bottom. It presented the perfect measure of potential danger. We could probably make it across, but it would be risky. There was just one obstacle.

Which one of us was going to jump first?

That's human nature, isn't it? Whether it's two kids jumping over a ravine or a married couple trying to resolve conflict, we naturally want the other person to take the first step. In marriage, that attitude often leaves us stuck. Blaming each other for conflict rather than taking responsibility for our own choices can erode trust and stunt growth in our relationship. It prevents us from finding solutions to our disagreements. And that's when human nature gets in the way . . .

Somebody has to jump first!

If your marriage is struggling, humility is essential. Instead of waiting for your spouse to change, consider what *you* can do to move your relationship in a positive direction. Then be courageous and take the first step.

After all, someone has to.

[Love] does not insist on its own way; it is not irritable or resentful; it does not rejoice at wrongdoing, but rejoices with the truth.
1 CORINTHIANS 13:5-6

God, grant me the humility to take the initiative in resolving conflict. Guide both of us along our journey of reconciliation, and lead us to unity and peace.

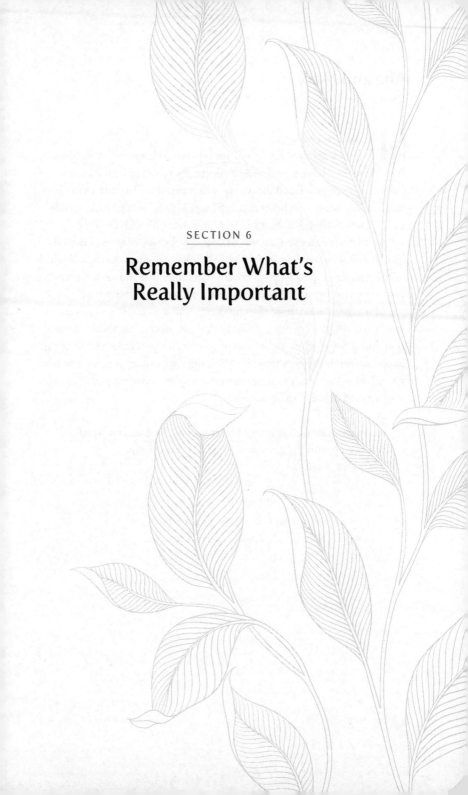

SECTION 6

Remember What's Really Important

Abe and Mary

Marriage can be tough.

Consider President Abraham Lincoln's relationship with Mary Todd Lincoln. She was reportedly a contentious woman with a vicious temper. Because of mental illness, she was institutionalized for a time later in life. Once she was so upset that she barged into a presidential meeting Lincoln was having with heads of state and threw his drink in his face.

Another time, a salesman was so upset by the way Mary had treated him that he went straight to the Oval Office to complain. Lincoln listened to the complaint, put his hand on the man's shoulder, and said, "Surely you can endure for fifteen minutes what I've endured for fifteen years."

Marriage is about more than just our happiness. It's about growing us into better people. I'm not suggesting that you tolerate an abusive situation, but if you're about to bail out of your marriage because you're not as happy as you think you should be, you might reconsider your view of marriage. Just as important as happiness is serving one another, giving to one another, and learning to be patient.

> I consider that the sufferings of this present time are not worth comparing with the glory that is to be revealed to us.
> ROMANS 8:18

God, give me grit to endure the trials in my marriage. Use them to transform me and to make me more like You.

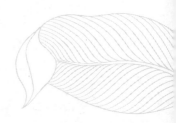

Two Men and a Donkey

Keep your marriage strong by keeping the main thing the main thing. The importance of that is illustrated in one of the classic fables attributed to Aesop. A man rented a donkey to carry him across a scorching desert. He also hired the donkey's owner to be his guide. Halfway through their journey, they stopped to take shelter from the hot sun in the donkey's shadow. But there wasn't enough room for both men.

They argued over who owned the donkey's shadow. The one man stated he had rented the donkey and its shadow as well. The donkey's owner claimed that the man had only rented the donkey's labor. Nothing else.

They argued so vigorously that both men forgot to keep hold of the donkey's reins. Frightened by all the shouting, the donkey ran off, leaving both men stranded in the desert with no shade to protect them.

The lesson for married couples? Bad things happen when you lose focus in your marriage. You'll fight over trivial matters. You'll turn little things into big things and escalate conflict.

Successful couples resolve their disagreements by working together in the same direction. They stay focused on finding common ground . . . and keeping the main thing the main thing.

Trust in the LORD with all your heart, and do not lean on your own understanding.
PROVERBS 3:5

Lord, how easy it is to lean on my own understanding and want my way in my marriage. Help me stay focused on You and working together with my spouse so we keep the main thing the main thing.

Contract or Covenant?

Divorce is a serious problem because society doesn't understand the true depth of the marriage relationship.

Most couples marry dreaming about love, romance, and happiness together. But what happens when conflict erupts? A lot of times the magic disappears. What was once beautiful turns ugly. But those difficulties actually reflect marriage at its most glorious . . . if you understand the difference between contracts and covenants.

Contracts define people's individual rights. A contract defines what is fair for each person and creates a way out if either person fails to hold up his or her end of the deal. It's a way of saying, "I'll go only as far as you go. If you mess up, I'm out." Marriage as a contract is all wrong, and it's why so many fail.

Marriage is a covenant. Biblical covenants seal relationships that are bound by love and trust, not individual rights. The marriage covenant treats couples as one, bonded together through sickness and health, for better or worse. They're a way of saying, "Even if you don't hold up your end of the deal, I'll hold up mine."

So if problems have erupted in your marriage, don't give up; get to work. That's when you'll discover the deep richness that marriage was meant to be.

> So will I ever sing praises to your name, as I perform my vows day after day.
> PSALM 61:8

Lord, keep me mindful that my wedding vows are a sacred covenant between the three of us: You, my spouse, and me. Kindle my mind and heart not to give up but to work on improving my marriage day by day.

My Spouse Has Changed!

Some of you are newly married, but already your spouse seems like a different person from the one you dated. It could be because your partner changed. But there's another possibility.

What if your spouse is the same, but you're seeing your mate through different eyes? More than likely you've taken off your rose-colored courtship glasses. Before the wedding, each partner often feels invigorated by their mate's differences. But it's usually not long into marriage before those character traits start becoming annoyances that drive the couple apart. It's a common problem.

That's actually good news because it means the solutions are common as well. You can begin by sitting down and listing all the reasons you chose to marry your spouse. Then start valuing those differences the way you used to. It really is a choice you can learn to make. Don't give in to negative and critical thoughts. Offer your spouse your appreciation and positivity instead.

It's possible your spouse *has* changed. But it's just as likely that your perspective could use a little readjustment as well. Give it a try. I think you'll find that a lot of what bugs you about your spouse will disappear once you change the way you look at him or her.

That their hearts may be encouraged, being knit together in love.
COLOSSIANS 2:2

Lord, encourage our hearts to see each other as You see us—beloved and accepted in You. Remove any blinders from my eyes that cloud my perspective on the reasons why I married my spouse in the first place.

A Husband's Sacrifice

How would you react if there was a good chance you only had moments left to live?

On January 8, 2011, seventy-six-year-old Dorwan Stoddard and his wife, Mavy, attended a public appearance outside Tucson by Arizona congresswoman Gabrielle Giffords. That's where a gunman opened fire on the crowd, killing six people and wounding thirteen others.

In the chaos, Dorwan shielded his wife from the rain of bullets and literally saved her. Mavy sustained gunshot wounds to her legs. Dorwan Stoddard, however, was hit in the head and died at the scene.

According to his pastor, Mr. Stoddard's final act symbolized the way he lived his entire life. He said, "Dory Stoddard didn't die a hero; he lived a hero." Even President Obama paid tribute when he said, "His final act of selflessness was to dive on top of his wife, sacrificing his life for hers."

Even in everyday life, we should follow Mr. Stoddard's example by putting our spouse and our family first. Hopefully we'll never have to take a bullet for them. But we need to make sure that our careers, hobbies, and interests take a back seat to those we love.

Greater love has no one than this, that someone lay down his life for his friends.

JOHN 15:13

Jesus, You made the ultimate sacrifice for us.
Help me live every day mindful of laying down
my own interests to love my family well.

Love Note from the Grave

If you suddenly died, what would your family discover on your smartphone?

One husband and father sadly passed away at age thirty-two from complications related to the coronavirus. A few days after his death, his wife opened his phone to retrieve the photos he'd taken of their family. In the process, she found an unsent message that he'd written to her and their two small children.

It began like this: "I love you guys with all my heart and you've given me the best life I could have ever asked for. I am so lucky."

His message reminded his children how precious and deeply loved they were and urged his wife to live her life with passion. What an incredible blessing in dark circumstances.

That story got me thinking. What would my wife and boys find on my phone if I died? Would they discover anything beyond work-related messages or grocery list reminders? I hope my digital footprint would mirror how deeply I loved them every day. After all, what greater gift can we offer our loved ones when we die than the certainty of how much we loved them while we were alive?

May the Lord make you increase and abound in love for one another and for all, as we do for you.
I THESSALONIANS 3:12

Loving God, what greater gift can I offer to my loved ones beyond telling them how much I love them? Bless our lives with unending times of sharing this sentiment: "I love you guys with all my heart."

When Things Don't Go as Planned

Weddings don't always go as planned. Brittany and Sean spent eleven months planning their special day. They booked a venue in Spokane, Washington, for late September and planned nearly the entire event to be outside. The changing fall colors would be a perfect backdrop for their wedding photos.

For months, the weather was warm and sunny. A week before the wedding, the sunshine turned to dark clouds and rain. The morning of the wedding, it turned to snow. Nearly twenty guests canceled because of the weather. The bride almost lost her veil in the wind, and one of the bridesmaids slipped and did a face-plant in the snow.

Yet Brittany and Sean refused to let the inclement weather ruin their special day. The important thing, they realized, wasn't their wedding day; it was their marriage.

Weddings don't always go as planned, but often neither do marriages. Every relationship is a journey into whiteout conditions. There are twists and turns that couples never see coming.

Good marriages aren't good because they're perfect or because they never face obstacles. They're good because spouses love each other and keep their relationship top priority even when things don't go as planned.

> The fig tree ripens its figs, and the vines are in blossom; they give forth fragrance. Arise, my love, my beautiful one, and come away.
> SONG OF SOLOMON 2:13

God, we thank You for meeting us in the obstacles. Continue to sustain us in those moments and remind us of what's true.

Love Isn't Self-Sustaining

Couples often assume their love will take care of itself. The truth is that you have to invest in love, or it'll die.

When Jean and I first started dating, I would occasionally drive ninety miles to where she was working to bring her dinner. During our courting days, I was willing to inconvenience myself to show my interest. But fast-forward to the early years of our marriage, and I couldn't be bothered to run an errand down the street.

That behavior change is common in relationships, and it illustrates that love isn't self-sustaining. The idea that love naturally stays alive on its own is one of the greatest relationship myths.

It's a serious mistake to stop nurturing your marriage and instead focus all your attention on other areas of life, such as work, church activities, and even your kids. One study showed that the average married couple spent an hour a week in connecting moments.

If you really want a vibrant marriage, you have to invest in it. Like so many other areas in life, it's the little things that make it successful.

Pursue righteousness, godliness, faith, love, steadfastness, gentleness.
I TIMOTHY 6:11

---

*Jesus, help me stay mindful about investing time
and commitment in my marriage. Remind me
whenever I get off course by thinking my marriage
partner doesn't need much time together with me.*

Making It Work

In our second year of marriage, Jean and I hit a little bump in the road. One night I found Jean sobbing in bed. I said, "What's the matter?" She said, "I'm not a good wife. I don't think you should be married to me." Immediately I thought, *What have I done?* And we sat in bed and talked.

She said, "I'm not good enough to be married to you." And I thought, *That's ridiculous. I'm nothing special.*

Jean shared about her depression, her lack of a healthy self-image. She was simply crying out from her heart. So I told her that I loved her so much, and that I was never going to let our marriage fail. I said, "Jean, we can only do this two ways—happily or unhappily." And then something blossomed in her. It was as if she knew that our relationship was solid.

Sometimes in our marriages, we each need to know that no matter what, the other one is there for us. Things in our past threatened to derail our relationship. Jean battled depression, and I came from a home with no father. But we determined to make our marriage work. We went to counseling. We had good friends around us. That was many years ago, and our marriage today is stronger than ever.

Many a man proclaims his own steadfast love, but a faithful man who can find?

PROVERBS 20:6

God, thank You that husbands and wives can be steadfast in love and faithfulness, even if we have negative past experiences or insecurities that threaten to derail us.

A Wedding in a Bathroom

Brian and Maria were at their county courthouse ready to say their "I dos" when Brian's mother had a severe asthma attack and rushed to the restroom. Sheriff's officers gave her oxygen while they waited for an ambulance to arrive.

Brian and Maria worried about Brian's mom while they faced another dilemma. If they didn't tie the knot that day, they'd have to wait forty-five days for a new marriage license. They didn't want to get married without Brian's mother present, but they couldn't wait, either.

The magistrate thought of a third option: Why not conduct the ceremony in the restroom where Mom was receiving care? Family video shows the bride and groom exchanging vows right there by the towel dispensers. At least their wedding was memorable, right?

By the way, the groom's mother recovered just fine, and the important thing to Brian and Maria wasn't the bells and whistles of a traditional wedding ceremony. All that mattered was their lives together afterward.

Brian and Maria have a solid grasp on what's really important. As long as they had each other, it didn't matter if they were surrounded by centerpieces and flowers . . . or paper towels and restroom stalls.

We know that for those who love God all things work together for good, for those who are called according to his purpose.
ROMANS 8:28

Father God, sometimes it's hard to see the good in the not-so-good. Thank You that You work all things together for the good of my life, my marriage, and my family. All praise to You!

How Does Your Marriage Grow?

Author Brian Lowe says he discovered an important secret to marriage in an unexpected place: his garden. He planted it one spring with big dreams and a commitment to work hard. He built four-by-four frames, mixed his own soil, and bought a variety of flower and vegetable seeds. He diligently watered and weeded.

The problem was, Brian lived in the Midwest. The weather there can be quite hot in July. Sure enough, by the end of summer Brian was waving to his garden from the comfort of his back window. And while he kept cool inside, his garden paid the price.

That experience taught him a lot about gardening—and about his marriage. He'd once had big dreams for that, too. But over time, he discovered that his relationship with his wife required the same dedication and hard work to thrive as his garden did. Without that, it wouldn't take long for weeds of conflict and the heat of resentment to overtake his marriage . . . and kill it.

Give your marriage the nutrients it needs to grow strong and healthy. Spend quality time together. Communicate. Your relationship can only thrive when you cultivate it.

> Whatever you do, in word or deed, do everything in the name of the Lord Jesus, giving thanks to God the Father through him.
> COLOSSIANS 3:17

Father, it pleases You when I take seriously the things You've given me to say and do, doing these things in Your name and with a heart of gratitude. Help me apply this principle to my marriage: to tend to my spouse and cultivate our relationship, knowing that this is pleasing to You.

True Happiness

"And they lived happily ever after." It's the stuff of fairy tales and epic stories, and it's the hope of every couple standing at a wedding altar. But is it wise to make happiness the primary goal of marriage?

Here's the problem: Happiness is an emotion—and a fickle one at that. It comes and goes with nearly every change of our circumstances. Which is the very reason that our spouse cannot make us happy all the time. No matter how hard he or she tries, over the course of life, a spouse will disappoint.

Plus, making happiness the primary goal for marriage shows we're in the relationship for what *we* can get out of it. And seeking to gratify ourselves at the expense of our spouse will destroy a relationship.

Am I suggesting we shouldn't want to be happy in our marriage? No. Of course we can be happy. But it's important to realize that true happiness comes from a deep commitment to place the needs of our spouse above our own. When a husband and wife devote themselves to each other in this way, they'll truly live happily ever after.

[Jesus] answered, "Have you not read that he who created them from the beginning made them male and female, and said, 'Therefore a man shall leave his father and his mother and hold fast to his wife, and the two shall become one flesh'?"
MATTHEW 19:4-5

Father, You didn't create marriage as a way for me to pursue my own happiness, but so I could experience oneness and union with my spouse. Thank You for the deep joy we can experience as we see our marriage—and each other—through Your eyes.

Don't Flush Your Relationship

About a year after my wife, Jean, and I got married, I came home from work and found her in the bathroom crying. When I asked her what was wrong, she said, "I flushed my wedding ring down the toilet." Back then, she kept her jewelry in a basket behind the toilet. That day, she'd hit the flusher and the basket at the same time. It had happened so fast—her wedding ring disappeared in a whirlpool before she could reach it.

I spent part of that weekend taking the toilet apart. I never found her ring. But you know what? All in all, in the greater scheme of things . . . it's okay.

The wedding ring is a symbol. A beautiful one and, might I say, expensive. But a symbol. The most important thing is the relationship itself. As long as we don't let *that* go down the toilet, we can survive losing a few other things.

Of all the things in life that can get flushed, don't let your marriage be one of them. Invest in it. Guard it. Protect it. It's far more important than even the most beautiful wedding ring.

Keep your heart with all vigilance, for from it flow the springs of life.
PROVERBS 4:23

Lord, help us protect our marriage with every fiber of our being. Especially, Lord, help us protect our hearts toward each other and toward You.

Learning to Overlook

Many couples allow every little annoyance to turn into conflict, which, of course, is not healthy for a relationship. That's why sometimes the best idea is simply to overlook minor problems and focus on your partner's positive traits instead.

Janet learned that lesson the hard way. She often complained to her friends, "John makes me so mad. I've asked him again and again to clean the bathtub, but he never does. I don't know how much longer I can take it!"

Then one morning the phone rang. "Your husband has been in an accident. You need to get down here right away!"

As Janet rushed to get dressed, she couldn't help but notice the bathtub. She started to cry. That dirty ring suddenly didn't seem so important. Instead, her mind was flooded with all John's wonderful qualities. She kicked herself for allowing something so minor to affect how she saw her husband.

What about you? Are you making mountains out of molehills? Step back and take a fresh look at your relationship. Are the things that bother you really that important? If not, maybe it's best to overlook them.

I press on toward the goal for the prize of the upward call of God in Christ Jesus.
PHILIPPIANS 3:14

Heavenly Father, let our annoyances never become the focal point of our marriage. Just as we press on toward the prize of the upward call of God in Christ, let us also press on toward another prize: a healthy and happy marriage.

Make Every Day Count

An angry bride-to-be went viral after she reportedly lashed out at her guests on social media. She complained that she wasn't getting the celebration of her dreams. She and her fiancé had saved $15,000, but the wedding they wanted cost $60,000. The bride sent a message to each of her guests: Cough up $1,500, or don't bother coming to the wedding. It probably won't surprise you to hear that most everybody declined her request. She eventually called off the wedding.

That angry bride is an extreme example of a common problem—planning a wedding, but not a marriage. The wedding industry did almost 75 billion dollars in business last year. That averages out to almost $35,000 per wedding. What's troubling about that number is that most couples will never invest a fraction of that amount in the health of their marriage.

A happy, fulfilling marriage isn't a by-product of an extravagant ceremony or an expensive honeymoon. A successful marriage is the by-product of a husband and wife who invest in their relationship daily. The marriage you're dreaming of isn't just about the "big day," it's about every day.

> Better is a little with righteousness than great revenues with injustice.
> PROVERBS 16:8

Lord, please help us focus on the most important things in marriage: the things that can be done, every day, to increase our appreciation of each other.

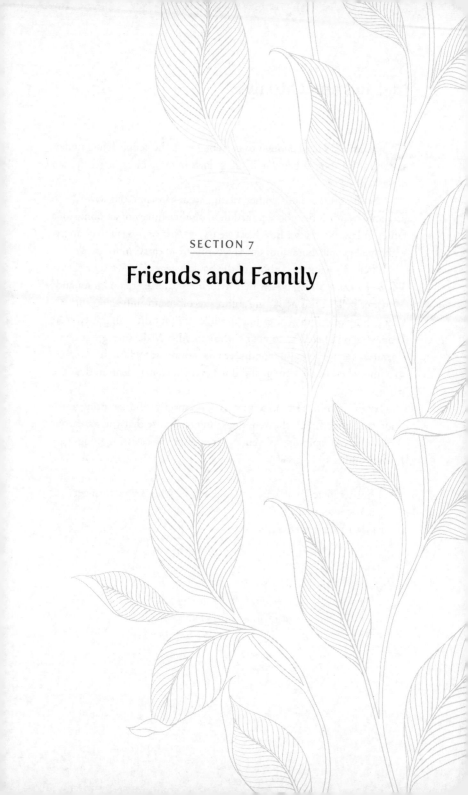

SECTION 7

Friends and Family

In-Laws and Outlaws

Sometimes it's hard enough to get along with the people living under your own roof. When you bring in-laws into the mix, the results can be downright scary.

Not all of us have difficulties relating to our in-laws. But we've probably heard stories about a meddling mother-in-law or an obnoxious father-in-law. No matter how hard we try, we just can't seem to connect with these people. Sometimes in-law conflict can carry on for *years*.

When this happens, I think of the book *Loving Your Relatives Even When You Don't See Eye-to-Eye* by David and Claudia Arp and John and Margaret Bell. In this book, the authors recommend embracing a few simple rules of civility. For example, smile, and not through gritted teeth. People respond better to someone who's smiling. Make sure you're considerate, practice restraint, and never raise your voice. Have the courage to admit when you're wrong, and don't ever ridicule or demean the other person.

Try to see things from your in-laws' perspective. Be accepting and understanding of their shortcomings, and recognize that you have your own faults and hang-ups as well. No matter how frustrating things get, just remember to be civil!

A hot-tempered man stirs up strife, but he who is slow to anger quiets contention.
PROVERBS 15:18

Heavenly Father, grant me the grace to love my family despite our conflict. Close my mouth when my heart is spewing hatred, and guide me into humility.

Is Your Spouse Your BFF?

Thinking of your spouse as your best friend is probably not as healthy as you think.

Spouses often refer to their partner as a "best friend" as a way to reflect the closeness of their marriage. That's good, but some couples mean it literally. They believe all their relational needs should be met in each other. That may sound romantic, but it's not healthy.

A strong husband-wife connection is certainly important. But it's impossible for one person to meet all our deepest relational needs. We were designed for community. Men, you need the influence of other men in your life. And ladies, you need some girlfriends who can enrich your world as well.

Expecting our marriage partner to satisfy every need for connection will smother the relationship. Both spouses will eventually feel overwhelmed by the burden of having to act as the be-all and end-all for their mate. That's where actual best friends come in. A good buddy can connect with a guy at a masculine level his wife simply can't. And the same holds true at a feminine level for a wife and her friends.

It sounds simple, but it's true: Healthy friendships won't threaten or weaken your marriage; they'll strengthen it.

A friend loves at all times, and a brother is born for adversity.
PROVERBS 17:17

Jesus, You are relational, and You know the value of close connection in marriage and friendship. Help me find a healthy balance of people who can meet my relational needs.

A Cord of Three Strands

The Bible says, "A threefold cord is not quickly broken" (Ecclesiastes 4:12). That's a simple concept to understand, but it's profound enough to transform your marriage.

A rope's durability lies in its construction. Strands of fiber work together, creating a strength they could never have on their own. That's a perfect analogy for the importance community plays in our marriages. Marriages are strongest when they're supported by three types of relationships.

The first is a couple who have been married longer than you. They're older and wiser and have the years of experience to mentor and advise you and your spouse.

The second is a couple in your peer group. These are usually friends in a similar stage of life with whom you give and receive support and encouragement. You journey through life with this couple.

The third is a younger couple whom you mentor. You're the older and wiser couple speaking into their lives. Your influence makes a positive impact in their marriage and will strengthen your own relationship.

Most couples need all the support they can get to build a thriving marriage. Surrounding yourself with three strands of support is a great strategy for strengthening your relationship for a lifetime.

When each part is working properly, [Christ] makes the body grow so that it builds itself up in love.
EPHESIANS 4:16

Lord, what a helpful way to consider our couple relationships! May our marriage grow stronger as we invest in the lives of other husbands and wives.

Marriage and In-Laws

Do you get along with your in-laws? If not, consider doing what you can to work out the kinks.

According to a national study, a man who is on good terms with his wife's parents is more likely than those who aren't to enjoy a lasting marriage. Terri Orbuch, the study's author, explained that men who bond with their in-laws send a message to their wives: "Your family is important to me because you're important to me."

My wife's dad and mom, Jerry and Pat, were married for fifty-eight years before Jerry passed away. We experienced many good times together. Neither Jerry nor Pat ever interfered in our marriage or with the raising of our boys. There was always a spirit of mutual respect between Jean's parents and me that I believe drew Jean and me closer together.

Movies and television routinely highlight in-law dysfunction. We're all familiar with stories of pushy mothers-in-law and grumpy fathers-in-law. But I wonder how often people allow those stereotypes to create division rather than ties that bind. If possible, build a solid relationship with your spouse's parents. You just might find it'll strengthen your marriage as well.

Children, obey your parents in the Lord, for this is right. "Honor your father and mother" (this is the first commandment with a promise), "that it may go well with you and that you may live long in the land."
EPHESIANS 6:1-3

Father God, thank You for my in-laws. While we may not agree on every little thing, I am grateful to have them in my life. Without them, I wouldn't have my spouse. Keep strengthening all our family bonds.

An Unexpected Way to Love Your Husband

Ladies, there's another woman in your husband's life—that's right, his mom!

It can be difficult to navigate the relationships between you, your husband, and the in-laws—and couples need to set appropriate boundaries with their parents, especially in the early years of marriage. But as you define those boundaries, don't send the message to "butt out!"

If you feel criticized every time your mother-in-law visits, do your best to neutralize the situation. Resist the urge to criticize back—even if she deserves it! She may be feeling threatened by you, and you don't need to add to her insecurity.

Instead, support your husband's relationship with his mom. My own mother passed away when I was young, but I know lots of husbands who wish their wives would reach out more to their moms. Many a wife doesn't realize that her role as a daughter-in-law is a critical part of how she can show love to her husband.

So how do you do that? Remind him to send flowers for his mom's birthday. Keep in touch on the phone or through email. And thank your mother-in-law for raising such a wonderful son. Who knows—you might just make a friend in the process.

> Strive for peace with everyone, and for the holiness without which no one will see the Lord.
> HEBREWS 12:14

Father, help me be an instrument of peace and encouragement within our extended family. You allowed my spouse to be born into his family of origin. Help me love and appreciate the people who have invested in the man who is my husband today.

A Couple's Leave of Absence

It usually takes longer than the span of a honeymoon for couples to settle into their new roles. That's why one of the best things they can do is to further the honeymoon escape and take a "leave of absence."

Dr. Greg and Erin Smalley had been married just two months when they went to England with Greg's family. It didn't go so well. Once in Europe, newlywed Greg reverted to acting like a son instead of a husband. Greg and his wife now realize they needed more time to learn their new roles and to form a unique identity as a couple.

In Greg and Erin's book *Before You Plan Your Wedding . . . Plan Your Marriage*, they suggest newlyweds take what they call a "leave of absence." This means leaving behind other areas of life for a time and giving priority to each other. This includes not only time-consuming hobbies but also regular get-togethers with friends and family.

When you emerge from this time, you'll be better able to interact with others as a husband or wife instead of settling into the familiar roles of your past. By doing so, you'll give your marriage its best chance to flourish for years to come.

For everything there is a season, and a time for every matter under heaven.

ECCLESIASTES 3:1

Lord, help us have the wisdom to leave behind
other areas of life for a moment in order
to cling to each other for a lifetime.

Double-Dating

Married couples need to spend a lot of one-on-one time together. But they also need to surround themselves with other couples who can positively influence their relationship and help strengthen it.

Your marriage is not an island. You need to interact with other couples—to invest in their lives and for them to invest in yours. How often? Well, there's no hard-and-fast rule, but making one out of every four dates a double date is a pretty reasonable goal. If you date your spouse once a week, that's one double date a month. If you and your spouse only go out once a month, you'll still squeeze in three double dates a year. That may not sound like much, but don't underestimate the impact they can make.

Relationships with other couples can help keep your marriage healthy, but they'll be especially valuable if your marriage hits a rough spot. During troubled times, couples tend to isolate themselves. Friendships will give your marriage a strong shoulder to lean on and help you get through the painful times you're facing.

We were designed for community. As individuals and as couples, we need the support and influence of others.

> Confess your sins to one another and pray for one another, that you may be healed. The prayer of a righteous person has great power as it is working.
> JAMES 5:16

Father, we need community in our lives for the good of our marriage. Please help us identify another couple that we may be friends with, confide in, pray with, and have community with. Thank You.

Help Others, Help Yourselves

Have you ever helped someone with a problem and found that you benefited more than he or she did?

James and Linda's marriage was on the verge of divorce when a counselor suggested they ask another couple to mentor them. They called Dewey and Lynne Wilson—friends they respected and who, they believed, shared a good, strong relationship.

Dewey was flattered, but embarrassed. He and Lynne had been simply coexisting for years. Their relationship looked intimate and respectable on the outside, but in reality, it was empty. How could they possibly impart to others what they didn't possess themselves?

With reservations, they agreed to mentor James and Linda. And that's when the miracle began. In the process of trying to save someone else's marriage, they were forced to reexamine and overhaul their own. What came out of that experience was a relationship grounded in substance and intimacy.

Dewey and Lynne's experience is by no means unique, and it speaks to the power of the mentoring process. So if your marriage needs strengthening, consider allowing a mentor to speak into your relationship. Then give of yourselves to other couples who are in need of help as well.

Let the word of Christ dwell in you richly, teaching and admonishing one another in all wisdom.
COLOSSIANS 3:16

Father, You created us to need each other. As we find other couples to encourage in their walks with You and with each other, let our marriage be strengthened as well.

When You "Get" Each Other

Sam and Alice had one of the great romances in television history. You remember them, don't you? Alice was the housekeeper on *The Brady Bunch*, and Sam was her boyfriend. And boy, did he take meat seriously. He owned a butcher shop. He attended the butchers' ball every year. And he finished almost every joke with a reference to some sort of meat.

So it's no surprise how he behaved in one episode when he and Alice had a misunderstanding. Sam brought Alice four lamb chops as a peace offering for the mistakes he'd made. He handed her the special cuts and said, "I just couldn't figure another way to say, 'I'm sorry.'"

Alice could have rolled her eyes at his gesture and held a dismissive attitude. But Alice "gets" Sam. She understood the significance of the four lamb chops. Which is what made her response so great. She smiled and told him, "Sam, it couldn't be better if it was 14 karat gold."

I know we're talking about a scripted sitcom here, but don't lose the significance of that moment. Giving someone a great cut of meat was a gesture from Sam's heart. And Alice knew that and honored it.

A lot of spouses don't look deeply enough into their mate's soul. They don't see the ways their spouse says "I love you" through everyday behavior. Sometimes marriage only changes when the perspective does. Through the eyes of love, even a slab of meat will look like a diamond ring.

> Love does no wrong to a neighbor; therefore, love is the fulfilling of the law.
> ROMANS 13:10

God, help me clearly see the heart of my spouse. For my part, let me view my spouse through the eyes of love.

When Young Couples Want It All

Today I have a few helpful tips for young couples who want it all—a family and a career. More than anything, remember this: *How* you handle opportunities that come your way over the next few years will either benefit your family or harm it.

Let's say your spouse is up for a big promotion, but it will require your family to relocate to another state. How will that impact *your* career? How will it impact your children? Those are big decisions. As you work through them, keep a few things in mind.

First, compliment each other. When I say *compliment*, I do mean that you should say nice things to each other. But I wish I could write both spellings at the same time, because I also mean *complement*. Work together as a team. Channel your competitiveness into your career, not your family. You and your spouse both bring something to the table that can help you decide how best to move forward.

Second, be flexible. Your responsibilities at home and at work will shift over time as the needs of your family change. Be willing to adapt.

Third, and most important of all, let the good of your marriage guide every decision you make. Career goals and a bigger earning potential are both important considerations. But more zeroes on your paycheck won't improve a bad marriage.

If you're a young couple, a healthy balance between your career and your family begins with the decisions you make today. Achieve all you can at work, but make the health of your marriage your top priority.

> This is the message that you have heard from the beginning, that we should love one another.
>
> I JOHN 3:11

Jesus, help us make the right choices today so
that our marriage will flourish tomorrow.

When Your Mate Is Different

You've probably noticed that you and your spouse don't always see eye to eye. If you're not careful, those differences can drive you apart. But it doesn't have to be that way.

When my wife, Jean, and I were first married, we discovered one of the biggest differences between us: She is a night owl, and I am a morning person. I've since learned how common simple differences like that are among couples. But at the time, it threw me. In fact, every morning for weeks I thought she was mad at me because she would barely speak until about ten o'clock. I'd wake up bubbly and excited to conquer the day. But my chipper attitude was often met with a grumbling response.

To be fair, by that evening, we had switched roles. She would be lively and ready to talk, and all I could think of doing was crawling into bed to sleep.

Differences often put a couple at odds with each other. Petty disagreements can easily turn into full-blown battles that bleed a relationship dry. That's why couples need to learn to compromise and find some middle ground. A large part of making marriage work is figuring out what hills are worth dying on and what issues are best overlooked. To do that, you have to work together to identify what's really important and find the right balance between each other's needs.

Let us then with confidence draw near to the throne of grace, that we may receive mercy and find grace to help in time of need.
HEBREWS 4:16

Lord God, we need You throughout our differences.
Let us never be split apart by our differences. Rather,
help us find balance between each other's needs.

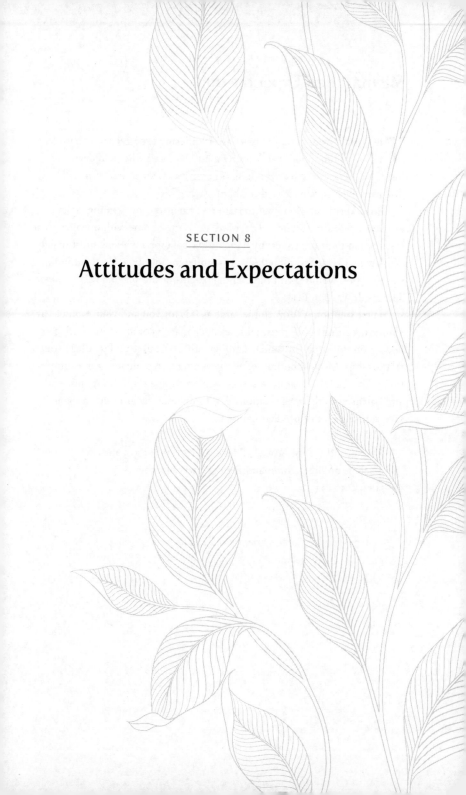

SECTION 8

Attitudes and Expectations

Mismatched Expectations

The number one pitfall in marriage is differing expectations. That's right: all those hopes and desires a husband and wife hold deep inside yet seldom discuss with each other. It's a major source of marital disharmony—as Bob learned the hard way.

An avid runner, Bob used to train for marathons by running eighteen or twenty miles at a stretch. Afterward, he'd come home with one very clear expectation in mind: to rest by lying on the sofa for a while. Unfortunately, Bob's wife, Leesa, had something quite different in mind. *Her* assumption was that Bob would spend the evening parenting and playing with the kids. The result was conflict.

Their solution was much the same as it is for you and your spouse: Lay your expectations out on the table and negotiate a compromise. And learn how to do this *before* misunderstandings stir up trouble and sabotage your relationship. Most important of all, be willing to reevaluate your assumptions. The reality is that both sides could probably be a bit more reasonable and balanced in their expectations. Find some middle ground, and you'll save yourself a lot of needless conflict.

The second is this: "You shall love your neighbor as yourself."
There is no other commandment greater than these.
MARK 12:31

God, reveal all my hidden expectations and help me
rightly evaluate their necessity. More importantly, show
me how to put my spouse's desires above my own.

Believe the Best

Picture this: You're a newlywed, but you hardly see your spouse because his or her career is just getting started. With an unpredictable schedule and eighty-hour weeks, you rarely share time together, let alone plan social events. If that was your marriage, what would you assume about your spouse?

Jackie remembers her reaction all too well. She automatically believed the worst about her husband, Jeff. She was convinced he cared more about work than he did about her. And it didn't take long for those negative assumptions to escalate into conflict. That's why she was caught off guard by his true motives for working so hard: "I love you," he said. "I just want to create a better future for us." It was a turning point in their marriage and a first step toward mutual understanding. Jeff recognized her need for affection and cut back on his workload, and Jackie learned to trust his love for her.

She also learned another valuable lesson that day: Many marital problems can be prevented by assuming the best about our spouse instead of the worst. It's a simple idea, but it can make the difference between a miserable home life and domestic bliss.

> Finally, brothers, whatever is true, whatever is honorable, whatever is just, whatever is pure, whatever is lovely, whatever is commendable, if there is any excellence, if there is anything worthy of praise, think about these things.
>
> PHILIPPIANS 4:8

Lord, I want to be my spouse's biggest fan.
Point out what is true and lovely about him
or her and help me assume the best.

Battling Boredom

Remember when you and your spouse first dated? Back then, you didn't need a list of exciting things to do. The relationship itself was the important thing, and it was enough that you were together. But after the wedding, something changed. Life settled into a routine, and over time, the excitement that once burned in your relationship slowly fizzled.

Every marriage has a case of the "yawns" now and then. But boredom, left unchecked, can easily take over a relationship. A bored couple will eventually grow apart and wind up living like roommates instead of husband and wife. He'll have his life; she'll have hers. Even worse, a spouse who feels his or her marriage has grown stale may look outside the relationship for excitement.

A couple's lifeless and gray marriage can sparkle with new color if they learn to reconnect emotionally. A good start is to find activities you both enjoy doing together. It's also important to break out of your own world and enter into your wife's or husband's. Rediscover where their interests lie. Just remember, it's not simply about *doing* stuff together. It's about reconnecting your hearts and coming alive to each other again.

How beautiful is your love, my sister, my bride! How much better is your love than wine, and the fragrance of your oils than any spice!
SONG OF SOLOMON 4:10

Rekindle the sparks that once brought us together.
Give us things to bond over, and help me find
enjoyment in putting my spouse's desires first.

A Winning Attitude for a Better Marriage

A negative attitude will keep you stuck in an unhappy marriage. Negativity doesn't look for solutions; it finds reasons why nothing will work. Maybe you've heard yourself say, "My marriage will never be any better. Too many problems have gone on too long." Those messages are destructive and stop even the hope of progress in its tracks.

A negative attitude leads to negative choices. If you think negatively *about* your spouse, you'll say critical things and act negatively *toward* him or her. Criticism will cause your spouse to pull away. Negativity is counterproductive to creating the marital happiness you want.

A positive attitude isn't magic and won't heal your marriage overnight. But it will open the door to new possibilities. If you think about the good qualities of your spouse and your relationship, you'll start to see things differently, and better choices will follow.

If you'll *speak* positively to your spouse, the odds increase even more that you can influence change in your relationship. Constructive comments are much more likely to help your spouse be willing to change.

My advice? Get rid of "stinking thinking." Positivity will move your relationship *away* from conflict and *toward* healing and intimacy.

As you excel in everything—in faith, in speech, in knowledge, in all earnestness, and in our love for you—see that you excel in this act of grace also.

2 CORINTHIANS 8:7

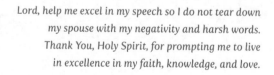

Lord, help me excel in my speech so I do not tear down my spouse with my negativity and harsh words. Thank You, Holy Spirit, for prompting me to live in excellence in my faith, knowledge, and love.

We See What We Want to See

Remember this: You often see in your spouse what you want to see.

That principle was illustrated in a nationwide physicians' study. The doctors were asked to look for a particular form of lung disease in a set of X-rays. The doctors weren't told that a picture of a gorilla had been embedded in the X-rays.

After their examinations, 83 percent of the doctors reported they never saw anything unusual in the X-rays. Doesn't that sound crazy?

The study results shouldn't surprise us. Something similar happens every day in a lot of marriages. We tend to see what we're looking for. If you feel negatively about your spouse, maybe you're looking for the negative. You can turn that around by looking for the positive.

I know one wife who started writing down one thing every day that she was thankful for about her husband. One day it was "He helped me fold the laundry." Another time it was "He picked up the kids from school for me."

Within a few weeks, she wasn't seeing just one thing per day but ten, fifteen, or twenty. What changed wasn't her husband, but rather her view of him. She learned that we see what we want to see.

Be not wise in your own eyes; fear the LORD, and turn away from evil.
PROVERBS 3:7

So often, God, I see what I want to see in my spouse. Teach me how to be wise not in my own eyes but wise with eyes that see with Your perspective.

DAY 112

Different Doesn't Mean *Wrong*

Have you ever wondered how qualities you found so attractive in your spouse when you were dating became so irritating once you got married? If so, it's helpful to remember that *different* doesn't mean *wrong*.

One of the toughest challenges for newlyweds is accepting their spouse's personality. Dating couples are usually so busy impressing each other, they overlook their partner's quirks. But after the honeymoon, all those irritating habits can get pretty hard to live with.

That's where many couples make a fatal marital mistake. They allow their mate's personality to grate on their nerves. Left unchecked, resentment will build. Once resentment takes hold, marriage commitment can quickly erode.

There's a better path. It starts with having the right attitude toward your spouse. The key is to recognize that *different* doesn't have to mean *wrong*. Our personality is what makes us uniquely who we are. A marriage can handle two unique individuals and yet thrive.

True, learning to accept your spouse's personality quirks may take some patience and growth. But it's an important step in cultivating variety in your relationship. After all, variety is the spice of life—and a little spice can go a long way toward helping your marriage thrive.

Behold, how good and pleasant it is when brothers dwell in unity!
PSALM 133:1

Lord, You intend unity in all relationships within the body of Christ, particularly in marriage. Show me how to accept—maybe even greatly value—my spouse's personality quirks. I know that embracing each other's differences can infuse our love with the spice of life.

Where True Love Is Found

Marriage counselors Drs. Les and Leslie Parrott still recall the precise moment they realized they had found "true love." Care to guess where they were and what they were doing at the time?

If you guessed they were honeymooning in a beautiful place (in this case, the Oregon coast), you'd be correct. But if you thought they recognized their deep love for each other strolling on a moonlit beach or enjoying a candlelit dinner, you'd be well off the mark. In reality, they were sitting on a curb, waiting for a locksmith to retrieve the keys they'd accidentally locked in their rental car.

It's the sort of thing that could have pushed them into conflict. Instead, it became a defining moment in the Parrotts' marriage. As she sat on that curb, Leslie says, it hit her: Even when life's circumstances were less than ideal, "I had married a man who loved me deeply, just as I loved him. . . . We had committed ourselves to walking together forever."

Now *that's* true love! In fact, most people find "true love" in tough times—not in the sparks, fireworks, or dizzying passions of a new relationship. True love is when a couple draws close and connects with each other in the midst of life's challenging, often painful moments.

Love bears all things, believes all things, hopes all things, endures all things.

I CORINTHIANS 13:7

God, we love because of Your love for us. Please help my spouse and me weather every challenging time by holding fast to You and to our love for one another.

Recast Your Dreams

It's not too hard to find couples who grumble about what their marriage is compared with what they dreamed it would be. But what they often fail to consider is whether their expectations were realistic in the first place.

Marital bliss is a common dream when people are dating. In those early stages of romance, they can't imagine feeling discontent with their spouse. What disagreements?

But once a couple is married, those expectations usually hit a speed bump. There's the monotony of work and paying bills week in and week out. Then there are all the stressors. Maybe a spouse loses his or her job, or a baby is born, impacting the couple's finances. In other words, real life sets in, and the dream begins to fade.

All of this shows that good marriages aren't built on lofty expectations. They're formed through the ups and downs of day-to-day experience. So if your relationship isn't all you'd hoped for, take a look at what you originally wanted. Maybe some of your expectations were unrealistic. If so, cast a new vision for your marriage. But this time, temper your dreams with a little less fairy tale and a little more real life.

As it is written, "What no eye has seen, nor ear heard, nor the heart of man imagined, what God has prepared for those who love him."
I CORINTHIANS 2:9

God, we humans fall short with our limited vision and unrealistic expectations. Help my spouse and me navigate the realities of daily life while still believing You for incredible adventures.

Recipe for a Good Marriage

My wife, Jean, and I approach recipes entirely differently. Jean has a degree in biochemistry and sees recipes as detailed road maps to be precisely followed.

I, on the other hand, am more of a free spirit with recipes. I see them as "a few things to keep in mind." Which means I kinda, sorta measure ingredients, but not very carefully.

Despite our differences in the kitchen, Jean and I have learned that if we allow each other to bring our unique flair to a recipe, we usually end up with something that we both enjoy.

We approach our marriage that way too. We're different from each other. She's an introvert. I'm an extrovert. She's a night owl, and I'm a morning person. Nevertheless, we come together on this point: There is no detailed recipe for how to make a marriage work. Except this—fill up your relationship with as much *love* and *respect* as you can. When you get *those* ingredients in the correct proportions, your marriage will thrive despite any other parts of your relationship that could use some adjustment.

Like with recipes, when we honor each other's differences in our marriage, we usually cook up something that we both enjoy.

Let us consider how to stir up one another to love and good works.
HEBREWS 10:24

*God, You are a divine Creator, blending together
my differences with my spouse's. We are not exactly
alike, and that is a flavorful recipe. Guide us
both in how to honor our differences so we keep
cooking up a relationship that we both enjoy.*

The Power of a Wife

"**B**ehind every great man is a great woman." That saying is certainly true for Stephen King. He happily admits that it was his wife's encouragement that enabled him to succeed as an author.

In the early 1970s, Stephen was a public school teacher and wrote stories on the side. Money was tight, so he earned extra money selling his stories to magazines. One of his tales was about a bullied high school girl with special powers. Something about the story wasn't working, so Stephen threw its few pages into the trash can. His wife, Tabitha, found them there, read them, and encouraged Stephen to finish the story. He did, and *Carrie* became his first published novel.

Since then Stephen King has gone on to write more than sixty novels and has sold around 350 million copies. None of Stephen's success would have been possible without Tabitha, who saw something in him that he couldn't see in himself at the time. Her belief in Stephen enabled him to have confidence in himself.

That's the power of a wife on full display. No matter how tough and on top of things we men try to act, nothing propels us forward like an encouraging word from our wife.

An excellent wife who can find? . . . The heart of her husband
trusts in her, and he will have no lack of gain. She does him good,
and not harm, all the days of her life.
PROVERBS 31:10-12

God, thank You that You created each of us
with unique gifts to encourage and inspire
our spouses. May I be continually grateful
for how my partner brings out my best.

Love Is a Verb

It took a garden for Andy to learn that true love requires action. It happened one summer after his wife said she wanted to plant some vegetables in their backyard. Andy wasn't really interested in digging through the dirt, however. And more importantly, he worried it would interfere with what he hoped was one of his wife's biggest priorities—*Andy*! So he tried to talk her out of it.

But then it hit him: This wasn't a question of whether *he* enjoyed pulling weeds. Love required him to look out for *her* interests, not his. With that insight, it wasn't long before he was turning over his first spade of soil.

The truth is that most of us tend to treat love like a noun, a thing that we *get* from somebody else. And if it doesn't measure up to our starry-eyed expectations, we simply toss it aside. Is it any wonder divorce rates are so high in a culture with an "easy come, easy go" mentality?

Instead, we should train ourselves to think of love as a verb—in other words, as something we *do* rather than something we *get*.

Do nothing from selfish ambition or conceit, but in humility count others more significant than yourselves. Let each of you look not only to his own interests, but also to the interests of others.
PHILIPPIANS 2:3-4

God, grant me joy in considering my spouse's needs above my own. May I find more joy in serving my spouse than in serving myself.

The Need for Hope

The needs of the homeless might seem obvious—food, money, shelter. But there might be a deeper need: hope!

Dr. Jim Withers has cared for the homeless in Pittsburgh, Pennsylvania, since 1992. Every night, his team visits the city's destitute, providing free medical care and, most importantly, encouragement. As Dr. Withers says, "When [people] are shown that they matter . . . hope grows."

Most of us will never know the challenges of being homeless, but we all probably know what it means to feel hopeless. Unfortunately, too often our first instinct is to fix things: We're told of someone in need, so we pass on a few dollars. Or maybe a colleague is struggling in his marriage. But instead of allowing him to talk about his pain, we jump right to solving their problem.

Caring for the immediate needs of family and those in our communities is important. But let's remember that people long to be seen. They need someone to acknowledge them as a person. For someone wondering if he or she matters, a hug or a kind word is an important element for one of the most basic needs of all—the need for hope.

The needy shall not always be forgotten, and the hope of the poor shall not perish forever.
PSALM 9:18

God, You are our hope, and You willingly offer Yourself to restore us. Empower me to spread Your hope to my family and those around me.

Shaping Your Expectations

Most newlyweds view their marriage as an empty canvas. It's a perfectly blank surface upon which a beautiful portrait of their love will be painted. But the reality is usually far different. You see, each of us enters into marriage with color already splashed across our canvas. Those colors reflect a set of expectations we may not even realize we have. They're formed within us from our earliest years, and they determine what we'll expect from our spouse.

For Greg, it was the hot breakfast his mother cooked for him every morning when he was a kid. Naturally, when he got married, he assumed his wife would do the same thing. Boy, was he in for a surprise!

It could have been a serious problem. That first day his wife didn't agree to cook, Greg thought she was angry with him. She could have responded to his expectations with anger or frustration, but they managed to choose a healthier direction. Together, Greg and his wife learned how to communicate and shape their expectations into something realistic.

Remember, your marriage is not a blank canvas. Talk about the expectations each of you brought to the marriage, and those colors will start blending into something beautiful.

Do nothing from selfish ambition or conceit, but in humility count others more significant than yourselves.
PHILIPPIANS 2:3

God, reveal my expectations and help me lay them all at Your feet. May my spouse and I discuss our expectations openly, that our marriage might become a beautiful portrait of our love.

Honeymoon Horror Stories

One bride-to-be told her fiancé, "I've always wanted my honeymoon night to be in a cozy living room with a fireplace and surrounded by candles." Sure enough, when they arrived at their hotel after the wedding, a fire was burning in the hearth, and candles were bathing the room in a romantic glow.

Sadly, the evening went downhill as soon as the new husband carried his bride across the threshold. As he leaned her back for a dip and a kiss, her hair fell into one of the candles and caught fire! He did the only thing he could think of—he pulled her into the bathroom and stuffed her head into the toilet.

Stories like that are more common than you think—and too often a ruined honeymoon is the beginning of a ruined marriage.

I hope your special day went off without a hitch. But even if it didn't, don't let it overshadow the importance of your marriage. Turn your disappointment into a memory you can both laugh about later. With the right attitude, even a honeymoon horror story can launch a beautiful relationship together.

Anxiety in a man's heart weighs him down, but a good word makes him glad.
PROVERBS 12:25

Father, as we go through life, there will be plenty of opportunities to be weighed down by anxiety or disappointment. In those moments, give us words for each other that will bring encouragement, hope, and even humor—and most importantly, draw us closer together rather than drive us apart.

Moving past Misunderstandings

Every married couple has disagreements. But some of those arguments happen because one spouse misunderstands what the other is really thinking.

Take Dan and Barb for example. Barb asked her husband a couple of weeks ago to fix the kitchen sink, but Dan hasn't gotten around to it. Now Barb is tired of waiting, so she reminds him that the sink is still broken. And that's all it takes to spark misunderstanding and conflict.

Barb sees the situation her way: Dan has had plenty of time to get the job done, but he's lazy and hasn't taken the initiative to do the work.

Dan, on the other hand, has an entirely different view: He's not lazy. He's worked late every night, and there are a lot of other things around the house he's been trying to get done first.

When a disagreement like that pops up, a great starting place for resolving your differences is to consider whether you're seeing the situation accurately. You can't avoid conflict if you think the worst about your spouse. Give each other some grace. It'll reduce your conflict and increase your happiness.

When one of you has a grievance against another, does he dare go to law before the unrighteous instead of the saints?
I CORINTHIANS 6:1

King of kings, when my spouse and I get irritated, help us show patience, grace, and understanding to each other. In doing so we will avoid thinking the worst about each other and will instead see each other in a better light.

Perceptions Matter

Do you see your spouse through rose-colored glasses? Believe it or not, it might help. A common marital problem is what counselors call a *self-fulfilling belief.* That means the state of our marriage is often determined not so much by what's really true, but by our preconceived ideas. Let me give you an example.

Years ago, an experiment was conducted with three teachers, each assigned ninety students who were said to be especially bright. By the end of the year, the students had achieved far beyond their peers across the city. Only then was it revealed that the students didn't have high IQs. They had been selected randomly. So what led to such significant results?

Our beliefs look for evidence to prove them true. If you're convinced your spouse is untrustworthy, for example, everything around you will seem to support that conviction. Our perceptions can shape a marriage into something negative.

But this principle can be used in positive ways as well. To improve your marriage, develop a better mindset about your spouse and your relationship. Learn to look for the good. It'll open your eyes to qualities you otherwise wouldn't see.

Do not be overcome by evil, but overcome evil with good.
ROMANS 12:21

*Lord, it is so easy to let evil perceptions override
the truth. Help us always look for the good
in each other and, in so doing, see the many
wonderful qualities that drew us together.*

Understanding and Patience

Understanding and patience can go a long way in marriage. They can even transform burnt biscuits into an opportunity to shower your spouse with love.

There's a story told about a family gathered for dinner. The mother prepared the meal and set everything on the table. It all looked delicious until the kids noticed the biscuits. They were badly burnt. The weary mother apologized. But the father simply smiled at his wife, slathered the hockey pucks with some butter, and ate without complaining.

Later, one of his children came to him and asked why he hadn't thrown the nearly inedible biscuits away. The father said, "Your mom had a long, hard day at work. She's more important to me than whether my food was a little charred."

Much of having a successful marriage is learning how to be patient with imperfection. Each of us is prone to mistakes, after all, and could use a smile instead of judgment when things aren't going well.

So if your marriage serves you a burnt biscuit, slather it with some love, understanding, and grace. It'll make that hard circumstance a whole lot easier to swallow.

> Be not quick in your spirit to become angry, for anger lodges in the heart of fools.
>
> ECCLESIASTES 7:9

Help me always see the good in everything my spouse does for me, no matter what. When mistakes are made, help me avoid anger and show grace, love, and understanding.

Is Marriage Meant to Make You Happy?

Is marriage supposed to make you happy? I guess the answer depends on how you define *happiness*.

Some people think of happiness as a destination, a place where you feel good because all your circumstances line up correctly. That's only a useful goal for marriage if your spouse is perfect—and if you've been married for long, you know he or she isn't. What then? Kiss your happiness goodbye?

There's a better way: Recognize that happiness isn't a destination. It's a choice. Nothing is perfect, including marriage, which means happiness is relative. Some couples have everything and are miserable. Some couples have little and choose to be happy.

You create a happier marriage by choosing behaviors that make your relationship healthier and more deeply connected. Every couple wishes their relationship could be a little more *this* or a little less *that*—good news when you recognize you have the power to choose new behaviors that can create the relationship you want.

Let's go back and answer our original question: Is marriage supposed to make you happy? The answer is no. But you can choose behaviors that will create a happy marriage. And when your marriage is happier, you'll be happier.

I have set before you life and death, blessing and curse. Therefore choose life.

DEUTERONOMY 30:19

Father, You have always given Your people choices. I realize there are choices I can make that will bring death to my marriage, and other choices that will bring life. Empower me to make life-giving choices every day.

Three-Quarters of the Way

How far would you go to build a successful marriage? Part of the way? *All* the way? When former first lady Barbara Bush was asked that question, she answered, "Three-quarters of the way."

Her answer sounds strange until you understand her meaning. After her husband, George, served heroically in the navy during World War II, he considered pursuing business opportunities in Texas. That change promised to be life-altering for Barbara, who had spent her entire life on the East Coast. Nevertheless, if her future with her husband lay in Texas, she would happily go—even if it meant moving, as she put it, "three-quarters of the way across the country."

From that day forward, the phrase *three-quarters of the way* became George and Barbara's metaphor for going *all* the way—making their marriage work no matter what was required. And make marriage work they did. She and former president George H. W. Bush were married for seventy-three years.

The commitment to going the distance is something every marriage deserves. Fifty-fifty isn't a winning formula. Couples who only do their "fair share" rarely survive tough times. Because it's in those tough times that couples learn how to come together with full effort and work through their trials together as one.

For a marriage that will stand the test of time, how far will you go? Will you go—as the Bushes would say—three-quarters of the way? Will you go all in?

We rejoice in our sufferings, knowing that suffering produces endurance, and endurance produces character, and character produces hope.
ROMANS 5:3-4

Lord, help our marriage withstand the test of time.
May Your love be the unbreakable thread that weaves
through the fabric of our union and creates a tapestry
of enduring joy, resilience, and commitment.

Each Thread Strengthens the Whole

Spiderwebs can seem creepy, but they are truly masterpieces of design and engineering. They appear fragile—a child can obliterate one with a sweep of a hand, after all—yet they are actually quite strong. Spiderwebs are constructed from many tiny silk threads, each one like a steel beam in terms of strength relative to size. And each thread connects with the rest of the web, in turn strengthening the whole.

Good marriages are a lot like that. They're constructed of dozens of threads that connect a husband and wife together: There is a spiritual thread. A financial thread. There are physical and emotional threads. There are threads for hobbies, food preferences, musical choices, and dozens of other things. Each one by itself is a point of connection, and each one binds one aspect of the relationship to every other part, again strengthening the whole.

To spin a strong web for your marriage, find multiple ways to connect. Enter each other's world. Ask thoughtful questions, and listen carefully to the answers. As your relationship grows stronger in one area, it'll grow stronger in other areas as well—until, eventually, your marriage becomes a masterpiece of design.

We are his workmanship, created in Christ Jesus for good works, which God prepared beforehand, that we should walk in them.
EPHESIANS 2:10

Heavenly Father, strengthen our marriage through multiple threads of connection. Weave these threads together, and strengthen the bonds that make our marriage a masterpiece of Your design.

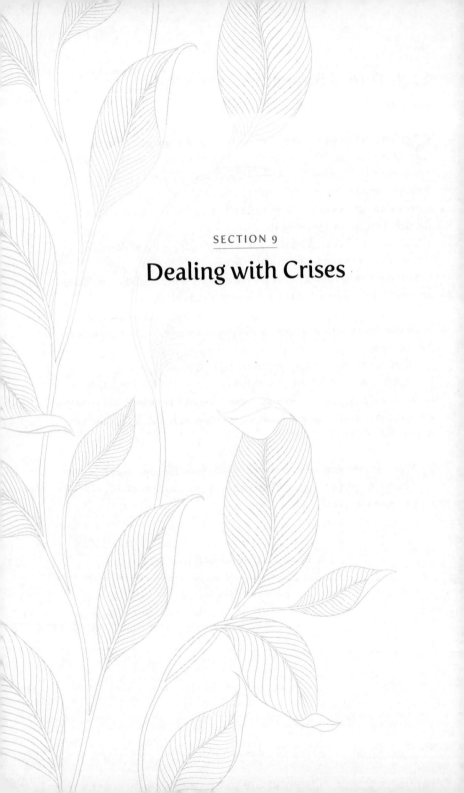

Dealing with Crises

Responding Properly

The easiest way out of a problem may not be the best way out.

When we encounter trials, how we respond matters more than we think. Responding well makes it more likely that the problem itself will get resolved and prepares us to better handle future crises as well. A healthy response to a serious issue bolsters our character and further matures us as individuals.

For example, some couples don't handle conflict well. They insult each other, act petty, or behave with a harsh, critical attitude that makes their problems worse. It's like cleaning up a spill with an oily rag. The whole mess gets worse, not better.

On the other hand, couples who treat each other with respect in a conflict stand a much better chance of healing their marriage. They're more likely to resolve the issue they're facing today, and they put themselves in a better position to correct issues down the road.

So remember, the next time you face a serious life challenge, the goal isn't simply to correct the problem by any means necessary. *How* we resolve problems is just as important. We'll either act in a way that enhances our character or in a way that diminishes it.

We aim at what is honorable not only in the Lord's sight but also in the sight of man.

2 CORINTHIANS 8:21

Lord, I want to honor You in how I honor my spouse. Remind me to respond with kindness and gentleness when handling conflicts in my marriage and beyond.

The Impact of Infertility

If you and your spouse are struggling with the pain of infertility, then you know the stress it can place on your marriage. Let me encourage you that infertility doesn't have to take a toll on your relationship.

Infertility can tax virtually every area of a couple's marriage—from the financial strain of exploring treatment options, to altered career decisions, to hopes and dreams put on hold. The emotional weight of it all can be especially devastating. In many cases, a husband and wife may both struggle with feeling inadequate, each believing they're letting down the other.

Often the disappointments compound until they begin to define a couple's relationship. That's why a husband and wife need to refocus their marriage in light of such a heartbreaking reality.

Couples need to mourn their inability to have children. Infertility is the death of a dream, and you and your spouse need time to grieve that loss. But out of the ashes will come new hope. Infertility opens the door for you to heal together and make new choices. Maybe you'll even experience the blessing of adoption. With time, your heartache can become a source of strength rather than a source of pain.

> You rejoice, though now for a little while, if necessary, you have been grieved by various trials.
> 1 PETER 1:6

Jesus, our hearts deeply ache over not being able to have a child together. You understand our sorrow. Uphold us and encourage us as we mourn and move forward with hope.

Would You Marry Your Spouse Again?

If you suffered from amnesia and lost all memory of getting married, would you want to fall in love with your spouse all over again?

As bizarre as that scenario sounds, it actually happened to Krickitt Carpenter in September 1993. Only ten weeks after her wedding, Krickitt was seriously injured in a car accident and went into a coma. After she woke up, her husband, Kim, discovered that Krickitt had lost all memory of him and their marriage.

With the help of family and photographs, Krickitt soon realized she was indeed married. Still, Kim seemed a complete stranger, and she felt no emotion for him. In the end, Krickitt chose to honor her vows to Kim, a commitment familiar to her only because she'd watched herself in a wedding video. She and Kim began to date again, and three years later they renewed their vows.

Very few marriages encounter circumstances as extraordinary as the Carpenters'. And yet many couples face the same question: Is it possible to fall in love with your spouse all over again? My hope is that you'll answer yes! No matter what may have stolen your love for each other, you can find it again. It'll take effort, but it starts with a commitment.

Husbands should love their wives as their own bodies. He who loves his wife loves himself.
EPHESIANS 5:28

Lord, let nothing steal my love for my spouse. May our marriage commitment stay strong in sickness and in health.

Wisdom in Pain

No other generation in history has enjoyed our level of comfort. But all that luxury comes at a high cost to our wisdom. Technology has made our lives so easy that we're losing our discernment.

Comfort has become our highest pursuit. We chase it . . . and we desperately cling to it once we get it. We avoid discomfort. And therein lies the problem. Past generations knew something that we're forgetting: Wisdom is more important than short-term comfort.

The book of Proverbs, the most popular collection of wisdom in history, was written in a culture that believed wisdom was the highest pursuit in life—not money, comfort, or luxury. Proverbs reminds us that wisdom usually requires a little pain. Your path forward is never a straight line. You get stuff wrong. Hopefully, you learn from your mistakes and do better next time.

The trouble is that we want wisdom without pain. I never want comfort to win out over my desire to do what's right. That's how you build a better marriage, become a better parent, or make better career choices. You live with the courage to do what's right.

Enjoy your comfort, but it's never wise to run from your pain.

Blessed is the one who finds wisdom, and the one who gets understanding.
PROVERBS 3:13

My wise and discerning Father, lead me on a path lined with wisdom and understanding. Direct my steps to seek Your truth and wisdom more than I long for money, comfort, and luxury.

Together in Grief

The death of a child can devastate a marriage. A high percentage of couples who lose children get divorced. The grief each parent feels is so deep that it's hard to come together as a couple.

Christian music artist Steven Curtis Chapman and his wife, Mary Beth, endured just such a trial. Their three young daughters were playing outside as their teenage son was returning home in the family Land Cruiser. He couldn't see one of his little sisters running to greet him, and the vehicle struck and killed her.

Steven and Mary Beth's grief was so agonizingly deep that it could have ended their otherwise happy twenty-five-year marriage. But they refused to turn on each other. They turned *toward* each other and worked through their pain together. They entered marriage counseling and invested in keeping the surviving family members together.

If your child has been taken from you, let your marriage be a reason that you feel the strength to carry on. You'll need support from your family, from your church, and maybe even from professionals. Don't let it take the rest of your family too. Survive the darkness together, and you'll build a family that will one day thrive again.

I am sure that neither death nor life, nor angels nor rulers, nor things present nor things to come, nor powers, nor height nor depth, nor anything else in all creation, will be able to separate us from the love of God in Christ Jesus our Lord.
ROMANS 8:38-39

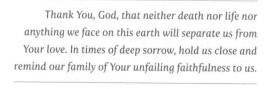

Thank You, God, that neither death nor life nor anything we face on this earth will separate us from Your love. In times of deep sorrow, hold us close and remind our family of Your unfailing faithfulness to us.

Do You Believe in Miracles?

Do you believe in miracles?

You should if you're clinging to hope. Success and victory often require something intangible that miraculously intervenes.

The "Miracle on Ice" is a classic example. In 1980, the Soviet Union was expected to win the Olympic gold medal in men's hockey. Their players were the world's best, and the Soviets had won the gold in five of the previous six Winter Games.

By contrast, the American team were college kids. They were good, but no one believed they stood a chance against the much more experienced Soviet team. Just two weeks before, the Soviets had embarrassed them in an exhibition game by a score of 10–3. But then in the Olympic medal round, the US defeated the "unbeatable" Soviets 4–3.

What enabled them to skate to victory? Hard work? Skill? Determination? All those things. But there was something else at work, something intangible that intervened against all odds.

Is something in your life too big to handle? A wayward child? A marriage that seems beyond repair? A career change?

The bigger question is, as legendary broadcaster Al Michaels asked in the final seconds of that historic hockey game, "Do you believe in miracles?"

God also bore witness by signs and wonders and various miracles and by gifts of the Holy Spirit distributed according to his will.
HEBREWS 2:4

God, You truly are a miracle worker. You know the divine intervention I need in my life. I ask You to keep me expectant of the intangible— the surprise answers from above.

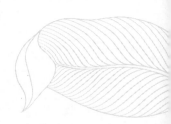

Facing the Empty Nest

According to an ancient legend, if all the ravens in the Tower of London fly away, England will fall. There's another kind of empty nest, and this one can bring down a marriage.

Life with teenagers can be a whirlwind with sports, orthodontist appointments, church youth activities—sometimes all in the same day! For many parents, life starts revolving around their kids, and the marriage gets pushed aside. Years later when the kids leave home, there's nothing to hold the couple's relationship together, and it crumbles.

Fortunately, you and your spouse can actively prepare for when it's just the two of you.

First, be intentional about strengthening your communication. Read a book together about relationships. Attend a marriage enrichment event. Or if needed, talk with a counselor.

Second, get involved in social activities or hobbies together. Gather with a church fellowship group. Volunteer at local charities. Or take up recreational activities. Finding common interests can help create new foundations for relating to each other.

The warning about the ravens in the Tower of London may be the stuff of legend, but empty nests in our homes are real. Strengthen your marriage now, and those years can be an enriching time of intimacy and connection.

By wisdom a house is built, and by understanding it is established; by knowledge the rooms are filled with all precious and pleasant riches.
PROVERBS 24:3-4

A home built on wisdom, understanding, and deep connection will stand steady once the nest is empty of children. Lord, this is the home I want to build now with my spouse as we are intentional about strengthening our relationship for today and tomorrow.

The Challenges of Deployment (Part 1)

Military deployment can be tough on couples. The good news is there are steps a husband and wife can take to prepare for their time apart.

In the days leading up to a deployment, remember that husbands and wives tend to handle stress differently. Men will often begin to detach emotionally. It's a coping mechanism that helps them function well under extreme pressure. Women are usually the opposite. Their need for emotional connection will increase as the time for separation draws closer.

Obviously, this inherent difference can lead to conflict—but it can also be a source of understanding and deeper intimacy if couples will openly communicate about what they're feeling. So talk with each other.

Furthermore, remember to make the most of the moments you have together. Instead of worrying about the months ahead and losing touch with your spouse, create good memories together right here and now. The more moments you enjoy before you're separated, the less stressful your time apart will be.

And finally, set aside time to be alone together before the deployment. Say goodbye to friends and family members early, and then devote the last few evenings to each other. Let those last moments be about your commitment to your marriage.

> Do not be anxious about tomorrow, for tomorrow will be anxious for itself. Sufficient for the day is its own trouble.
> MATTHEW 6:34

Lord, help my spouse and me live in the here and now as we wait for deployment. Bless us with rich, beautiful memories together before we are apart. Settle any of our anxious emotions, and draw us closer together than we've ever been.

The Challenges of Deployment (Part 2)

To help military couples prepare for deployment, I'd like to offer a few suggestions.

For the spouse waiting at home, the pain of the separation is often made worse by fear that something may happen to his or her deployed spouse. If children are involved, the parent at home shoulders the full brunt of the household responsibilities for a while.

That's a lot of stress, so it's critical to surround yourself with a supportive community. Time alone can be helpful here and there, but it's important to connect with other people who can come alongside you in meaningful ways.

Also, communicate with your spouse as often as you can. Technology makes it easier to stay in touch. But be careful. Never end a conversation in anger. And don't try to resolve big problems if they can wait. A frustrating situation will be twice as hard to manage over the miles between you. So try to stay positive: Keep your spouse updated on home life, send packages he or she will enjoy, and keep family photos coming.

Finally, don't put your life on hold while your spouse is away. Take care of yourself physically, emotionally, and spiritually. Your spouse will be relieved to know you're doing well.

Fear not, for I am with you; be not dismayed, for I am your God; I will strengthen you, I will help you, I will uphold you with my righteous right hand.
ISAIAH 41:10

Deployment separations are tough, Lord. I pray that my spouse and I will stay steady in our love and commitment while we are apart. Thank You that I don't need to fear because You are with me and You are strengthening and helping me.

Back Together Again

The end of a long military deployment can be challenging for service-men and women, as well as for their spouses at home.

For months, the partner at home has acted as a single parent, caring for all the household responsibilities. Once the military spouse returns, settling into a steady routine where each spouse knows his or her role can be tough. And that confusion can lead to misunderstanding and conflict.

A solution is for couples to ask and answer this basic question: Who should be responsible for what? Some couples may prefer to sit down before a tour of duty even begins and discuss how they want things to go when the deployment ends. Other couples may decide to wait until after the spouse returns. That allows them to make plans based on how things have changed over the months.

Either strategy gives the couple the opportunity to talk through their expectations, understand each other's needs, and come up with a plan they agree on. Like a lot of areas in marriage, it all comes down to good communication.

So if you're facing a deployment, make time for a good talk. It'll keep that long-awaited reunion from breaking down into conflict and friction.

There is one whose rash words are like sword thrusts, but the tongue of the wise brings healing.

PROVERBS 12:18

Jesus, guard our marriage from conflict and friction as we reunite as a cohesive team. Our words and communication truly do matter even in the small, everyday choices we face.

Coping with a Spouse's Unemployment

Unemployment often puts an emotional strain on a marriage. Here are some practical suggestions for alleviating that stress.

If your spouse is unemployed, it can feel as though the job search will never end. But it's important not to get discouraged. Keep a healthy perspective, and try to remember that this difficult challenge is only temporary.

It's beneficial to keep life as normal as possible. Maintain a routine. Take life one day at a time, and understand that there will be good days and bad. Also, carve out time for yourself and as a couple. Most importantly, don't overlook the value of staying engaged with the people closest to you. When life gets tough, it's easy to hunker down and isolate ourselves. But those are the times we need the love and support of a community of friends and family.

Finally, don't let daily life become consumed with seeking work. Plan activities that have no other purpose except to have fun. It's good to set aside your worries, even if just for a short time, and refresh yourself and your marriage.

So whatever you do, in the midst of your spouse's unemployment, make your marriage your top priority.

Be strong, and let your heart take courage, all you who wait
for the LORD!
PSALM 31:24

*Lord, waiting is not easy for me, especially
when I'm trying to keep my spouse encouraged.
Help us both rest in Your unfailing provisions
and in Your faithful presence each day.*

When Love Is Tough

One of the biggest reasons many marriages collapse is that couples want love to be easy, and they don't stay committed to each other when things get tough.

Anyone can show love to a spouse when life is clicking along smoothly or when they feel their needs are being met. But to have a marriage that endures, couples need a love that's selfless and goes much deeper.

A relationship can only thrive when the love you give isn't dependent on how perfectly your spouse loves you first. Love only shows its true colors when it's tested. Love isn't tested until a problem crops up and it becomes difficult to give love to your spouse.

But those rough patches are what give marriage a chance to deepen to an even more meaningful level. You don't stay married for decades without a few complications along the way. A strong marriage isn't about the absence of conflict. It's about weathering life's storms and working through those troubles together.

Genuine love is committed to the well-being of someone else. When a crisis happens, you'll either demand your own way or try to understand your spouse's needs and do what's best for the relationship.

> Love bears all things, believes all things, hopes all things, endures all things.
> I CORINTHIANS 13:7

Lord, help me when my love for my spouse is tested and I feel like giving up on us. Strengthen us with Your love that bears all things and endures all things.

From the Ashes

The Thomas Fire was, at the time, the largest wildfire in California history. Don and Julie were forced to evacuate their home and barely escaped with the clothes on their backs. A few days later when they were allowed to return, they found a pile of charred rubble where their home once stood. As you can imagine, they were devastated. They had lost everything. Forty years of memories had been reduced to ashes.

But then, in the midst of the ruin and heartache, came a glimmer of hope. There, in the blackened debris, was Julie's wedding ring. Suddenly, Don's and Julie's lives seemed clearly in focus. They had lost everything, but they still had . . . well, everything. They wept together—as much out of happiness as out of pain.

Then Don knelt down in the ashes of his former life and proposed to his wife all over again. It was his way of saying, "Honey, as long as we have each other, that's what really matters."

Don and Julie knew that the beauty of marriage is fully revealed when it survives a threat that could have destroyed it. As long as you have each other, your marriage is complete.

Count it all joy, my brothers, when you meet trials of various kinds.
JAMES 1:2

Reprioritize my thoughts and my desires,
Lord. Remind me of the gift of my marriage
and help me find joy in the trials.

Suffering Together

Taylore Woodard never thought she would beg God to take her child. The fact that she did gives you an indication of how sick her twelve-year-old son, Keith, was. He was suffering from a form of soft tissue sarcoma. The symptoms began when Keith was five years old. Despite several rounds of aggressive treatment, his cancer spread throughout his body. Sadly, Keith didn't live to see his thirteenth birthday.

There are no easy answers for terrible situations like that, but Taylore and her family took an approach that's inspiring. Instead of allowing sadness to darken their last days together, they attempted to create as many memories as possible.

Before Keith died, he wanted to create one last, very special memory. He asked to walk his mother down the aisle for her wedding. What a gift he gave to his mother in one of their darkest hours!

There's no cure for tragedy and suffering, but we can move through it in a way that brings something good. Keith's family carried each other through their pain. Suffering together doesn't erase the pain, but it does strengthen the family bond, and it infuses our lives with profound significance and meaning.

This light momentary affliction is preparing for us an eternal weight of glory beyond all comparison.

2 CORINTHIANS 4:17

God, You've obtained the victory. Let me live in Your victory, choosing to grow through suffering and not be broken by it.

Forgiveness, Not Revenge

In 2004, an Iranian woman was horribly disfigured when a man, angry that she had refused his marriage proposal, threw acid into her face. According to the laws of that country, victims like this woman have the right to receive justice through eye-for-an-eye retribution. In this case, the woman's attacker was ordered to have acid dripped into one of his eyes.

However, at the last minute, the woman stunned her countrymen by requesting that her attacker be spared. Though her life was forever altered by the cruel action against her, she decided against seeking revenge. She later explained, "I forgave him. It is best to pardon when you are in a position of power." The woman's actions demonstrated the power forgiveness holds.

Forgiveness is not about excusing the wrongs against us, nor does it water down the awful nature of an offense. In fact, it really has little to do with the offending person at all. Forgiveness releases our hearts from the resentment that keeps us trapped in emotional pain. It sets us free and allows us to move forward through life with peace.

Do not repay evil for evil or reviling for reviling, but on the contrary, bless, for to this you were called, that you may obtain a blessing.

1 PETER 3:9

*Father, help me see that You ask me to forgive because
You want to bless me with peace and freedom.*

An Endless Capacity to Love

It happened one warm and sunny May afternoon when Heather and Gary were driving home from a family wedding. A truck driver lost control of his vehicle and crashed into them. The results were devastating. The couple's two-year-old son was killed. And Heather, who was eight months pregnant at the time, went into premature labor. She gave birth to a baby boy, who died just a few days later.

Some of you understand Heather and Gary's loss. You might even relate to their feelings of guilt. Heather and Gary were in such a dark place. They felt they'd be betraying the children they'd tragically lost if they chose to have more children. Choosing to move forward felt like choosing to leave their deceased children behind.

But Heather and Gary eventually felt peace about their desire to rebuild their family. What they discovered was that there are no limits to a mom and dad's capacity to love their children.

If you've lost a child, gently remind yourself of that truth. Give yourself plenty of time to grieve, and give yourself permission to live again. Love for one child never means less love for another.

Cast your burden on the LORD, and he will sustain you; he will never permit the righteous to be moved.
PSALM 55:22

Loving Father, please hear my cry and take my burden. Help me grieve well and experience Your peace through this tragedy.

The Relationship Recession

The National Marriage Project released a report outlining the heavy toll that economic crisis takes on married couples.

It's not hard to imagine how this could happen. Statistics show that 75 percent of layoffs associated with a recent recession happened to men. Psychologists have found that when a male primary breadwinner is cast adrift, he can suffer from depression, hopelessness, and a reduced sense of self-worth. And these feelings, coupled with the hard realities of trying to get by on a reduced income, can have devastating effects on the marital relationship.

In the years immediately following the Great Depression, the divorce rate steadily increased, reaching higher than it had been before the Depression started. And researchers are concerned that the same thing could happen again.

If you're among the millions of married Americans who have been impacted by economic crisis—maybe even to the point of losing your job—let me encourage you to stick it out. There are organizations and resources available to help you, not only with the financial challenges you're facing, but also with the stresses and strains that those challenges place on your marriage.

I tell you, do not be anxious about your life, what you will eat or what you will drink, nor about your body, what you will put on. Is not life more than food, and the body more than clothing?
MATTHEW 6:25

Dear God, no matter what happens in life, please help my spouse and me remain faithful to You and each other.

In Sickness and in Health

When I broke my ankle in a motorcycle accident, my doctor told me to stay off my feet. My wife was great to me, but I felt bad for her. She had to help me with everything from bringing me glasses of water to helping me get up and down the stairs. I discovered that even simple requests can become a burden when you feel you're needed all day, every day. And I was only off my feet for a short time.

That's why my heart goes out to those of you who take care of a spouse who's ill. Your love and commitment should inspire the rest of us. Every day you're honoring your vows, in which you said you would remain united "in sickness and in health." You're taking on your spouse's struggles as your own.

Our circumstances will never stop changing. Sooner or later, we're all forced to answer the question "What is my marriage really about?" The couples who endure are the ones who say, "Marriage is about commitment and love put into action." If you're caring for a spouse who's ill, thank you for reminding the rest of us what honoring marriage really looks like.

> Faith, hope, and love abide, these three; but the greatest of these is love.
>
> I CORINTHIANS 13:13

Help us remember our vow to love each other in sickness and in health, no matter the circumstances we face. Love is the greatest of all; help us honor it in our hearts throughout our marriage.

When Your Spouse Says, "I Don't Love You"

Here at Focus on the Family, we routinely receive heartbreaking messages like this one. It reads: "My spouse just told me he (or she) doesn't love me and we shouldn't stay married. What can I do?"

Maybe your marriage has encountered a similar problem, and you have the same question. The answer, according to counselor and author Dr. David Clarke, is to implement an aggressive strategy of tough love as soon as possible.

That means you have to show strength and take decisive action. Typically, that includes steps such as confronting the problem, setting up healthy boundaries, and insisting you receive marriage counseling.

But above all, remember this: Never chase, beg, or plead. You see, if your relationship has deteriorated to the point where your spouse is ready to take action, you have to be willing to take action as well.

Standing firm when your emotions are fragile can be tough. That's why you need to surround yourself with friends and family who can help you find the courage to stand your ground. It's also a good idea to seek out a counselor who can help you make good, strong decisions.

If you love me, you will keep my commandments. And I will ask the Father, and he will give you another Helper, to be with you forever, even the Spirit of truth, whom the world cannot receive, because it neither sees him nor knows him. You know him, for he dwells with you and will be in you.

JOHN 14:15-17

Jesus, please help me keep Your commandment to love, even when I feel unloved. Please also help me stay levelheaded and make wise, strong decisions in the face of adversity. Ultimately, Lord, please help my marriage be healthy and whole.

Immerse Yourself in Recovery

Is your marriage in trouble? Don't give up hope! You can turn things around. But to do it you'll have to immerse yourself in the process of recovery, not just dabble in it.

I'm not much of a gardener, but I know a few things. Like getting seeds to germinate, for example. Seeds will never grow if you dip them into a patch of dirt every so often. You also can't be impatient and give up on a seed if it doesn't push through the soil after a day or two. A seed is transformed into a thriving plant when you bury it in the soil and allow the process of sun, light, and water to take its course.

A troubled marriage isn't much different. You can't heal a broken relationship overnight or with an occasional visit to a counselor. Struggling couples must immerse themselves in a process of recovery and give helpful resources time to breathe life back into their relationship.

I believe willing couples can turn almost any situation around. I've seen it happen again and again. Commit yourself to the influence of helpful people and do the work that needs to be done.

Humble yourselves before the Lord, and he will exalt you.
JAMES 4:10

Father, it is a Kingdom principle that humility precedes great things. As we humble ourselves before You—and humble ourselves before each other as we embrace this season of recovery—we ask that You will exalt, strengthen, and heal our marriage.

In Praise of My Wife

Back in 1985, when I was still single, I had a strange experience at church. In the middle of his sermon, the pastor walked right up to me and said, "I believe God has your wife picked out for you. She'll be your crown."

Three days later, I met Jean for the first time at a friend's wedding. With no thought of what the pastor had said, I told my friend, "I think that's the woman I'm going to marry." On our very first date, we both felt that we were going to marry each other.

Married life hasn't always been rosy, of course. Both of us had things in our pasts that threatened to derail the relationship. Jean had battled depression. I had come from a broken home with no positive male role models. But we were determined to make it work, with God's help. We decided to go to marriage counseling, which helped untangle the knots that were tying us down.

As a result of prayer, good counsel, and determination, our marriage today is stronger than ever. Our lives are filled with many blessings, including two wonderful sons. That pastor was right—Jean truly is my crown.

Have I not commanded you? Be strong and courageous. Do not be frightened, and do not be dismayed, for the LORD your God is with you wherever you go.
JOSHUA 1:9

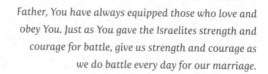

Father, You have always equipped those who love and obey You. Just as You gave the Israelites strength and courage for battle, give us strength and courage as we do battle every day for our marriage.

Is Your Marriage Drenched?

The trees in the northern Cascade Range teach us a valuable lesson. The majority of them are hundreds of years old. It's amazing they've survived so long when you consider that forests in the American West are under constant threat of fire from lightning strikes.

So what is it that has kept trees in the Cascades growing strong for centuries? Well, that area of Washington State routinely experiences drenching rains. The lightning still comes, but the trees remain safe because the forest is saturated with water.

The application to marriage is simply this: Every marriage will be struck by lightning of some kind—whether it be financial trouble, a long-lasting illness, or some other hardship. Many marriages erupt in flames, while others survive the challenges—or even thrive through them.

The primary difference is the absence or the presence of drenching rain. In marriage, drenching rain is found in things like maintaining good communication, being willing to forgive, and taking the time to laugh together.

Drenching your marriage with love takes time, commitment, and sacrifice. But the storms are coming. So protect your marriage from the lightning and flames. Let it rain, and your relationship can survive for decades.

You, O Lord, are good and forgiving, abounding in steadfast love to all who call upon you.
PSALM 86:5

Father, just as You are good and forgiving and loving to me, help my spouse and me reflect those same characteristics to each other. And in doing so, help our roots of love grow deeper, equipping us to withstand the storms of life.

The Four Horsemen of Divorce

The most reliable data place the divorce rate somewhere between 40 and 50 percent. But you can significantly improve the odds for success in *your* marriage by avoiding what Dr. John Gottman calls the Four Horsemen of Divorce.

In the Bible, the Four Horsemen of the Apocalypse symbolize destruction. Dr. Gottman adapts that imagery to describe four negative communication patterns most associated with marital conflict and divorce. They are

- criticism,
- contempt,
- defensiveness, and
- stonewalling.

Each behavior attacks your spouse's character and weakens the overall stability of your relationship. The antidote is to replace each of these negative communication patterns with a positive counterpart. Instead of criticism, be kind. Instead of contempt, respond with patience, love, and grace. Instead of defensiveness, validate your partner's feelings. Instead of stonewalling, engage your spouse and be responsive.

If the Four Horsemen of Divorce have already trampled your relationship, even to the point that you're considering divorce, a program like Focus on the Family's Hope Restored can work wonders in helping you unlock a whole new future for your family.

What therefore God has joined together, let not man separate.
MARK 10:9

Lord, rescue our marriage from destructive communication patterns. Free our hearts to offer each other kindness, validation, connection, and love. Fortify our marriages with stability and grace.

Scratches, Cuts, and Lacerations

Married couples often think about conflict in black-and-white terms—resolving their latest problem is all or nothing. Every issue, no matter how small or insignificant, is debated for days or even weeks. Or perhaps no issues get resolved, no matter how destructive they are to the relationship.

There is a better way. Counselor and author Dr. Randy Schroeder encourages couples to view marital conflict in terms of scratches, cuts, and lacerations.

Scratches are superficial wounds caused by things like misunderstandings or thoughtless words. Scratches sting, but they generally heal with just a little care. In most cases an apology is all that's necessary to help heal a scratch.

Cuts are deeper and more serious. They shouldn't be ignored. When cuts aren't given proper attention, they can fester and become infected. Relational cuts require more than a simple apology to truly heal. They require time, humility, and a willingness to address whatever created the wound in the first place.

Lacerations are the most severe. They're inflicted by egregious behavior such as adultery, physical abuse, or verbal abuse. These wounds can put a marriage in the emergency room, where professional intervention is usually required. If your marriage is dealing with a laceration, be sure to seek outside assistance.

One of the best ways to foster a healthy marriage is to avoid all-or-nothing extremes. Don't race to the emergency room over a simple scratch, but also don't ignore cuts and lacerations. Nurture your relationship, heal your wounds, and deepen your connection together.

> When the righteous cry for help, the LORD hears and delivers them out of all their troubles.
>
> PSALM 34:17

Lord, heal the wounds in our relationship. May Your grace strengthen our connection and foster a renewed commitment to restoration and healing.

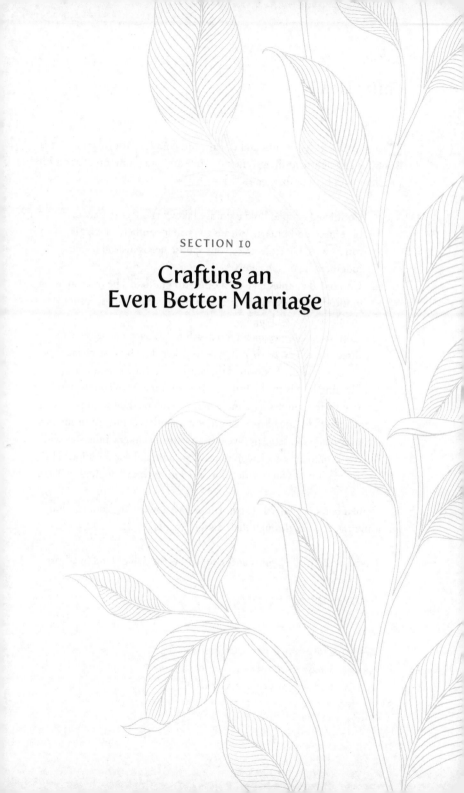

SECTION 10

Crafting an
Even Better Marriage

Four Fixes

Every marriage has its ups and downs. But couples with *great* marriages work through their disagreements. Here are four common relationship problems and how to fix them:

1. Conflicted couples hold a grudge, allowing anger to become bitterness, and bitterness leads to greater conflict. The fix is forgiveness. Give the grace your spouse needs instead of the judgment he or she deserves.
2. Conflicted couples take each other for granted. The fix is showing gratitude. Express appreciation, even for small things. A simple thank-you goes a long way.
3. Conflicted couples spend too much time apart, or they're disconnected even when they're together. The fix is to create times of togetherness. Renowned therapist Dr. John Gottman says, "Lasting love is fed by little, everyday moments of connection."
4. Conflicted couples have more negative interactions than positive. The fix? Flip the script. For every thoughtless comment or moment of impatience, serve up five or more positive interactions—a kiss, a compliment, or a few minutes of meaningful conversation. The more positive your relationship, the greater your happiness will be.

Remember, every marriage has its ups and downs, but couples with great marriages work through their disagreements.

Give thanks in all circumstances; for this is the will of God in Christ Jesus for you.

1 THESSALONIANS 5:18

Thank You for creating and divinely introducing
me to my spouse. Create in me a heart of gratitude
that remembers the joys even in the hardships.

Better Individually, Stronger Together

Watch closely the next time you visit a home improvement store. You will probably walk out with what you need to build a better home, and you might learn something to help you build a better marriage, too.

Home improvement stores have mastered good customer service. If you have a question or need help locating something, you can ask anybody who works there. But the employees don't just *advertise* their help; they deliver. Their focus is on you and your experience. That's why you usually walk out of the store feeling good about your shopping experience.

But think of how your opinion would change if, instead of helping you, the employees expected *you* to make *their* job easier. What if they told you to find that gadget you're after by yourself, or complained because you asked so many questions? I'd avoid shopping there, wouldn't you?

A lot of couples act like that. They focus on what their *spouse* can do for *them* to improve their marriage. But a great relationship takes two people who are willing to ask, "What can *I* do to be a better marriage partner?" Work on yourselves individually, and you'll grow stronger together.

Let all things be done for building up.
I CORINTHIANS 14:26

Lord, what can I do to be a better marriage partner?
Show me how to improve my weaknesses and use
my strengths to build up my spouse every day.

Marriage Isn't Static

If you want to improve your marriage, move your gaze off your spouse and look in the mirror.

Many spouses can list things they wish were different about their mate. But according to Dr. Greg Smalley, improving your marriage by trying to change your spouse is wasted effort. Why? Because you can't change other people. Instead, consider what you can do to be a better partner.

"But it's my spouse who needs to change," you say. Maybe you're right, but you have to start with yourself. The changes you make in yourself will influence your spouse to respond differently.

Dr. Smalley explains the concept using the game of ping-pong. Picture you and your spouse lobbing the ball to each other exactly the same way game after game. Neither one of you changes your approach because every shot is identical. But imagine placing just the slightest spin on the ball. That subtle difference requires your spouse to make some kind of change to return the ball.

The point is this: Marriage is never static. It's a living system of action and reaction. Changing how you interact within your marriage, even slightly, can automatically influence your spouse to make a few positive changes as well.

> If anyone is in Christ, he is a new creation. The old has passed away; behold, the new has come.
> 2 CORINTHIANS 5:17

Jesus, making changes for the health of my marriage is both exciting and a bit daunting. Thank You that I am a new creation and can rely on Your Spirit to help me embrace change.

Affirm Your Husband

Ladies, here's a simple idea that'll help you create a happier marriage: Affirm your husband.

Researchers followed more than three hundred happy, successful couples for twenty-two years. Their goal was to discover what those couples did *right*. The study's most important takeaway was that wives who affirmed their husbands had happier marriages. That's right: If you encourage your husband, your marriage will be happier for *you*. That's because the more you value *him*, the more he'll connect with *you* emotionally.

You may be thinking, *Where's my affirmation?* I know praising your husband can be challenging when he's not meaningfully reaching out to you. I'm sure he has some things he could improve in that area. We all do. But affirmation is the key that unlocks your husband's heart. He *craves* respect—from his boss, from his kids, and from you. Tell him he's a good husband, a great parent, or a hard worker, and the shell around his heart will crack. Say something encouraging daily, and it'll transform your marriage.

Watch for what he's doing *right*. When you catch him doing something well, tell him about it. Your affirmation will open his heart and fill his soul with love . . . for *you*.

Finally, brothers, whatever is true, whatever is honorable, whatever is just, whatever is pure, whatever is lovely, whatever is commendable, if there is any excellence, if there is anything worthy of praise, think about these things.

PHILIPPIANS 4:8

God, my husband is worthy of praise. He does so many things right and well, and I'm sorry that I don't always affirm him. Give me attentive eyes and ears to see and hear all the loving things he does for me—and remind me to thank him.

Three Qualities of a Healthy Marriage

Every marriage is unique, but every *healthy* marriage embodies the same three qualities:

1. *Reciprocity.* Marriage never works when good stuff in the relationship only flows in one direction. Healthy couples invest in their relationship equally. They're honest, they're caring, and they show love and respect to each other.

2. *Cooperating rather than controlling.* The couple shares power and responsibility in the relationship. When one spouse exercises too much control, the other spouse's freedom is limited. Your relationship will thrive if you become servant leaders—mutually submitting to each other and striving to "out-sacrifice" the other.

3. *A "we" attitude instead of a "me" attitude.* Individual freedom is important to relationships. But your individuality must also be harnessed and put to work on behalf of your marriage. Your freedom isn't only about the ability to do what *you* want. It's about supporting each other to grow and to thrive as individuals.

Any marriage can prosper. Both husband and wife must be willing to do what it takes. This might mean changing up a regular schedule, or even spending some of the food budget on a date night. Whatever you do, make it count!

[Submit] to one another out of reverence for Christ.
EPHESIANS 5:21

Jesus, teach me how to submit to and out-sacrifice my spouse. Help me put aside my selfish attitude and invest only the positive in my marriage.

Strength and Fragility

Marriage is one of the strongest relationships. But if you don't care for marriage properly, it can become one of the weakest.

A Prince Rupert's drop is an anomaly in glassblowing. It's created when a blob of molten glass is dropped into cold water. The glass instantly cools and forms a tadpole shape—a teardrop head with a long, wispy tail.

This object is so strange because of its strength yet utter fragility. The teardrop portion is virtually indestructible. It can be squeezed with pliers or hit with a hammer without cracking. But if the thin tail is simply snapped between your fingers, the entire piece will explode into dust.

The physical properties of the Prince Rupert's drop provide a clear metaphor for marriage. Among all the expressions of human relationship, the bond between a husband and wife is one of the most powerful. The connection is so deep and meaningful, it'll carry a couple through life's harshest experiences.

Yet if not properly nurtured, marriage can become utterly fragile. When people enter into this sacred institution, it's crucial they also choose to treat their marriage with care and respect. If they don't, the marriage—and the lives it represents—can easily shatter.

Walk . . . with all humility and gentleness, with patience, bearing with one another in love, eager to maintain the unity of the Spirit in the bond of peace.
EPHESIANS 4:1-3

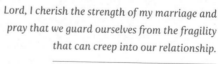

Lord, I cherish the strength of my marriage and pray that we guard ourselves from the fragility that can creep into our relationship.

Like a Skyscraper

Skyscrapers survive because they have the right balance between strength and flexibility.

For example, New York City's One World Trade Center (initially called the Freedom Tower) is the tallest building in the Western Hemisphere, built to replace the twin towers destroyed on September 11, 2001. In honor of our nation's birthday—1776—the tower stands at 1,776 feet.

For a skyscraper that high to survive, it has to remain strong against tremendous forces like gravity and wind. But a tall building also needs to be flexible enough to bend when facing those same forces. One World Trade Center is designed to sway four to five feet from center.

Strength and flexibility. You need both in a skyscraper. You need both in marriage as well. The healthiest couples are those who can stand their ground when necessary. But they also compromise for the sake of their spouse and their relationship.

If you have a strong personality, you may need to soften a bit and become more flexible in approaching your relationship. If you have an easygoing personality, you may need to be strong with better boundaries and be willing to confront wrong.

Reach for the sky in your marriage. But remember that you'll need strength and flexibility to build a loving, happy union.

As each has received a gift, use it to serve one another, as good stewards of God's varied grace.

1 PETER 4:10

Father, I love the blend of strength and flexibility in marriage. My spouse and I are stronger because we flex with each other, and we are flexible because of our combined strength. Keep us steady in You, Lord, as we reach for the sky in our relationship.

The Tingles

Bestselling author Dr. Gary Chapman hears about "the tingles" a lot. When couples come to him for premarital counseling, he asks, "Why do you want to get married?" And the one reason every couple includes is "We love each other."

What they *mean*, according to Dr. Chapman, is they *feel* something—some sort of emotional flutter for each other. In other words, they have "the tingles."

The tingles play an important role in a relationship. They motivate people to pursue a deeper connection with each other. The tingles turn a simple hello into a lunch date, and a lunch date into a romantic dinner together.

There's only one problem: The tingles fade. It's science. Long-term studies show that intense feelings in a relationship last, on average, just two years. Which is usually about the time Dr. Chapman says he hears about the tingles again—this time from couples who say they're on the verge of divorce. The intensity of their love is gone, and their feelings have faded.

Dr. Chapman routinely reminds couples that as wonderful as the tingles feel, you shouldn't rely on them. Good feelings aren't enough to sustain a relationship. Marital intimacy takes a lifetime to fully discover.

Blessed is the man who remains steadfast under trial, for when he has stood the test he will receive the crown of life, which God has promised to those who love him.
JAMES 1:12

God, thank You for the gift of feelings and the role that they play. More importantly, thank You for the intimacy that comes from steady pursuit and commitment.

Avoiding the Doldrums

Thanksgiving is replete with leftovers. But day after day with no variety isn't just a problem during the holidays. It can affect a marriage, too.

When you first pull that Thanksgiving bird out of the oven, and the table is set with stuffing, gravy, and pumpkin pie, you feel like you could eat it all. By evening, you've already made your first turkey sandwich and had seconds of everything else. But fast-forward a few days. You're losing interest in the Thanksgiving meal remnants, and the leftovers are pushed farther and farther toward the back of the fridge.

Marriage can be a lot like that. Right after the wedding, couples usually can't wait to spend all their free time together. But sooner or later, life settles into a routine, and you're left with . . . leftovers. The passion and excitement are replaced by the same ol' same ol'. From there, the relationship gets pushed farther into the background of life and, sometimes, thrown out altogether.

Let leftovers in the fridge serve as a reminder: Take action in your marriage. Don't let it slip into the doldrums. Do something outside your normal, everyday routine to revive the freshness of your relationship.

Strive together with me in your prayers . . . so that by God's will I may come to you with joy and be refreshed in your company.
ROMANS 15:30, 32

Heavenly Father, just as the apostle Paul longed for
refreshing times with dear friends, I long to be refreshed
in my marriage. Revive our passion and excitement,
and keep us from growing stale in our love.

Every Day Like the First

What if you loved your spouse every day like it was your first day together?

Becky's dad told her that that was *his* secret to a happy marriage. "Every morning," he said, "I wake up with your mother, and I treat her like it's our very first day together."

Becky remembered expressing love to her husband on their first day together. Instead of day one, her marriage now felt like day five thousand six hundred and something. Her marriage was good but not great.

Now, Becky often waited for her husband to express love to her first. When he didn't, she became resentful and refused to reach out herself. They began drifting apart.

After her dad's advice, Becky felt inspired to work her marriage forward . . . by working it backward. She wanted her relationship to be more like day one.

So she chose to love first. She didn't wait to hear "I love you." She said it. She initiated hugs. She didn't wait for her husband's forgiveness. She chose to forgive him.

Don't wait for your spouse to change. Work your marriage backward and love your spouse every day like it's your very first day together.

We love because he first loved us.

I JOHN 4:19

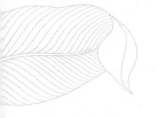

Lord God, teach me to love as You love. You loved me and my spouse long before we fell in love with each other. I recommit to loving my partner the way I did on our wedding day.

Churchill on Marriage

Are you too busy for your marriage? Winston Churchill would say that you should never be too busy to let your spouse know that you love them.

The late, great prime minister of England was a World War II hero who helped stop the spread of evil throughout Europe. His time-consuming job required him to often be away from home.

Even though Churchill's mind was preoccupied with the troops, his heart was with his beloved wife, Clementine. They wrote letters to each other continually throughout their fifty-seven-year marriage.

Each letter shows that they were as committed to each other apart as they were together. They shared little things about their days and spurred each other on when things were tough. Once when a stressed Churchill's attitude soured, Clementine told him, "You're not so kind as you used to be." She advised him to calm down and be nicer to his staff.

Winston and Clementine invested in their marriage. Instead of making excuses for growing apart, they took the time to write each other.

What about you? Are you making excuses or making commitments? Unless you're busier than Winston Churchill, surely you have time to let your spouse know: "I love you."

Husbands, love your wives, and do not be harsh with them.
COLOSSIANS 3:19

---

*Lord, we all get wrapped up in our own responsibilities
and schedules. Winston and Clementine Churchill
remind me that I, too, can communicate with
kindness and love to my spouse. Help me
never get too busy to say "I love you."*

Get Out of Jail

A Lawrence, Kansas, man was arrested after he robbed a bank. Court documents say the seventy-year-old handed a bank teller a note that read, *I have a gun. Give me money.* The teller complied.

The man took the money and calmly sat down in the bank lobby waiting to be arrested. It turns out he wasn't after the money. He just didn't want to go home to his wife anymore. In fact, the man told investigators that he'd written his demand note right in front of his wife and then walked out the door saying, "I'd rather be in jail than at home."

Wow. I know marriage can be tough, but I hope to convince *you* that there are better answers for a troubled relationship than getting yourself arrested. A conversation with a friend is sometimes enough to get through a rough spot. Other issues may require the help of someone like a pastor or a professional counselor who can bring clarity to your relationship.

Whatever problems you face, there's no reason for your marriage to feel like a jail sentence. Reach out for some help, and build something you're happy to go home to.

> Let us not grow weary of doing good, for in due season we will reap, if we do not give up.
> GALATIANS 6:9

Guide us through our challenges and back into rich relationship. Bring wise people around us who can point us back to Your plan for our marriage.

A Passion for Marriage

Men, does your marriage need a greater sense of duty . . . or greater passion?

Write down everything you do in a typical week. Your list might include working at your job, enjoying a hobby, or making repairs around the house. Next, place a check mark by the tasks you do out of duty and a heart next to the activities you do from a sense of passion. Chances are that the majority of your weekly activities are defined by duty.

Now obviously, some things simply have to get done, but often, the responsibilities overshadow our deeper passions. That's where the problem begins. Duty and chores are to the soul what bread and water are to the body—they allow us to survive physically, but not to thrive.

And so it goes with marriage. We marry for love, romance, and dreams, but the practical demands of life often overtake us. Before long, intimacy is replaced by busyness, and the passion we once knew is lost.

The good news? Passion *can* be restored to your marriage. Try spending time with your wife for fifteen minutes a day. Hold hands on a walk together. Find ways to connect with your wife's heart, and watch her—and your marriage—come alive with passion.

> I slept, but my heart was awake. A sound! My beloved is knocking. "Open to me, my sister, my love, my dove, my perfect one, for my head is wet with dew, my locks with the drops of the night."
> SONG OF SOLOMON 5:2

Thank You that You delight when we delight in each other. Rekindle our passion, for You are a passionate God.

Thriving through Symbols

For cultures to thrive, they need strong symbols. Symbols ground people in core values that enable them to prosper.

Take the American flag, for example. Its stars and stripes represent all fifty states and the original thirteen colonies. But the flag represents so much more. It's an enduring symbol of democracy and freedom.

A wedding ring is another powerful symbol in our culture. It not only communicates that the wearer is married but also symbolizes the nature of unconditional love itself—an unbroken circle with no beginning and no end.

Wedding rings also symbolize a couple's vow to love each other till death parts them. That's why wedding rings are usually fashioned out of precious metals and gemstones. Not only are diamonds and gold inherently valuable, but they also last because they've been purified through fire and intense pressure.

We don't always live up to our ideals as couples or as a nation, but when we fail, the answer isn't to abandon those ideals. It's to work even harder to reinforce them. For couples, that means honoring their commitment to faithfully love and sacrifice for each other.

Walk in love, as Christ loved us and gave himself up for us,
a fragrant offering and sacrifice to God.
EPHESIANS 5:2

God, when our marriage goes through fire, sustain
us and purify us. Give me the courage to sacrifice
for my spouse and the commitment we've made.

Giving Your Best

A guy selling cable TV service tried to get author Dave Willis to be satisfied with his company's leftovers. He wanted Dave to pay more for less. That's not how the guy pitched his offer, of course. The company would take care of him. The best channels at the best price.

Then Dave started asking questions. And the more he learned, the more he realized that the cable company would give him as little as necessary to keep him as a customer. Leftovers are a lousy model for a marriage, too. When couples are first together, they give each other their best. They're romantic. They call, they text, they care about what the other person thinks and feels.

But after the honeymoon ends, many couples abandon their pursuit. Instead of chasing each other, they chase schedules, money, titles, and children. Those are all great things—in balance. But when your priorities shift away from your marriage, your relationship gets your leftovers.

So if your relationship feels dull, know this: You can change it. Invest in your relationship with a renewed sense of passion. Don't settle for leftovers. Give your marriage your best.

The point is this: whoever sows sparingly will also reap sparingly, and whoever sows bountifully will also reap bountifully.
2 CORINTHIANS 9:6

Jesus, Your Word teaches us to sow bountifully. Please show us how to sow passionately into our marriage, never settling for leftovers. Thank You for Your blessings.

Fall in Love More Every Day

At his nephew's wedding, Ken Blanchard said something unusual. He told the young couple he hoped that their special day would be the moment they loved each other the least.

To understand Ken's words, you have to start in India, where he was traveling. A tour guide explained that his parents were arranging his marriage. Curious, Ken asked what the differences were between arranged marriages in India and typical American relationships. The man replied that couples in India assume they'll fall in love with each other after they marry. In America, people tend to fall in love before marriage, then out of love during it.

Many young couples enter marriage focused entirely on their intense emotions for each other. But eventually, infatuation disappears, and couples question whether they married the right person.

And that's the deeper meaning behind Ken's hope that the couple's wedding would be the moment they loved each other the least. He followed up those words with this beautiful blessing: "May your life together be one of falling in love with each other more every day." May that be true of all our marriages.

> But Ruth said, "Do not urge me to leave you or to return from following you. For where you go I will go, and where you lodge I will lodge. Your people shall be my people, and your God my God. Where you die I will die, and there will I be buried. May the LORD do so to me and more also if anything but death parts me from you."
> RUTH 1:16-17

Lord, just as Ruth said she would remain committed unto death, help us remain committed to each other, deepening in our love each day, no matter what life throws our way.

Extending Kindness

There's a simple way you can make a good marriage great or bring a struggling marriage back to life. It's kindness.

Sound too good to be true? Researchers studied more than seven hundred husbands and wives to find out the effect kindness had on their marriages.

For thirty days, each spouse focused on three behaviors: They eliminated their own negativity, they affirmed and praised their partners, and they performed simple acts of kindness.

The results were impressive. Ninety percent of the couples reported a dramatic reduction in relational negativity. An equal number described significant improvement in their romantic connection and in the overall well-being of their marriage.

Such dramatic benefits shouldn't come as a surprise. What we consider "simple" kindness is actually a very strong gesture. It can move any marriage in the right direction because genuine kindness communicates to your spouse how deeply you treasure him or her.

Extending kindness benefits you, too. It enables you to be patient when there is conflict to work through. It'll help you recognize your own negative behavior and soften your heart in ways that will strengthen your marriage.

Best of all, kindness isn't a help only a few can afford. It's available to anyone.

He has told you, O man, what is good; and what does the LORD require of you but to do justice, and to love kindness, and to walk humbly with your God?
MICAH 6:8

Father, how can I love kindness if I am unwilling to show it daily to my beloved? Help me embrace this facet of what pleases You and shower my spouse with kindness today.

Loving with Attitude and Action

One summer Greg was trying to get his family's vacation underway. But first, he had to deal with four-year-old Murphy, who refused to leave without her toy bunny. Greg tried to outsmart his daughter. He suggested the bunny needed to stay home to guard the house.

But Murphy wasn't buying it. She loved her bunny so much she said, "I want her to have fun. I'll stay here and watch the house so she can go with you on the trip."

Needless to say, Murphy got to go on vacation—with the toy bunny.

And Greg learned a lesson about loving others. His daughter loved her toy bunny so much she was willing to sacrifice good things for herself. In other words, she combined attitude with action.

It's an approach that can transform your marriage. Start with the right attitude. Discover what's important to your spouse. Then, remember to follow that up with action. In other words, ask your spouse what you can do to help him or her feel loved. Then do it.

Sound simple? It is, but you'll be amazed at the difference it makes.

If a brother or sister is poorly clothed and lacking in daily food,
and one of you says to them, "Go in peace, be warmed and filled,"
without giving them the things needed for the body, what good
is that?

JAMES 2:15-16

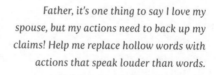

Father, it's one thing to say I love my spouse, but my actions need to back up my claims! Help me replace hollow words with actions that speak louder than words.

Seven Opportunities

If you'd like a happier marriage, then you have some choices to make. In fact, you have about *seven* choices to make. And that's just today.

Research indicates that couples disagree on average almost 2,500 times per year, which comes to about seven times a day. That's seven opportunities a day to push you and your spouse further apart . . . or draw the two of you closer together. Which path you take depends on *you*. You get to choose.

You might believe the myth that conflict in your marriage is the result of your differences. It's not. It's the result of how you *handle* those differences. Unhealthy couples put individual goals above the health and well-being of the relationship. They dismiss their partner's feelings and seek after *me* and *mine*. Healthy couples, on the other hand, work together as a team. They put *we* before *me*, and they choose what's best for the relationship even when it requires self-denial.

A good marriage is about channeling your differences in a positive direction and coming together in unity. Progressive romantic attraction might be known as *falling* in love, but a relationship that endures is no accident. It must be nurtured through selflessness, sacrifice, and the pursuit of unity in almost every situation possible.

It's not enough to proclaim on your wedding day that you will love your spouse "for better or for worse, till death do us part." It's a choice you continue to make every day thereafter—often several times a day.

> Be kind to one another, tenderhearted, forgiving one another, as God in Christ forgave you.
> EPHESIANS 4:32

Father, grant us the wisdom to navigate our differences
with patience and understanding. Give us the humility
to compromise for the sake of our relationship.
May Your love foster unity in our marriage.

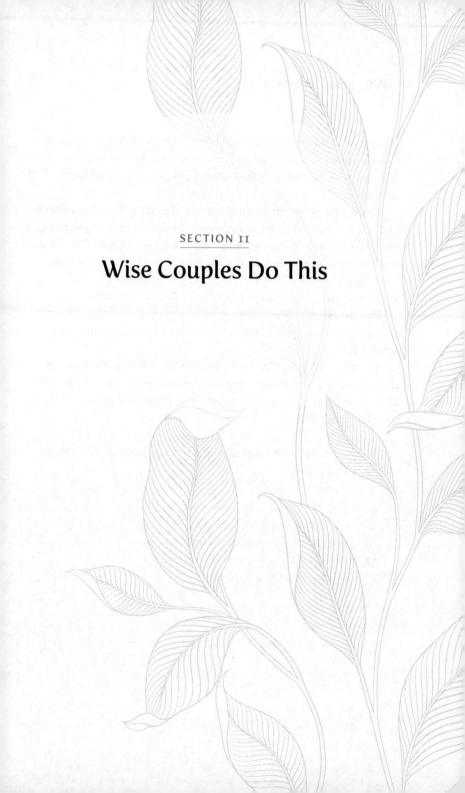

SECTION II

Wise Couples Do This

Love and Cherish

Author Gary Thomas once asked a group of women if they felt their husbands loved them. All of them raised a hand. Then he asked, "How many of you feel like your husband *cherishes* you?" Every hand dropped.

There is a difference between loving and cherishing. Love focuses on sacrifice, service, loyalty, and commitment. To cherish a person means to respect them, honor them, and hold them in high regard. Sometimes that involves minimizing your own presence in order to elevate your spouse.

To better cherish your wife, Gary suggests the following tips in his 2017 book *Cherish*:

First, recommit to your wedding promise to cherish her. Even if your vows didn't include a commitment to cherish each other, commit to this practice anyway.

Second, avoid comparing your wife with other women. Comparison, after all, can lead to contempt. You will surely see other women's strengths and your wife's weaknesses at times, but always treat your spouse like she is the one—the *only one*.

An excellent wife who can find? She is far more precious than jewels.
PROVERBS 31:10

Heavenly Father, remind me daily how to truly love and cherish my wife. She is far more precious than jewels and deserves to be treated as a royal daughter of the King of kings.

Can Your Spouse Meet All Your Needs?

Only in romance novels and poetry do couples believe *My spouse is my everything*. In real life, it's impossible for one person to meet our every need. I learned that the hard way.

In the first years of our marriage, Jean and I spent a lot of time together traveling to high schools around the country. Being an extrovert, I loved the constant interaction.

But Jean is an introvert. She enjoyed the work we did in schools as much as I did, but she felt drained by all the people. One afternoon, she headed out the door for some groceries. I asked to tag along, but she said, "Jim, I love you, but I'd really like to be alone." Initially, I was hurt that she didn't want me to go with her, but I soon realized that she *needed* time alone. Once I learned to give Jean some breathing room, our marriage reaped the benefits.

Your spouse *cannot* meet your every need, so fill those spaces with other healthy activities. Have good friendships, pursue a hobby, or enjoy a little solitude. Give your spouse room to breathe in his or her own way, and you'll find your time together growing even richer.

My God will supply every need of yours according to his riches in glory in Christ Jesus.
PHILIPPIANS 4:19

Thank You for providing for all my needs. Give me grace for my spouse when he or she needs space, and teach us to understand each other's needs.

An Expert in Her

Guys, if I asked you to tell me about your favorite hobby or sport, how long would it take? Some of you could talk to me for hours.

Now, what if I asked you to tell me about your wife? How long would *that* take? Some of you might do all right, but a lot of you would run out of stuff to say in about thirty seconds.

The truth is that we give our attention to things that matter to us. So if you'd have a hard time saying something insightful or meaningful about your wife, maybe it's time for you to discover more about her.

Of all the things you're striving to be an expert in, let your wife be at the top of your list. Learn her love language. Remember her likes and dislikes, and take note of the little quirks that make her uniquely her. Or try this: Ask her questions about her dreams or her biggest fears. Then sit back and really listen.

Your wife is a bottomless well of discovery. If you'll take a little time and dig, there's always something more to know about who she is. Become an expert . . . in *her*.

You have captivated my heart, my sister, my bride; you have captivated my heart with one glance of your eyes, with one jewel of your necklace.

SONG OF SOLOMON 4:9

Captivate me with the beauty and the mystery
of my wife. Guide me in understanding and
truly knowing the depths of her heart.

Forgiveness Isn't Fair

*F*airness is one of the worst things you can do to a relationship.

Fair is all about keeping things even between two people. That sounds good in theory, but it doesn't work so well in practice. *Playing fair* means, "If you treat me right, I'll treat you right. But if you cross me, I'll hurt you right back." That's exactly how a lot of married couples treat each other. They call each other names or act disrespectfully.

The best thing you can do is to forgive. Forgiveness offers your spouse what he or she *needs* instead of what your mate *deserves*. Forgiveness meets mistakes with grace instead of judgment. *That* is how you heal your relationship and empower it to grow stronger and become more loving.

The reason you don't forgive is that forgiveness isn't fair. Forgiveness requires you to give up the right to hurt someone who has hurt you. I'm not asking you to excuse or minimize wrongs. Forgiveness doesn't do that. Instead, it sets you free from *your* hurt and allows *you* to move through life in peace.

Forgiveness isn't fair. And it isn't always easy, either. But it can transform a marriage.

If you forgive others their trespasses, your heavenly Father will also forgive you, but if you do not forgive others their trespasses, neither will your Father forgive your trespasses.
MATTHEW 6:14-15

Jesus, You are serious about forgiveness. You died to grant us forgiveness. Help me not to look for fairness in my relationship with my spouse but to seek and model true forgiveness.

Married Eighty-Six Years

There's a reason we seek advice from people who've been around awhile. They have the hard-earned wisdom that only comes from experience.

Before his death at age 104, Herbert Fisher and his wife, Zelmyra, held the record for the world's longest marriage. They were just a few months shy of eighty-seven years together! With a history like that, it'll come as no surprise that people far and wide clamored for their secret. Their answer, however, may have surprised some.

"There is no secret," Herbert and Zelmyra both pointed out. Their shared advice went something like this: "Marriage is not a contest, so never keep score" and "Above all else, be willing to stick it out. God has put the two of you on the same team to win together."

Words like *commitment* and *hard work* don't exactly ring with fairy-tale charm. But they reflect the hard-earned wisdom couples need to hear. Successful marriages are too often considered the result of "chemistry" or "fate." After all, love should be easy, right? The truth is that there is no secret to a successful marriage. As Herbert and Zelmyra would have agreed, it all boils down to investing in your marriage and doing what you have to do to make it work.

> My son, do not forget my teaching, but let your heart keep my commandments, for length of days and years of life and peace they will add to you. Let not steadfast love and faithfulness forsake you; bind them around your neck; write them on the tablet of your heart. So you will find favor and good success in the sight of God and man.
>
> PROVERBS 3:1-4

Lord, thank You for Herbert and Zelmyra's marriage and wisdom. I want to invest in my marriage with the same steady commitment and faithful love.

Cheer Him On

Applaud your husband. That's right—cheer him on.

Just about every guy has had people cheering for him from boyhood. His parents, coaches, teachers, buddies. They clapped when he scored a touchdown, or mastered a musical piece, or brought home an A. Now as a grown-up, he's looking for pats on the back from his boss, his coworkers . . . and from you. He wants *you* to be his biggest cheerleader.

But some guys come home to a wife who's almost booing. Pointing out a husband's flaws is not helping him but pushing him away. What he *hears* is how unsatisfied you are with him: He's not a good husband and father and doesn't provide well for the family.

Your husband needs to know that you believe he can be as successful at home as he is outside it. He craves your respect. He'll step up when someone spurs him on as a father, as a husband, and in his career. When you speak words of encouragement into his heart and believe in him, he'll transform. He'll strive to become the great guy you already believe he is.

So if you want to draw closer to your husband, cheer him on.

May the God of endurance and encouragement grant you to live in . . . harmony with one another, in accord with Christ Jesus.
ROMANS 15:5

Thank You for being the God of endurance and encouragement. I want to reflect Your encouragement as I exuberantly cheer on my husband. He deserves more praise and thankfulness from me. Remind me to express how much I do believe in him and see great things ahead for us.

Fill It to the Brim

I s your marriage "filled to the brim"? It can be, *if* you've got the faith to keep doing what's right.

Let me illustrate with a story about Jesus' first miracle when a wedding party ran out of wine. Jesus told the servants to fill six stone jars with water—each one holding twenty to thirty gallons.

Note the faith of the servants. Remember, this was first-century Judea. There was no plumbing or garden hoses. Filling stone jars that size would have required repeated trips to a well.

At any point, the servants could have looked at the water in the jars and decided, "This isn't working." They could have given up and only filled the jars partway. Instead, they kept doing what they knew was right until the jars were filled to the brim. And because they did, everyone at the wedding witnessed a miracle.

The secret to a strong marriage? Keep doing what's right even if it's taking longer to see results than you want. Do not stop halfway or do just enough to hold your relationship together. Day after day, keep filling your relationship with love, intimacy, and connection . . . until it's filled to the brim.

> Give, and it will be given to you. Good measure, pressed down, shaken together, running over, will be put into your lap. For with the measure you use it will be measured back to you.
> LUKE 6:38

Jesus, it's so encouraging to know that Your first miracle led to such abundance. You are a God of abundance, and I want my marriage to brim over continually with love, intimacy, and connection.

Stand by Your Man

Ladies, do you want your husband to be a success? Then it's important for you to understand the crucial role you play.

Authors and relationship specialists Bill and Pam Farrel can tell you all about that. Early in their marriage, a mentor advised Pam never to embarrass her husband in public. "Stand by your man," the older woman said. "Be his biggest cheerleader." At the time, Pam scoffed at the idea. But it wasn't long before she learned the influence she had in building his confidence.

She and Bill were dancing at a party when Bill suddenly backed away. "I ripped my pants," he said discreetly. Since Pam could easily laugh at her own shortcomings, she shouted to everybody in the room, "Look! Bill ripped his pants!" Everyone laughed—except Bill. Not only that, but at speaking engagements later that week, Bill's usually strong presence seemed timid and insecure.

It was then that Pam understood her mentor's advice. If a man's wife isn't his biggest fan, it can strip him of his confidence with others. You can help his confidence soar, or you can shackle him with self-doubt. So stand by your man and cheer him on!

An excellent wife is the crown of her husband, but she who brings shame is like rottenness in his bones.

PROVERBS 12:4

God, give me eyes to see my husband as You see him. Guard my mind and my tongue from speaking ill, and help me encourage him toward Your greater purposes for his life.

Mending the Holes

A fishing net with giant holes in it is useless. So is a marriage with giant holes.

Leslie has been a commercial fisherwoman with her husband for forty years. They've had plenty of disagreements. Sometimes the boundaries between husband and wife and skipper and crewman get blurred. But an important skill set from their profession has helped Leslie and her husband keep their marriage strong.

Their day doesn't end when the fishing is done. They spend hours every week mending the holes in their nets. They cut away the netting around the hole and leave behind a neat square or rectangle. Then they cut an identical-sized piece from another net. That new piece is then sewn into the first net. After the repair, the net is even stronger.

Leslie says keeping your marriage healthy is similar. Life can tear holes in your relationship. But there is hope. You mend your marriage in much the same way you mend a fishing net. You cut away the frayed, unhealthy parts, and you replace them with something good.

Cut away dishonesty, contempt, and jealousy, and weave back in trust, love, and respect. It'll mend the holes in your relationship and make your marriage even stronger.

No one puts a piece of unshrunk cloth on an old garment, for the patch tears away from the garment, and a worse tear is made.
MATTHEW 9:16

Father God, patch up any holes in my marriage. Let me look to You—the One who really knows how to mend the frayed places in my relationship with my spouse.

Cherish Your Wife

You love your wife. But do you *cherish* her? Some guys don't seem to understand what it means to cherish their wives.

Let me explain it this way: If money were no object, what would your dream car be? From the shiny paint to the finely tuned engine, I bet you'd devote yourself to that car. You'd protect it from dents and potholes. You'd keep it washed and waxed. You'd be so proud of your car, you'd want everyone to see how much you valued and cared for it. You'd probably even think about your car when you were busy doing other things.

Investing that much zeal in a car is all in good fun, but devoting that kind of passion to your wife can transform your marriage. When your wife feels cherished by you, her heart will come alive, and she'll be much more willing to invest in your relationship.

Cherishing your wife is a skill you can develop. You can learn how to make your wife the center of your attention and affection. You can learn to take pride in your marriage and to build a relationship that's deep and meaningful.

Don't settle for less.

Husbands, love your wives, as Christ loved the church and gave himself up for her.
EPHESIANS 5:25

Jesus, I love my wife, but I really want to know how to cherish her well. Thank You for this incredible woman who deserves my best. Teach me how to make my beloved the center of my attention and affection.

Cherish Your Husband

I talk with husbands about the value of cherishing their wives, but ladies, your husband wants to be cherished just as much as you do. A friend told me about a former elite swimmer, a champion in both high school and college. The man's training and dedication to compete were woven so deeply into his life that he lost an important part of himself after he retired.

What got him through that confusing time of life was the way his wife cherished him. She didn't antagonize him, belittle him, or unfairly compare him with male family members, friends, or coworkers. She cherished him for who he was and reminded him of all the good he had to offer. Her support and encouragement helped him move forward with strength and confidence into new opportunities.

As that story illustrates, cherishing your husband will probably take patience and a little grace. Every one of us has areas of strength and areas where we need to improve. So be your husband's biggest fan. Build him up. Offer him respect and believe in him, both for who he *is* and for all that he can *become*, and he'll open his heart to you.

> Let each one of you love his wife as himself, and let the wife see that she respects her husband.
> EPHESIANS 5:33

Gracious Lord, I want to be kind, patient, and supportive of my husband, especially when he is struggling. As I do this, I know this shows him how much I respect and cherish him. He deserves to know that I believe in him and stand with him through everything.

Love Is Strong, Not Weak

Guys, when you hear the word *love*, what images come to mind? Thanks to Hollywood, it's probably stuff like a bouquet of roses, beautiful weddings, or strolls along the beach at sunset. We've been conditioned to associate love with things that are tender and nurturing.

Love *is* all those things, of course, but frilly ideas like that don't usually resonate with men. So guys tend to consider love a topic best left to women. That's really unfortunate because love has a strong side that transcends all the soft imagery that traditionally characterizes it.

As British author and apologist G. K. Chesterton famously said, "A true soldier fights not because he hates what is in front of him, but because he loves what is behind him." In other words, it's love that drives soldiers forward into battle. And it's love that gives parents the courage to make difficult choices to steer their children in the right direction.

At its core, love is strong. It empowers us to take a stand against anything that would threaten the well-being of the people we care about. It doesn't matter whether it's people or bad choices coming against a member of our family. Love is courageous.

> "Because the poor are plundered, because the needy groan, I
> will now arise," says the LORD; "I will place him in the safety for
> which he longs."
> PSALM 12:5

*You protect and You love ferociously. Lord, make
me more like You in how I love those around me.*

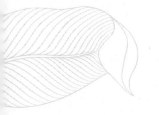

Try New Things

Every marriage hits a lull sooner or later. One day, the excitement gives way to the dullness of routine. It's okay to say it because it's true: Husbands and wives get bored with each other. Relationships get stuck, and we don't always know how to break free. We need a strategy that we can return to in order to navigate the different stages of our marriage.

Here's a helpful tip: Try new things. Studies show that experiencing something new together is like opening a window to your relationship and letting in fresh air. One study tested the effect of different experiences on marriages. One group shared a typical date night together—like a nice dinner and a movie. Another group spent ninety minutes a week trying new things. Some went hiking for the first time or took dance lessons. The couples who tried new things reported higher levels of connection, intimacy, and feelings of romance than those who enjoyed a routine date night. They talked more. They touched more. They looked each other in the eyes and connected at a deeper level.

Give it a try. Get out of the rut you're in and carve a new groove, one that breathes life into your marriage.

If any of you lacks wisdom, let him ask God, who gives generously to all without reproach, and it will be given him.

JAMES 1:5

God, I invite You into my marriage. Give me wisdom and creativity to love my spouse.

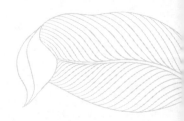

My Sweet One

In the Broadway musical *Man of La Mancha*, the main character, Don Quixote, falls in love with a barmaid named Aldonza. Everyone else mistreats her, but to Don Quixote, she is—and will always be—his Dulcinea, which means "sweet one."

While on his deathbed, Don Quixote asks her why that name, Dulcinea, matters to her. She says that his unconditional love completely transformed her life. It helped her rise above her abuse, and it taught her how to love herself. The beauty is that Don Quixote's relationship with Aldonza was rooted as much in unconditional love as it was in romantic feelings.

Romance is good for a marriage, but romantic feelings have a shelf life. They feel good, but they can fade. They're not enough to sustain a relationship for five, ten, or fifty years. Romantic love is conditional.

But unconditional love is transformative. It extends love to your spouse, your child, or a friend, not for what they can do for you, but simply because of who they are.

Man of La Mancha is just a story, but it points us to an ideal that's worth pursuing. Whoever your "sweet one" is, give him or her your love—unconditionally.

I will have mercy on No Mercy, and I will say to Not My People, "You are my people"; and he shall say, "You are my God."
HOSEA 2:23

God, thank You for loving me unconditionally.
Help me be a reflection of Your love to my spouse.

Don't Miss the Trees for the Trail

Consultant Peter Bregman led a group on a mountain trek—and realized at one point that they weren't where they were supposed to be. They'd followed what seemed to be the right trail. But they hadn't paid attention to nearby landmarks and distant points that could have kept them on the actual path.

A dangerous thing happens when we follow a trail, Bregman says. We stop paying attention to the environment. Since the trail is easy to follow, we let our minds wander and stop paying attention to where we are.

That's a valuable lesson. Daily routines can make the trail seem clearcut. But they can also set us up for complacency and a false sense of security. We miss the drop-off ten feet ahead because we're looking down at our own two feet. Or we don't notice dangers creeping from behind because we only see the worn stones underneath.

Sure, we need to watch where we're walking. But we also have to keep long-distance goals for healthy marriage in view. Wherever our journey takes us, though, we'll be a lot less lost if we remember to look up.

> Look carefully then how you walk, not as unwise but as wise, making the best use of the time, because the days are evil.
> EPHESIANS 5:15-16

God, please help us stay focused on where we are and where we need to go relationally. Help us lift each other up as we walk this journey of life together.

Kindness Is Key

What if someone could accurately predict whether your marriage will succeed or fail? Dr. John Gottman, a widely respected marriage therapist, estimates he can predict with better than 90 percent accuracy whether a newly married couple will go the distance.

A claim like that gets my attention. If there's an objective way to gauge my marriage's health, I want to know about it. Gottman's secret isn't a crystal ball. It's extensive research he's conducted that examines how couples communicate.

Dr. Gottman has observed a number of factors that predict how well a marriage will do. In happy couples, both spouses show a lot of affection toward each other. They practice healthy conflict resolution and are respectful of each other's needs and desires. They show interest in what their mate says—even when he or she makes little comments about a pretty sunset or shares a nice moment from their day.

Unhappy couples behave just the opposite. They look for reasons to criticize each other. They ignore or dismiss those little comments about sunsets. And when one spouse has a bit of good news from the day, the other spouse either doesn't acknowledge it or doesn't share in the happiness.

Simply put, marriages flourish or perish depending on whether the relationship is fueled by kindness or contempt. Genuine kindness can move any marriage in the right direction.

I know how to be brought low, and I know how to abound. In any and every circumstance, I have learned the secret of facing plenty and hunger, abundance and need.

PHILIPPIANS 4:12

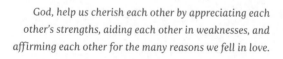

God, help us cherish each other by appreciating each other's strengths, aiding each other in weaknesses, and affirming each other for the many reasons we fell in love.

Thoughtful Caretakers

I love old homes. There's something special about a structure that's stood unmoved for a century while everything around it changes. It reminds me a lot of strong marriages.

Old homes have unique character. The walls usually aren't square, and the floors roll and dip. But what they lack in precise construction, they make up for in charm. They're like stepping into a time machine. You can imagine generations of families running up and down the staircase or laughing at the dinner table.

That rich history would disappear if not for thoughtful caretakers. A home can't withstand decades of sun, rain, and wind without some attention. Cracks have to be fixed, siding repainted, and the roof kept weathertight. Because if the home deteriorates and is lost, the memories can also be lost.

Which brings me to marriage. It's an identity, a sense of belonging in a world full of strangers. But for a marriage to endure, it needs thoughtful caretakers. Give it the loving care it deserves to restore it back to health. Because when a marriage ends in divorce, it's like an old house with all its history being torn down.

> Restore to me the joy of your salvation, and uphold me with a willing spirit.
> PSALM 51:12

Lord in heaven, please help me do my part as a thoughtful caretaker of my marriage. As I willingly do what it takes to restore this marriage with loving care, please instill a joyful spirit within me.

When Your Spouse Needs a Change

A lot of people are struggling with obesity these days—and your spouse may be one of them. So how do you tactfully encourage him or her to lose weight?

There is absolutely nothing you can do to make your spouse lose weight. Slimming down has to be your spouse's idea. If he or she perceives it as your idea, your spouse may go out of the way to prove that he or she is in control of his or her own choices.

The best strategy is to have *one* caring conversation about weight. Tell your spouse that you are concerned about his health, but you recognize that it is his decision. Then close your mouth about the topic.

Do your best to cook healthy meals and maintain an active lifestyle. But if he buys cookies and potato chips, leave him alone. No hints, jokes, or cold shoulders.

Your spouse may never choose to change his eating or exercise habits. On occasion he'll make choices you don't agree with. This makes marriage the most difficult and amazing relationship in the world—a commitment to love even in the midst of disagreement and disappointment.

> By this all people will know that you are my disciples, if you have love for one another.
> JOHN 13:35

Precious God, I ask that You help me engage in wise, selective conversations with my spouse in areas where I am concerned. Help me refrain from badgering or giving cold shoulders if my spouse's opinion is different from mine. Please help us remain committed in love, even when we disagree.

What Really Matters— and What Doesn't

Author Jim Burns remembers the day he confronted his new bride about her outlandish behavior. He led her into the bathroom and pointed at the toilet paper holder. Instead of properly installing a new roll, she had simply set it on top of the dispenser. Jim demonstrated how to install a new roll correctly.

"Really, sweetie," he asked, "how long does this take?"

Jim expected his wife to be happy that he'd shown her a better way. She wasn't.

At that moment Jim realized something: His wife didn't need to learn a lesson—*he* did! He realized there are behaviors that matter, and there are behaviors that don't. Abuse matters. Addiction matters. So do infidelity and dishonesty. But does it really matter if the toilet paper is sitting on top of the dispenser? Or if the toothpaste gets squeezed in the middle?

Anything can turn into conflict if you let it. Happy marriages require two people who serve each other. Servanthood takes a lot of work as you deny what you want and allow your spouse to have some things his or her way. Yet serving your spouse does something for your heart as much as your spouse's.

Even the Son of Man came not to be served but to serve, and to give his life as a ransom for many.
MARK 10:45

Father, Your very own Son served those around Him—to the point of sacrificing His life on the cross. What a small thing it is for me to serve my spouse by not demanding that his or her every behavior meets my expectation.

The Kiss Still Works

D r. Richard Selzer told a story that illustrates what growing together in marriage is all about.

One of his patients was a young woman who underwent surgery to remove a tumor from her cheek. The complicated procedure severed a nerve, paralyzing the left side of her face and leaving her smile crooked. The young woman was devastated. When she broke down in tears, her husband offered reassurance in a beautifully touching way. He altered the shape of his own lips to match hers . . . and kissed her. Then he looked deep into her eyes and said, "Don't worry, our kiss still works."

There comes a time in every marriage when something turns out differently than you'd hoped. In countless ways, the person you married will not be the same person five, ten, or twenty years from now. Neither will you be.

Marriage changes us—and so do raising children, pursuing a career, and every other significant event in our lives. In those moments, love calls us not to turn away, but to alter something about ourselves that meets our spouse at his or her point of need.

If I have prophetic powers, and understand all mysteries and all knowledge, and if I have all faith, so as to remove mountains, but have not love, I am nothing.

I CORINTHIANS 13:2

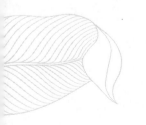

Father, it's tempting to see my spouse the same way I've seen him or her all along—and yet by doing that, I'll miss out on one of the greatest gifts, which is to truly see what my spouse's heart needs today and to willingly meet that need with love.

Background Singers

A good marriage is like good music.

To understand what I mean, think about your favorite song. One reason it likely moves you the way it does is the voice of the lead singer. Yet the backing vocals also help bring a song's melody to life, perhaps more than you realize. Background singers harmonize with the lead vocal, supporting the song's melody with a richness that the lead singer might never achieve alone.

In a similar way, couples who make beautiful music together are those who surround themselves with harmonious background singers—family members, close friends, or a marriage counselor. These are people who can support and encourage them when the marriage journey gets difficult.

With the divorce rate hovering near 50 percent, lots of marriages are clearly under immense pressure. Many couples feel isolated. They might socialize, but do they have anyone with whom to open up about the true state of their marriage? Isolation can turn every struggle into an obstacle to overcome alone. As a result, many couples don't survive. And those who do might never find a fulfilling rhythm together.

To protect your relationship from losing its rhythm or sounding out of tune, don't sing alone. Surround yourselves with a chorus of background singers who will help your marriage become a melody that will sweep you off your feet.

> Be filled with the Spirit, addressing one another in psalms and hymns and spiritual songs, singing and making melody to the Lord with your heart.
> EPHESIANS 5:18-19

Lord, turn our marriage into a beautiful song.
Surround us with background singers who harmonize
with us, enrich the melody of our union, and create
a chorus of encouragement in our marriage.

Make the Moments Count

Some folks think the number thirteen might cause bad luck, but the number ten can completely transform your marriage for the better.

First, set aside ten minutes a day for you and your spouse to talk. Sit together on the couch. Look each other in the eye. Then talk about anything you want. The only goal here is to get beneath the surface—to make a heart-to-heart connection. Discuss something more meaningful than your busy schedules or the weather.

Second, make a ten-second physical connection with each other, such as a hug, before you head out the door. Do it again when you're both back at home. Grab each other for ten seconds when you pass in the hallway. Make it random, lighthearted, and fun.

Third, give each other a ten-second kiss—or two five-second kisses. The point is to plant one on each other and linger a bit. Give your spouse a smooch that reconnects you and reminds you of the love you share.

Marriage isn't self-sustaining. It requires constant focus and attention. If your schedules keep you from spending quality time together for days or even weeks at a time, then grab a few moments whenever you can. A ten-minute talk, a ten-second hug, and a ten-second kiss can give your marriage a quick injection of love when life is moving fast.

Steadfast love and faithfulness meet; righteousness and peace kiss each other.
PSALM 85:10

Father, transform our marriage through deep,
meaningful connection. Be present in our
conversation and our physical touch. Help
these brief moments of interaction translate
to lasting intimacy when life gets busy.

SECTION 12

Temptation

The Power of Inner Weakness

Contrary to Hollywood's portrayal of Samson and Delilah, they were anything but a love story. They're a warning, among other things, about the dangers of not controlling sexual passion.

Samson is described as a warrior who is supposed to deliver the Hebrews from their enemies. His incredible strength is mysteriously connected to the length of his hair. If he cuts it, his power evaporates.

Enter Delilah. Samson falls in love, but Delilah seduces him for her own selfish goals. She tricks him into revealing the secret of his strength and gives that information to Samson's enemies.

Samson's outer strength meant nothing against the power of his *inner* weakness. His obsession with Delilah became his downfall.

That ancient story is just as relevant today. In one study, four thousand married couples who had suffered adultery were interviewed. Virtually all the offending partners said they were blindsided by their own sin. Men and women alike weaken themselves through small compromises and are caught up in dangerous behavior before they fully realize it's happening.

Sexual desire is glorious. But it can also be dangerous. As with anything that powerful, sex can only be healthy when you channel it toward what is true, good, and right for your marriage.

[The Lord] said to me, "My grace is sufficient for you, for my power is made perfect in weakness." Therefore I will boast all the more gladly of my weaknesses, so that the power of Christ may rest upon me.

2 CORINTHIANS 12:9

Jesus, You fully understand where true strength lies. Empower my marriage with what is true, good, and right. Help my spouse and me surrender our weaknesses and strengths fully to You.

In Love with a Fantasy

Infidelity has been described as a nuclear bomb detonating within a marriage. The effects on everyone involved are devastating.

The euphoria and excitement of infidelity are intoxicating. *Intoxication* is a perfect descriptor because, at their core, affairs are similar to alcohol and drug addiction. Neither addiction nor infidelity is a rational, logical solution to life's challenges. They're both ways to escape reality.

We all have legitimate desires for love and significance. But filling those needs with the emotional high of an affair is an illusion. You're not in love with a human being; you're in love with the fantasy of what you wish your relationships could be. The other person doesn't know the real, authentic you and therefore can't truly love you. It's love on the surface versus being known through years of healthy, intimate relationship. As with every addiction, you'll end up feeling empty.

Maybe you're struggling in your marriage, and the idea of an affair has crossed your mind. Or maybe you're already in one, and you feel trapped. I urge you to seek the help of a professional counselor now. There is still hope. Your marriage and your life can be restored.

[God] is able to keep you from stumbling and to present you blameless before the presence of his glory with great joy.
JUDE 1:24

Lord, I ask You to help me stay faithful to my spouse. It's tempting to look elsewhere to feel loved and significant. Guard and protect my marriage starting today, and keep me hopeful for Your best.

The Point of No Return

Some people enjoy flirting with danger. They love the thrill of getting right up to the edge without going over. But all it takes is one wrong step—just one toe over the line—and your life is never the same.

Locals around Niagara Falls consider the North Grand Island Bridge the "point of no return." Beyond this point, the force of the current is so powerful that it's impossible to alter your course and return to safety. You're going over the falls.

Flirting with danger is costly in marriage as well. Toying with feelings of attraction outside of marriage or flirting with a coworker might seem like innocent fun. But sooner or later, you'll cross a point of no return. Just one toe over the line, and it's too late. Before you know it, you're emotionally sucked in, and there's no escape. No amount of regret or good intentions will be enough to overcome the consequences of your decisions.

To enjoy a healthy, happy marriage, the wise choice is to avoid the point of no return. Invest yourself instead in building a marriage so intimate and loving that you fall in love with your spouse all over again every single day.

Watch and pray that you may not enter into temptation. The spirit indeed is willing, but the flesh is weak.
MARK 14:38

Lord, guard me from the temptation to flirt with danger in relationships outside my marriage. Thank You for giving me Your Spirit to stay firm against putting one toe over the line.

Social Media: Blessing or Burden?

According to author Neil Postman, "Every technology is both a burden and a blessing." This is certainly true with social networking, especially when it comes to building a strong and lasting marriage.

Married couples ought to be mindful of common pitfalls with social media. With online friends of the opposite sex, for example, it's wise to keep a close eye on your own behavior and attitudes. It's even good for spouses to list appropriate boundaries and agree to abide by them. The best way to keep technology from interfering with your marriage is to prevent problems from developing in the first place.

But technology can help a couple enhance their marriage as well. Husbands and wives can post photos and simple messages that celebrate their relationship. Or use social media to maintain a healthy connection during the workday or while a spouse is traveling. It's also helpful to network with other couples, discover common interests with friends, and plan get-togethers. Marriages are strengthened when they're plugged into a strong, marriage-affirming community.

When it comes to marriage, cell phones, iPads, and platforms like Facebook and Instagram can be either dangerous or enriching. The difference is whether they're used with wisdom and discernment.

Whoever brings blessing will be enriched, and one who waters will himself be watered.
PROVERBS 11:25

Father God, social media can be a blessing to strengthen our marriage, family, and friendships. Guard us with Your wisdom as we seek wholesome ways to use technology.

Friendship or Flirtation?

Counselor and author Dave Carder has studied the causes of infidelity for more than thirty years. He says most people don't wake up and decide, *I think I'll ruin my marriage today.* Affairs usually come about slowly, without people realizing they're drifting into dangerous emotional territory.

To protect your marriage, keep on the lookout for danger signs that your emotions are drifting—signs such as saving topics of conversation for somebody other than your spouse because, in your mind, he or she *understands* you better. Or you might be sharing intimate details about your marriage with that person. Your feelings have definitely gone too far when you look forward to seeing the other person more than your spouse.

These indicators are often subtle, but they're important. So much so that Carder offers this stern warning: You cannot resist infatuation once it's taken hold! When your marriage goes through a dry spell, you can easily become infatuated with someone else. You may lose all sense of reason, where almost nothing will prevent you from having an affair.

So to avoid making one of the biggest mistakes of your life, keep an eye on your relationships, and keep your emotions in check.

The lips of a forbidden woman drip honey, and her speech is smoother than oil.
PROVERBS 5:3

God, guard us from the temptation to find intimacy outside our marriage. Give us the courage to flee from sexual temptation and instead rush into each other's arms.

High Fidelity

We hear about it more and more these days—a politician or religious leader caught in a sex scandal. A man turning his back on his family to pursue an affair. A wife engaging in an online romance. How do we avoid disasters like this?

Marriage counselor Dr. David Sanford points out that infidelity can take root in the heart and mind long before someone commits the physical act.

Sanford outlines several steps to strengthen marital fidelity. These include affirming your spouse, listening to your spouse, and seeking to meet his or her needs. It also means setting healthy boundaries for your relationships outside the home.

On the other hand, marital fidelity weakens when you devalue your spouse, when you minimize the time you spend with him or her, and when you focus on meeting your own needs.

Even for those who have broken the bonds of marital trust, there is hope for healing and restoration. But the path is long and painful. It's so much better not to start down that road in the first place.

If I speak in the tongues of men and of angels, but have not love,
I am a noisy gong or a clanging cymbal.
I CORINTHIANS 13:1

Dear God, let us never start down the path of infidelity.
Rather, help us strengthen our marriage with things like
purposeful time, active listening, compassionate empathy,
and meeting each other's needs. Thank You, God.

Control Your Appetites

When it comes to food, you've probably been told the importance of controlling your appetite. But that isn't just good advice for physical health.

Dr. Juli Slattery tells of the time her husband was placed on a seven-day fast for medical purposes. To restart his diet, their doctor suggested Juli make chips out of the leafy vegetable kale. The problem is that many people don't think kale chips taste very good. So she handed the bowl to her husband, figuring he'd turn up his nose at them. He devoured the whole bowl. She learned a vital lesson that day. When someone is starving, almost anything will taste good.

Our sexual appetites aren't much different. Men crave intimacy. But instead of pursuing authentic connection with their wives, many feed their appetites with pornography. It holds true for women as well.

The effect is the same in either case. Escaping into fantasy strips men and women of the genuine desire they would otherwise invest in their marriage. The good news is that we can learn to control our appetites. But to do that, we have to pursue authentic romance, not a cheap imitation.

A man without self-control is like a city broken into and left without walls.

PROVERBS 25:28

Heavenly Father, please help me and my spouse have self-control. Help us live a life of authentic romance.

The Dangers of Pornography

If you've been married for a while, then you already know how hard it can be to keep your romance alive. That's why many couples look for creative ways to get a spark of intimacy going. It's a great idea. But beware: Some ideas will harm your marriage, not strengthen it.

Pornography is more prevalent than ever. Popular women's magazines even go so far as to suggest regular pornography use will help spice up your marriage. What many people don't realize is that porn can be powerfully addicting and can cause a severe breakdown in a marriage.

Authentic relationships take hard work; pornography is easy. That distinction is a key part of what keeps a person returning to pornography again and again and again. Before long, a man may lose interest in his wife because their relationship no longer provides the same level of excitement. Simply put, the erotic images the couple hoped would spice things up begin to drive a wedge between them.

Pornography is *not* a positive addition to a healthy marriage. It has the potential to seriously wound not only the marriage but the entire family as well.

Beloved, let us cleanse ourselves from every defilement of body and spirit, bringing holiness to completion in the fear of God.
2 CORINTHIANS 7:1

Jesus, we desperately want to have a life-giving marriage.
Please help us keep ourselves pure for each other as
we strive for a marriage that is healthy and whole.

Trouble Spots in Marriage

Most people who have an affair say the same thing: They never saw it coming—as if their infidelity materialized out of thin air. More likely, the couple neglected their marriage so severely that they never noticed the precarious position it was in. Not until it was too late.

To protect your marriage, learn to keep your eyes open for trouble spots—like unmet needs. If you and your spouse aren't connecting at an emotional level, you're at risk. Once loneliness or feelings of rejection kick in, the door is wide open for someone outside the marriage to swoop in and fill the vacuum.

Another trouble spot is past relationships. With social media, old flames are now just a click away. And they're especially dangerous because—unlike everyday connections that merely hint at the potential for romance—former relationships have passionate feelings already in place.

A third trouble spot is spending time alone with members of the opposite sex. Although this behavior is often characterized as innocent, coming together to share mutual interests is another open doorway to deeper and riskier emotional connections.

Infidelity doesn't spring out of thin air. It develops slowly, filling cracks in a relationship that many couples never see forming. Protect your marriage by developing healthy boundaries and keeping your eyes wide open for traps that could ensnare you.

Flee from sexual immorality. Every other sin a person commits is outside the body, but the sexually immoral person sins against his own body.

I CORINTHIANS 6:18

God, we ask You to strengthen the bond between us. May Your love be a beacon in our hearts, guarding us against temptation and fostering trust and loyalty in our journey together.

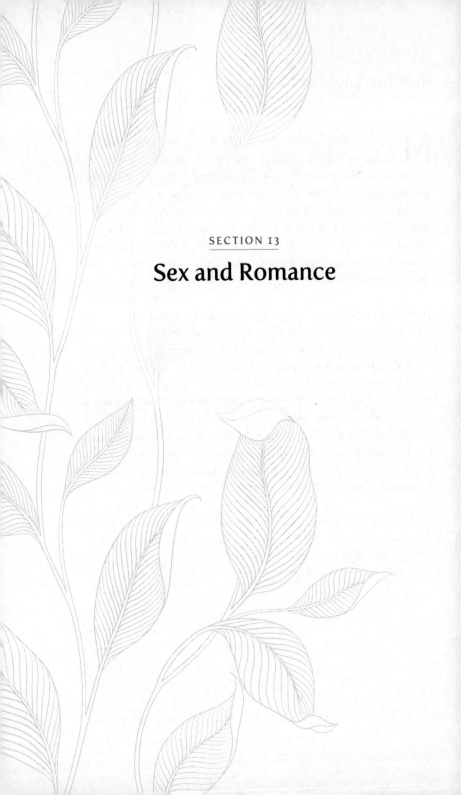

SECTION 13

Sex and Romance

Don't Settle for Leftovers

The sad truth for many couples is that their wedding ceremony is the high point of their marriage. They stand at the altar, light a unity candle, and pledge to love and honor each other till death do them part. They get married with eager anticipation.

Yet sooner or later they begin to feel as though marriage isn't what they expected.

The reason? Too many couples stop pursuing each other. Sometime after the honeymoon ends, romance goes by the wayside. Instead of chasing each other, they chase schedules, money, titles, and rambunctious children. All those are great things—in balance. But as a couple's priorities shift away from their marriage, their relationship drifts. Before long, romance fades, and instead of offering their spouse their best, they offer their leftovers: leftover time, leftover energy, and leftover commitment.

If the passion you once had in your relationship feels dull and flat, know that you *can* change it. Don't settle for leftovers. Invest in your relationship with a renewed sense of passion. Your wedding ceremony doesn't have to be the high point of your marriage. It can be a memorable first step on a long, exciting journey together.

> Your lips drip nectar, my bride; honey and milk are under your tongue; the fragrance of your garments is like the fragrance of Lebanon.
>
> SONG OF SOLOMON 4:11

Father, renew in us the desire to pursue each other's company, heart, and well-being. Passion and romance are not just for the young, but the young at heart. Help us not let the beautiful gift of romancing each other fall by the wayside in the busyness of life.

Scheduling Sex

Here's a question you probably haven't been asked before: Do you and your spouse have sex scheduled on your calendar for tonight?

Before you laugh, give that question some thought. Like most things in marriage, intimacy requires work and intentionality. That's why the solution for finding those important moments together is often to—you guessed it—sit down with your calendars!

Does that sound too contrived? It doesn't have to be. Planning ahead for sex can defuse a lot of problems. Take issues surrounding a couple's sex drive. Most nights, he's in the mood but she isn't, or vice versa. When one spouse feels he or she constantly has to ask or even beg for sex, fear of rejection can set in. Scheduling does away with that insecurity.

Thoughtful planning can even increase desire by engaging the most important sex organ in the human body—the brain. The calendar reassures the higher-sex-drive mate that their time together will happen, but it still leaves plenty of room for freedom and spontaneity.

So give it a try. I think you'll be surprised what a little planning can do to build confidence and trust between you and your spouse.

May he grant you your heart's desire and fulfill all your plans!
PSALM 20:4

God, sexual pleasure in marriage is Your design.
Keep me open to planning ahead for sex while
also staying spontaneous with my spouse.

Everyone Benefits from a Good Sex Life

Sex is good. In fact, sex was created to be one of the most pleasurable physical experiences a husband and wife can enjoy together. But sex brings that same level of intensity to a couple's emotional bond too. Husbands and wives both benefit immeasurably when their sex life is good.

Sex plays such a crucial role in the health and well-being of a marriage that disagreements about sex can be especially complicated for couples to resolve. It doesn't take much for a minor disagreement about your sex life to feel like an attack against the relationship itself. After money, sex-related disagreements are one of the most common reasons couples get divorced.

That's why one of the best things you can do for your marriage is to guard your sex life. Guarding your sex life means avoiding the bad, like pornography and extramarital affairs. But it also means strengthening the good. Find new ways to keep the romance in your marriage alive. And learn how to discuss sex in respectful ways that move your relationship forward and help you find common ground.

When you guard your sex life, you're guarding the very heart of your marriage.

I am my beloved's, and his desire is for me. Come, my beloved, let us go out into the fields and lodge in the villages.
SONG OF SOLOMON 7:10-11

God, You created sex, and You created it with purpose. Increase the intimacy between me and my spouse, and help us know each other more through Your delightful creation.

Love Doesn't Demand

I was intrigued a number of years ago by a *Reader's Digest* article sharing eight lessons from "the world's happiest couples." My wife, Jean, and I are pretty happy together, but what couple doesn't have room to improve?

The ideas listed were pretty basic: Be kind to each other, have good communication, and so on. But one point really jumped out. According to the study, 60 percent of extremely happy couples have sex three or four times per week.

My first impulse was to share that article with Jean, but many years of marriage have taught me a few things. I knew how she'd respond, reminding me that most of the women in that study probably weren't mothers of young children, as Jean was at the time. Physical intimacy for moms of youngsters can be challenging because they're running all day and fall asleep from exhaustion the minute they lie down.

In that season of life, Jean was going from sunup to sundown investing in our boys. Sharing that article with Jean would have been unwise—and unfair. Highlighting my own interests at the expense of hers is not what love is about.

Love doesn't demand its own way. It denies itself and focuses on the needs of others.

Do nothing from selfish ambition or conceit, but in humility count others more significant than yourselves.
PHILIPPIANS 2:3

Lord, I am grateful that our love life is not dependent on expectations from the world. Thank You that my spouse and I can enjoy our intimacy as we choose not to selfishly demand our own interests.

Initiating Sex with Your Wife

Okay, guys, if you want a better sex life with your wife, you're going to want to read closely today. Take some initiative. Pursue your wife, not to get something from her, but to offer your heart to her.

Your wife will be more willing to connect with you physically if you're taking the initiative to connect with her emotionally. Your wife should feel treasured, not objectified. So if you plan to initiate sex with her later, initiate relationship with her throughout the day, not just at night when you're ready to go.

Your question shouldn't be *How do I get my wife interested in sex?* If she doesn't seem interested, then become more interesting. If she's too tired from a long day of work, then help out with the children and around the house to lessen her load. Also, face it, brother: There may be some nights when she's just too tired. Instead of sex, she needs a night of attention, cuddles, and good sleep.

Guys, don't try to control how your wife will respond to you. Just pursue her and focus on strengthening your relationship.

Do not deprive one another, except perhaps by agreement for a limited time, that you may devote yourselves to prayer; but then come together again, so that Satan may not tempt you because of your lack of self-control.

I CORINTHIANS 7:5

Dear Lord, let us never deprive each other. Help us focus on the other spouse so intentionally that we forget our own needs in an effort to satisfy the needs of our beloved.

Preparing for Sex: Women

Ladies, the previous devotion was aimed at helping your husbands understand how they should treat you if they hope to enjoy a better sex life. Today, I have a helpful idea for you. Not only will this suggestion improve intimacy with your husband, but it will also help your marriage become much warmer and more connected.

What I told your husbands was that they should take initiative with you, pursuing you in ways that make you feel loved and cherished. Ladies, my idea for you is the same: Pursue your husband. Prepare your heart and mind throughout the day so you can be available to him emotionally and physically.

Preparing yourself for your husband is a beautiful expression of your willingness. In many marriages, a husband can be ready for sex at a moment's notice. But you might need time to warm up to the idea. That's okay too. Just keep those differences with your husband in mind.

If you each take the initiative and pursue each other, you'll create an intimacy in your marriage you might feel you can only dream of right now.

A man shall leave his father and his mother and hold fast to his wife, and they shall become one flesh.
GENESIS 2:24

God, help me never forget—and help me respect—the importance of understanding the differences between my spouse and me. Help me do this so we can continually become intimately closer with each passing day.

Romance Realities

Ladies, are you looking for a little romance in your marriage? I have a simple idea that I think will help: Teach your husband how to romance you.

It's perfectly normal for you and your husband to think differently about romance and what it ought to look like in your marriage. So tell him. Spell it out for him if you have to. Let him know, in terms he can easily understand, exactly what romance means to you and how he can offer it. Give your husband the tools he needs to build the marriage you want.

Don't confuse him with mixed signals. A guy once told me that his wife would nudge him during romantic movies and ask, "Why don't you ever sweep me off my feet like that?" So one day he did. But instead of melting into his embrace as the leading lady always did, she complained that her hair and makeup were getting ruined.

Ladies, you've got to help your husband out. Your knight in shining armor may have gotten a little rusty, but with some help, he can learn to sweep you off your feet all over again.

I am my beloved's and my beloved is mine.
SONG OF SOLOMON 6:3

I desperately desire romance with my beloved. I also know that I need to provide structure so he isn't guessing what I need. Please help us be open and honest about each other's expectations so that we can experience waves of romance once more in our marriage.

Intimacy vs. Sex

Here's a fact that may come as a surprise to a lot of couples: Intimacy and sex are not necessarily the same thing.

Most couples enter marriage thinking sex will be the *easy* part of their relationship, yet struggles related to sex are among the top reasons for marital conflict.

There are a lot of potential challenges, including unrealistic expectations, the couple's ages, busy schedules, and the hurdles of finding privacy with children around.

But as important as sex is to intimacy in marriage, it's only one part of the equation. Connecting emotionally is equally as vital, and you can still achieve that even when other factors are interfering with your sex life.

It takes a little creativity, but you can come up with a lot of ways to connect emotionally. Enjoy a cup of coffee together while you watch the sun come up. Snuggle on the couch and watch a movie, or have a heart-to-heart conversation around a candlelit dinner after the children are in bed and asleep.

Almost anything will work as long as you remember that sex is not the only way to achieve intimacy in your relationship.

Set me as a seal upon your heart, as a seal upon your arm, for love is strong as death, jealousy is fierce as the grave. Its flashes are flashes of fire, the very flame of the LORD. Many waters cannot quench love, neither can floods drown it. If a man offered for love all the wealth of his house, he would be utterly despised.

SONG OF SOLOMON 8:6-7

Father, strengthen our love for each other and our connection with each other. Let the intimacy of our hearts not be dimmed when the busyness of daily life gets in the way of physical intimacy.

The Post-Wedding Blues

Do you remember what life was like for you and your spouse before you got married?

If you're like my wife, Jean, and me, your courtship was a whirlwind of romance. There were long walks in the moonlight. Late-night talks. Lingering looks across a crowded room.

All too often, though, once a couple actually ties the knot, the romance fades. It's tough to plan a date with someone when he or she lives under the same roof with you. Once you add kids into the mix, you and your sweetheart might have very little time together at all. And so you settle into a routine, and by the time your kids leave home years later, you realize you're living with a stranger.

It doesn't have to be that way, though. I believe it's possible to keep the flame alive in your marriage, even with the demands of children and career vying for your attention. It might not sound very romantic to schedule a date night on your calendar. But you know what? If that's what it takes to allow you and your spouse some alone time, then do it! Don't let your hectic pace of life push the intimacy out of your marriage.

May mercy, peace, and love be multiplied to you.
JUDE 1:2

Father, I don't want love in our marriage to diminish, but to grow and multiply. Teach us what we need to do in order to keep passion and romance alive in our marriage, even when family life feels busy and distracting!

Sex-pectations

Sex is one of the greatest blessings married couples can experience with each other. It can also be one of their greatest sources of conflict.

Consider this: A reported 80 percent of couples—that's four out of five—experience some kind of conflict about sex. Most of that is fueled by what authors Gary Thomas and Debra Fileta call "sex-pectations," which are beliefs individuals have about sex. These beliefs could be good or bad, healthy or unhealthy, wise or unwise.

For example, unhealthy, unwise beliefs see sex as nothing more than a physical act. A wise view of sex, on the other hand, views it as an expression of love that helps knit a married couple together at a *soul* level. And when a couple connects on a soul level, physical connection falls into place more easily.

To help align your sex-pectations, try to focus on your relational intimacy *before* you focus on physical intimacy. Connect *emotionally* before you connect *physically*.

Equally important is to humble yourself. Sexual issues can admittedly be embarrassing to talk about, but the worst thing you can do is struggle in isolation. Reach out for help. Speak to a counselor, therapist, or medical professional. There *are* answers.

The more you and your spouse connect to each other's soul, the more your marriage—and your sex life—can thrive. What happens *above* the sheets fuels what happens *under* the sheets.

Love is patient and kind; love does not envy or boast; it is not arrogant or rude. It does not insist on its own way.
1 CORINTHIANS 13:4-5

Father, we pray for Your wisdom as we align our expectations with a holistic view of our marital union. Help us prioritize our emotional connection over our physical connection. May our intimacy deepen to a soul level and foster a fulfilling sex life with each other.

A Gateway to Romance

Many couples say physical appearance is what initially attracted them to their spouse. But when it comes to making a relationship last, studies rank physical attraction toward the bottom of the list of important factors. Above it are intelligence, a sense of humor, and kindness. Spirituality and healthy family dynamics also score above physical attraction.

So is physical attraction important or not?

Maybe the best way to explain the role of physical attraction in a relationship is to say that it's a natural gateway to romance. Two people see each other. Something clicks. They say hello, and they begin the process of getting to know one another.

That couple will inevitably run into trouble, however, if they rely too heavily on physical attraction to build a solid relationship. Physical attraction is temporary at best. It fades as time passes. Sooner or later, we all turn gray and lose whatever youthful beauty we had.

Fortunately, physical attraction is only one dimension of a relationship. "Becoming one" didn't happen the moment you said "I do." It's a journey that unfolds as you get beneath the surface and bond emotionally, mentally, and spiritually.

Do not judge by appearances, but judge with right judgment.
JOHN 7:24

Lord, form genuine bonds between us that enable us to engage more deeply with each other—emotionally, spiritually, and physically. Create a love in us that transcends physical appearance and fosters a romance that withstands the test of time.

Put Your Wife First

In the early days of marriage, most guys grasp the connection between emotional engagement with their wives and a good sex life. A man pursues his wife romantically. He shows her affection and engages her in meaningful conversation. He limits his time with friends and hobbies and prioritizes time at home.

But somewhere along the way, many a husband's thinking goes sideways. His primary interest becomes satisfying his own needs instead of his wife's. He works a lot. He spends more and more time hanging out with buddies or in his man cave or garage. He neglects meaningful conversation with his wife. Bring all that baggage into the bedroom, and sex is often reduced to a physical act that has lost its rightful place as an integral part of the marriage *relationship*.

Men, *emotional* connection is what fuels your wife's *physical* desire for you. A deep relational bond helps transform sex into what God designed it to be: emotional intimacy that overflows into physical intimacy.

For a better sexual relationship with your wife, try rethinking your approach—not just to sexual intimacy, but to your entire marriage. Invest in your relationship with your wife. Put her need for love, connection, and nurturing at the top of your list of priorities. Put your wife first.

[The Lord Jesus] said, "It is more blessed to give than to receive."
ACTS 20:35

God, I humbly seek your guidance in fostering
a strong and sacrificial bond with my wife. Help
me deepen our emotional connection and honor
Your sacred design for sex as an expression of
intimacy within the sanctity of our marriage.

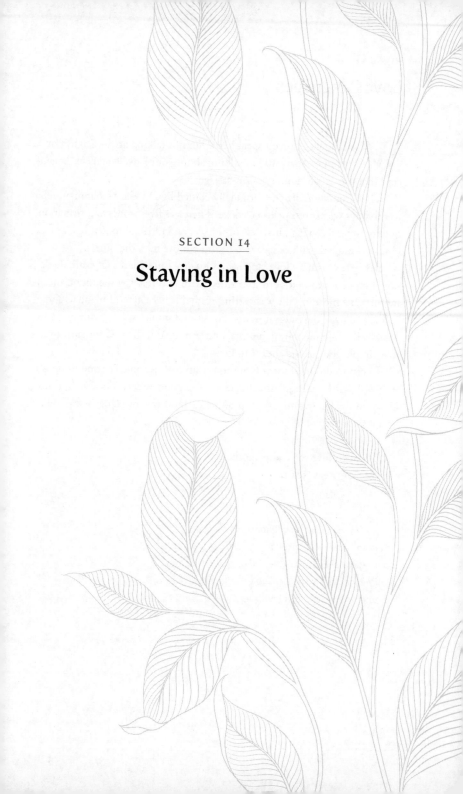

SECTION 14

Staying in Love

Love Languages

What language do you speak? No, I'm not talking about English or German or Spanish. I'm talking about your "love language," a concept that can revolutionize your marriage.

The term *love languages*, originally coined by Dr. Gary Chapman, refers to the ways we express or receive love. There are five: words of affirmation, quality time, receiving gifts, acts of service, and physical touch. Each of us tends to resonate with one or two of those more than the others.

My wife's primary love language is quality time. Here's an example of how I tapped into that need to connect with her in a way she found meaningful. One morning she was getting ready for her day, so I made us some coffee and took the mugs upstairs. For several minutes, I sat with her, and we talked while she put on her makeup. Afterward, she told me how much that simple gesture had meant to her.

I need to do that more often for a couple of reasons. For one thing, sitting with her for a short time made her feel good and significant. But more importantly, I'm learning that speaking each other's love language should be a regular way of life.

Through love serve one another.
GALATIANS 5:13

Loving God, You model how to love others
deeply and well. Throughout each day, I want
to speak the primary love language that uplifts
and blesses my spouse. Show me how to give
and receive love that builds up my marriage.

Laugh Together

I've got a simple idea that will help you build a great marriage.

Laugh together.

Studies show that couples who laugh together are healthier, happier, and more connected. Even little giggles between you and your spouse create relational bonds that draw you closer together. That's because laughter is a powerful connector.

In fact, laughter is *mostly* about connection—only partially about humor. Studies show that we laugh more when we're with someone than when we're alone.

My wife and I have sure discovered that to be true. Some of our greatest memories together involve laughing. A few times it's been tough to stop. We've laughed so hard for so long that we started laughing at each other's laughing.

And the more the better. Author Ted Cunningham encourages couples to strive for a laughter-to-conflict ratio of one hundred to one. The important thing is that you want your marriage to have as many points of connection as possible. Laughter is a great one.

Don't worry about telling jokes to each other. Connection is about finding the humor in everyday life. It's about enjoying your life as much as possible—together, and with a smile on your face.

A joyful heart is good medicine, but a crushed spirit dries up the bones.

PROVERBS 17:22

Laughter is such good medicine, God. Thank You for creating laughter and joyful hearts. I long for more laughter to enliven my marriage. Keep me smiling at the little everyday things that lighten my load.

Keeping the Spark Alive

When was the last time you told your spouse "I love you"? Do you wait for special occasions to declare your affection?

For Valentine's Day, many of us buy flowers or chocolates. There's nothing wrong with those things. It's fun to have a day set aside to proclaim our love for our spouse.

But it's also important that we make an effort to inject that same passion into our marriage on a regular basis. Husbands and wives have the opportunity to create romance every day of the year. We all have busy lives, so I know it's not easy. But if we're intentional, there are countless ways we can express our devotion—maybe a date night, or a nice card, or just a quick "I love you" email. I can almost guarantee that something along those lines will mean more to your spouse in July or September than it does on February 14!

This is something that my wife, Jean, and I try to keep in mind, even when we're running at a frantic pace. All of us can endeavor to keep the spark alive—to make our marriages the best they can be on Valentine's Day and every day.

> Little children, let us not love in word or talk but in deed and in truth.
>
> I JOHN 3:18

Lord, help me show my spouse my love every day not just with my words but also with my kind, caring actions.

The Dangers of Craving Control

Here's a riddle: Everybody wants it. But if you use it in your marriage, you could lose everything. What is it?

The answer is *control*. Whether it's having the right sweetener for our coffee or keeping our home at a certain temperature, we all want life to function in a way that suits us. If something doesn't work the way we like, we try to control it. Unfortunately, many people employ a similar strategy in their marriage.

Controlling behavior can occur because one spouse doesn't feel loved and validated by the other. The hurt spouse tries to control the other's actions to get the relationship he or she wants. But taking charge over a spouse erodes partnership and oneness.

If you control your spouse, you're in danger of losing your marriage. A spouse who feels controlled will try to escape. That may be through an affair, a divorce, or just staying at a distance.

The solution is to give up the role of "boss" and to begin cultivating a relationship of warmth and openness. It may take a counselor's help, but when a couple learns healthy ways to connect and become equals, a stronger marriage is just over the horizon.

> Where jealousy and selfish ambition exist, there will be disorder and every vile practice.
> JAMES 3:16

Thank You, God, that I can put aside my selfish ambition and attempts to control my spouse. Shower our marriage with Your peace, kindness, and gentleness.

Date Your Wife!

Guys, do you remember the excitement over that first date with the girl of your dreams? Wouldn't it be great to feel that way again, even though you're married now?

I'm talking about pursuing your wife with passion, even if you've been married for twenty years. Trust me, she still wants to be pursued. You should never grow tired of trying to win her heart.

I know it's not easy with long work hours, school activities, and countless commitments. But the busier we get, the more important it is to set aside time for each other. Plan a date night as often as possible. Sit down with your wife after the kids are in bed and just talk, heart to heart.

Marriage counselor Dr. David Clarke asks every client couple in crisis to hold hands after leaving his office. Those who take his advice—and who find other small ways to rekindle romance—will likely experience healing in their marriage. Those who don't are more likely to have problems.

No man ever says, "I'm passionate about my wife, but I want a divorce." Marriages go sour when we allow our passion for our spouse to die. It doesn't have to be that way.

Enjoy life with the wife whom you love.
ECCLESIASTES 9:9

Lord, fan the flames of my love for my wife. Help me truly enjoy my life with her again, and keep us steady in our romance today and always.

Drifting Apart

Divorce is especially sad when two people simply feel they're no longer in love. There is no adultery. No abuse. "We just drifted apart."

It takes work, prayer, and commitment, but there are some practical ways couples can keep the lines of communication open and the embers of romance burning. Consider some of these suggestions:

1. *Become a better listener.* Pay attention to your spouse's needs and desires.
2. *Take responsibility for your own actions and feelings.* If you're avoiding your spouse or harboring resentment about something, be honest about it.
3. *Be more affectionate and considerate.* Wives, when was the last time you gave your husband a kiss when he came home from work? Husbands, when was the last time you surprised your wife with flowers just because?
4. *Parent as a team.* The challenges and distractions of parenting can often cause husbands and wives to neglect their marriage. So make sure you are parenting as a team.

Too often, we take our spouses for granted and live our lives on auto-pilot. Marriage is a sacred commitment, and we need to invest time and energy in making it the best it can be.

May the Lord make you increase and abound in love for one another.
1 THESSALONIANS 3:12

Lord, help us deepen the communication, romance, and togetherness in our marriage. Increase my love and respect for my spouse beyond anything I can hope for or imagine.

What If My Marriage Isn't Perfect?

Sherri and Mark hadn't been married long before they started questioning why they had ever decided to tie the knot. He couldn't understand why she didn't want to spend every Saturday at his parents' for dinner. She was hurt because he preferred football games to picnics in the park on Sunday afternoons. And a mismatch in their sexual expectations left both of them frustrated and angry. It didn't take long for Sherri to wonder whether other people's marriages were like hers. She even began fantasizing about what it might be like to be married to someone else.

If you feel as disillusioned in your marriage as Sherri did, there's an important truth you need to know: There is no such thing as a perfect relationship! From the outside, other marriages may seem like something out of a fairy tale. But if you could peek behind closed doors, you'd see that every marriage has its challenges.

So don't allow dissatisfaction to creep into your marriage by comparing yourselves with other couples. The "secret" to a happy life together is not finding a perfect mate—it's the two of you embracing commitment and hard work. While that doesn't sound romantic, putting in the effort is worth it.

Whatever you do, work heartily, as for the Lord and not for men, knowing that from the Lord you will receive the inheritance as your reward. You are serving the Lord Christ.

COLOSSIANS 3:23-24

God, thank You for my spouse and for his unique design. Remind me of the things that I adore about him.

Staying Awake and on Course

One year, while working as a camp counselor, Craig Jutila grabbed a canoe for a quiet afternoon on the lake. There wasn't a cloud in the sky, and there was almost no breeze, so the water was completely still. As Craig let the canoe come to rest in the middle of the lake, it dawned on him: It was after hours, and no other boats were out. So he did the only sensible thing. With an extra life jacket for his pillow, he nestled in for a short nap.

An hour later, he woke up to voices, and his canoe beached along the shoreline of a camping area. There was a current in the water and a breeze in the air Craig hadn't sensed. They'd caused him to drift, and he ended up somewhere he had never intended to be.

Like that canoe, marriages often go off course. There's no obvious conflict or struggle, just subtle distractions that lull couples asleep. Spouses hardly notice they're losing interest in each other until they end up somewhere they never intended to be.

Fortunately, there's an easy solution. Stay alert and give your relationship the attention it deserves. It takes a bit of effort, but it can make all the difference in keeping your marriage on course.

Teach us to number our days that we may get a heart of wisdom.
PSALM 90:12

Father, each day You have given me with my spouse is precious. I don't want to be found asleep at the helm, having let our marriage drift into trouble. Fill me each morning with new appreciation and gratitude.

Creating a Masterpiece

You're probably familiar with the well-known French artist Claude Monet. His paintings are considered masterpieces for their detail and bright colors. But in the latter part of his life, his work became more abstract. Brushstrokes got wider. Images lost their definition. Colors started to blur.

At the time, the art world thought Monet was creating a distinctive new style. But he wasn't. Not intentionally, anyway. It turned out he'd developed cataracts and was simply painting the world as it appeared through his distorted vision. After surgery, his sight was partially restored. Horrified at what he'd painted, he began destroying many of his canvases. Only a few works from this period were saved by family.

Monet's story reminds me of how couples often view marriage. Their vision for a relationship filled with intimacy and deep connection gets skewed. And once that distortion takes hold, spouses zero in on each other's flaws and criticize each other endlessly.

The good news is that blurred perceptions *can* be brought back into focus. That clearer vision will help you have a deeper appreciation for your spouse and your marriage. And in the process, you just might create a marriage masterpiece.

You are altogether beautiful, my love; there is no flaw in you.
SONG OF SOLOMON 4:7

*Lord, give us eyes to clearly see the love
we should have for each other.*

A Bad Feeling with a Good Meaning

Not every negative feeling is bad. In fact, an unpleasant emotion can often point to something very good.

Consider the late President Ronald Reagan and his beloved wife, Nancy. Even during the demanding eight years they spent in the White House, their marriage remained a priority. When Mrs. Reagan was away, the president would often stand at the windows of the White House watching for the lights of the car that would bring her home. This couple's deep and unflagging devotion to each other endured through family challenges, the presidency, and Mr. Reagan's long battle with Alzheimer's.

I've been blessed to be married to someone I miss when she's away. I'm typically the one who's on the road—and I'm usually so busy that I don't have a chance to be lonely. But when Jean is the one who's traveling, I count the hours until she returns.

The next time the miles separate you and your spouse, be encouraged. When you enjoy your spouse's presence so much that his or her absence is difficult, it's a sign that you recognize just how fortunate you are to have that special person in your life.

Continue steadfastly in prayer, being watchful in it with thanksgiving.
COLOSSIANS 4:2

Lord, I am so appreciative of my spouse. Help me never forget how special this person is to me. Let me cherish this person with all my heart.

A Strategy for Resolving Conflict

Whether it's something minor like where to go for dinner, or a serious issue like the family budget or disciplining a child, sometimes husbands and wives don't see eye to eye. Authors Ron Blue and Jeremy White have developed an effective strategy for resolving conflict in marriage.

First, stick to the problem at hand. Don't bring up past issues or accuse your spouse of *always* or *never* behaving a certain way.

Second, get on the same side of the fence. Don't think about "my way" or "your way." Identify the core issue. Get to the heart of the problem, not just the symptoms.

Next, don't be a mind reader. Don't try to interpret your spouse's thoughts or motives; instead, ask direct questions.

If you haven't reached a consensus by bedtime, agree to resume the discussion the next day. No matter how strongly you disagree, attacking your spouse's personality or character is never acceptable.

Never forget that your relationship with your spouse is far more important than winning or being right.

And finally, be quick to forgive, quick to admit your own mistakes, and quick to move on from the conflict.

> If we confess our sins, he is faithful and just to forgive us our sins
> and to cleanse us from all unrighteousness.
>
> I JOHN 1:9

---

*Father, I need Your help to avoid pointing the finger
at my spouse. Let us never forget that we should
concentrate on the core issues that we need to
address to make our marriage healthy. Help us do so
without assuming motives or accusing each other.*

How Did We Get Here?

Someone once told me, "If you want to make God laugh, tell Him your plans." While it made me chuckle, it's really true. After all, how many of us set the course of our lives and marriages and then followed that path perfectly?

It's just not the way life works.

The good news is that the path God charts for our lives and marriages is always better than what we could ever plan. That doesn't mean God's course is easier, but it does mean that He is the one in the driver's seat.

A marriage dedicated to staying in the center of God's will is always in the best place it can be, even if that means difficult times. Challenges faced in the will of God are better than comforts and luxuries gained outside His plan.

In Psalm 23, David said that the Lord leads us into green pastures and beside still waters. As couples, we rejoice in those seasons. But David also said that we go through "the valley of the shadow of death." In those times, God is still with us, guiding, comforting, and protecting us and our marriages.

Even though I walk through the valley of the shadow of death,
I will fear no evil, for you are with me.
PSALM 23:4

---

*Father, when life doesn't go as we plan, we submit
ourselves to Your better ways and purposes, and
we ask You to be the one who brings Your work in
us to completion in Your way and Your time.*

Where Do We Go from Here?

Loss rocks our world. Financial trials, broken relationships, illness, even death. Loss can take many forms.

And the toll that loss takes on a marriage can be catastrophic unless we're grounded in a foundation that sustains us through the myriad emotions and times of pain. It can drive us apart as couples, or it can cement our resolve to stand when others might fall. The outcome depends on whether we do three things:

1. Trust that God is never taken by surprise. The losses we experience often sneak up on us and catch us unprepared. But God is never unprepared, and therefore He is always ready with the answers.
2. Know that God's love for us cannot be changed. Even the worst loss we experience does not change God's heart for us or His character. We need to cling to that truth like a spiritual lifeline.
3. Be assured that in spite of loss in this life, victory always awaits those who know Jesus. Loss and pain don't get to win in the end.

Fear not, for I am with you; be not dismayed, for I am your God; I will strengthen you, I will help you, I will uphold you with my righteous right hand.

ISAIAH 41:10

Father, we realize that loss is a part of our journey in this life. We thank You that You stand with us in times of loss, and we trust You with our future, for better and for worse.

Stuck in Your Marriage?

A groom named Brandon Valdez got stuck inside an elevator on the way to his own wedding. To honor the tradition of not seeing one another before the ceremony, Brandon and his bride-to-be, Misty, had spent the night in separate hotels. In the morning, Brandon and his groomsmen boarded an elevator for the lobby.

Somewhere between floors two and three, the elevator jolted to a stop. One of the groomsmen pressed the alarm button, and the front desk said they would be right up to help. Sometime later, when help still hadn't arrived, another groomsman called the fire department. Eventually Brandon was freed, safe and sound but nearly two hours late for his wedding.

Sometimes weddings don't go as planned. Sometimes marriages don't go as planned either. Relationships can be a journey into the unknown, filled with twists and turns you never saw coming. Successful couples are committed to each other but remain flexible in their approach to life's circumstances.

When your marriage seems stuck between floors, turn your challenges into opportunities for growth in your relationship. Strong couples make their marriage a priority and commit to sticking together—even when life doesn't go as planned.

> You have need of endurance, so that when you have done the will of God you may receive what is promised.
> HEBREWS 10:36

Father, help us face life's challenges hand in hand. Grant us the resilience to weather storms together, the wisdom to find solutions in times of adversity, and the strength to support and uplift one another through every trial.

SECTION 15

Parenting

Blenders and Crock-Pots

Becoming a stepparent can be rewarding. But if your stepchildren resist building a relationship with you, I have a suggestion.

Very few stepfamilies begin to jell immediately after marriage. It takes time for parents and kids alike to feel comfortable with their new living arrangement. So don't hurry or try to force relationships to grow.

Forcing relationships is something author Ron Deal calls the "blender strategy." Blenders are what chefs use to force ingredients together. It works well with food, but relationships? Not so much. If you push a child to connect with you, it'll backfire.

A more effective approach is what Deal calls the "Crock-Pot strategy." The idea is to allow family members to slowly find their place with one another. That means giving your stepchildren time and space to build a relationship with you. Be present in their lives, but don't push them to connect.

For example, your stepdaughter may be okay with your attending her soccer games, but she won't share her feelings with you. That's still an open door. So show up and cheer her on, but don't get impatient. Let her ease into a relationship with you at her own pace. Over time, she'll likely soften.

Rejoice in hope, be patient in tribulation, be constant in prayer.
ROMANS 12:12

God, help me be patient as I show up and cheer on my stepchild. Thank You that I can rejoice in hope and be constant in prayer as our family begins to trust and grow together.

Babies Change Everything

Maybe you're a married couple about to have your first baby. To that I say, "Congratulations! Children are a blessing!" But I also encourage you to take steps now to strengthen your marriage, because a baby changes everything.

Most new parents believe their marriage will get stronger after the baby arrives. Unfortunately, a baby can challenge every aspect of a marriage.

A new baby forces a couple's time and attention away from their marriage. In the first months after a baby's birth, marital conflict is eight times as frequent, while marital satisfaction declines for both the wife and the husband. A baby dramatically alters a couple's entire way of life—from sleeping patterns to economic stress to schedule changes.

Sound hopeless? It doesn't have to be. New parents adapt. But for their marriage to thrive, they must learn new ways to connect in the midst of life's changes. Perhaps enjoy coffee together while the baby naps. Or swap babysitting duties with another family and have a date night.

Just keep it simple. All it takes is a few moments a day to strengthen your marriage . . . despite the dramatic changes that come with bringing home that little bundle of joy.

Behold, children are a heritage from the LORD, the fruit of the womb a reward.
PSALM 127:3

Heavenly Father, we rejoice over the gift of children.
Be our strength and counselor as we navigate
the challenges of parenting. Uplift our marriage
with special times just for the two of us.

Prioritizing Your Marriage (Part I)

Remember when you and your spouse were first married? You scheduled the demands of life around the time you spent with each other.

Things have changed. Now that you're a parent, marriage may have slid down the priority list. Every moment is busy with your children. Your home has become *child-focused*. A child-focused home seems like a good idea, because parenting is one of the most important jobs in your life. Children require a lot. They need your attention, your affection, and your affirmation. They need you to be engaged in their lives.

But if everything—including your marriage—revolves around your children, your home is out of balance. The desire to be a great parent becomes counterproductive when it overshadows your desire to be a great spouse. A strong marriage is one of the greatest gifts you can offer your children. It's the foundation of their stability and confidence in life and will benefit them throughout their lives.

Protect your marriage. Love each other. Serve each other. Make time for your spouse, even while you're working hard to raise your children together. Secure, confident children don't come from *child*-focused homes, but from *marriage*-focused homes.

Grandchildren are the crown of the aged, and the glory of children is their fathers.

PROVERBS 17:6

Focus my eyes on my spouse, Lord. Let the richness of our marriage overflow and bless our children in abundance.

Prioritizing Your Marriage (Part 2)

Family psychologist John Rosemond says the best parenting advice he ever got came from his wife, Willie. When she was pregnant with their second child, Willie said, "We are not going to make this child the center of our lives. This child is going to adapt to *us*, not the other way around."

Why did she feel so strongly about this? Because the Rosemonds had adopted the exact opposite approach with their first child—with disastrous results.

Here's what they learned through that challenging experience: Marriage is the foundation of the family. That's why a husband and wife's first priority should be the health of their relationship. As a matter of fact, Rosemond says that couples should spend 80 percent of their time strengthening their marriage, over and above the demands of their schedules or the needs of their children.

If 80 percent sounds extreme to you, remember this: Your kids are only as safe and nurtured as your marriage is. They'll be most content when their parents' relationship is solid.

So it's marriage first, and then kids—in that order. That's the way it all begins, and that's the way it works best.

A man shall leave his father and mother and hold fast to his wife, and the two shall become one flesh. So they are no longer two but one flesh.

MARK 10:7-8

God, unite us as one, and bless our children through that unity. May we all know more of You through one another.

It's about Choices, Not Fate

My father was an alcoholic, and in his drunken stupors, he would threaten my mother and scare the living daylights out of me. My dad walked out on us when I was just five, and for years he floated in and out of my life. He was never a positive influence, and he didn't model for me what good fathering looked like.

Was I destined to follow in my father's footsteps as a parent to my two boys? Research does seem to indicate that most of us parent the way we were parented. But we can break the chains of dysfunction.

Learning to be a good dad hasn't always been easy for me, and it may be tough for you, too, if you didn't have a father who was invested in your life growing up. The most important lesson I've learned is that being a good man and a loving father isn't about fate; it's about choices.

Maybe you hope to be a different parent from the one you had growing up. If so, just remember that new choices aren't always easy, but they are possible. Your kids are counting on you.

Do not be deceived: "Bad company ruins good morals."
I CORINTHIANS 15:33

Lord, help me know and understand that I am not destined to follow a dark path. No matter how influential others may have been in my life, I ask that You help me be like You, not like those from my past.

Who's on First in Your Family?

If you're married with children, who's your first priority—your spouse or your kids?

Entertainment reporter and reality TV personality Giuliana Rancic sparked controversy when she said she puts her marriage first over motherhood.

One supportive commenter said, "Putting your marriage first gives the child a stable, loving home to grow up in." Critics on the other side say couples should make their children the center of the home. "Husbands can take care of themselves," they say. "Kids can't."

Now, nobody is suggesting letting young kids fend for themselves over a weekend so a husband and wife can escape to a romantic getaway. It comes down to this: Are the two of you acting as a team, looking out for each other, and lifting each other up in the eyes of your children?

As Jean and I were raising our boys, we tried to find a good balance. Here's a paradox: If you're becoming consumed with worry about being your spouse's priority, you're going to make yourself miserable. Instead of worrying about what you're going to get, spend your time actively loving your spouse and your children, and give everything you've got.

This is his commandment, that we believe in the name of his Son Jesus Christ and love one another, just as he has commanded us.

I JOHN 3:23

At the end of the day, Lord, we want our family to be in a good, godly rhythm. Please help us actively love one another and find the rhythms associated with caring for each other's needs above our own.

Let's Not Talk about the Kids

Before having children, my wife, Jean, and I would go to restaurants and spend hours talking about interesting topics like culture, books, and our childhoods.

As we raised our children, a lot of things changed. Like date nights. Not only did they happen less often, but when we did go out, our talks shifted from profound ideas to superheroes; from breaking world news to the latest big news from school.

That season of life made us realize that if we're not careful, something else important can slip—the depth of our relationship as husband and wife. While being great parents is incredibly important, so is having a great marriage.

Guys, it's important to carve out some time for deeper conversation with your wife. That may mean watching a little less football or turning off the phone while a mini crisis brews at the office. But the moments are there—if you'll look for them.

I am my beloved's and my beloved is mine.
SONG OF SOLOMON 6:3

Father, thank You for the gift of children! And because this gift can feel consuming at times, help us continue carving out time as husband and wife. Our relationship, after all, provides the foundation for our family. Help us keep that foundation intimate and strong.

Somehow Form a Family

In 1969, *The Brady Bunch* became the first sitcom in television history to depict what was then a fairly new trend in America: a blended family. Mike and Carol Brady, who each had three children from previous relationships, strived hard each week to—as the theme song said—"somehow form a family." Most of the problems the Bradys faced were humorous and easy enough to resolve by the end of each episode.

Unfortunately, things are rarely that simple in real life. For most couples, blending and rebuilding a family is more like Gil and Brenda Stuart's experience than Mike and Carol Brady's. Gil and Brenda entered their marriage with each other hoping they'd left the troubles of their first marriages behind. But just days after their honeymoon, wounds from the past bubbled into the present.

They went for a walk one day and wound up feeling angry and hurt. Gil thought they were headed one direction, while Brenda assumed they were going another. They got separated and lost sight of each other. By the time both made it home, they were so upset with each other that they nearly lost sight of their new marriage as well.

It's a common scenario. Old wounds can easily derail new families. Couples can step too quickly into the future before they've adequately settled their past. And they find themselves adrift.

To get your new, blended family on solid footing, focus on your marriage most of all. As much as possible, pull in the same direction. Make life about *us* and *ours* instead of *me* and *mine*.

Let each one of you love his wife as himself, and let the wife see that she respects her husband.

EPHESIANS 5:33

Lord, help us love, understand, and support each other through our challenges. May we cultivate a joyous and harmonious marriage that blooms into a joyous and harmonious family. Radiate Your love and grace throughout our home.

When Marriage Feels Too Hard

See the Deeper Value

Y ou may feel there's no hope for your marriage. But your relationship can heal if you learn to see past the problems to the true value of your relationship.

Before speaking at a marriage conference, Dr. Gary Smalley borrowed a friend's recently purchased old violin. One of the strings was broken, another was missing entirely, and the finish was faded and dull. In the middle of his talk, Dr. Smalley passed the violin through the crowd. Each audience member took a quick, dismissive glance, then passed it along to the next person.

Overall, the crowd was unimpressed. But that changed when Dr. Smalley pointed to a spot on the violin where faded ink read *Stradivarius*. *Oohs* and *aahs* immediately swept through the audience. Everyone realized they hadn't been holding a worn-out violin someone had picked up for a bargain at a garage sale. It was actually a finely crafted instrument from the seventeenth century worth several hundred thousand dollars.

When you truly understand the value of something, your perception of it changes. The dirt and grime of conflict may have tarnished the sheen your marriage once had. But it can be restored. It starts with seeing past the complications to the deeper treasure beneath.

Precious treasure and oil are in a wise man's dwelling, but a foolish man devours it.

PROVERBS 21:20

Lord, You place immeasurable value on things that I may not even notice. Teach me to treasure my spouse and our marriage, especially when we face conflict together.

The Heart of Partnership

If you went into business, what kind of a partner would you look for?

You'd look for someone whose strengths and working styles complement your own, and even make up for where you're weak. In fact, those differences could be the things that help make your partnership strong and effective.

So it is with the *ultimate* partnership: marriage. Husbands and wives have differences that can create friction. But they can also create great opportunity. Like business partners, couples who learn how to harness their differences and put them to use *in service of* their relationship can conquer anything together.

The one quality you *do* want to share with your partner is devotion—in other words, your spouse should be as committed to the relationship as you are. Commitment is an act of the will, a decision to approach your differences in a way that draws you together instead of driving you apart. Commitment empowers you to face challenges head-on and create a marriage that is rich, intimate, and meaningful.

Couples aren't successful because they're the same, but because they're committed to finding a way through their differences.

The LORD God said, "It is not good that the man should be alone; I will make him a helper fit for him."
GENESIS 2:18

Lord God, I love that my spouse is not exactly like me. We have our differences, but through Your help, we are committed to blending our differences together to be even stronger life partners.

Affirming Your Mate

The spoken word is incredibly powerful, especially in marriage. Our words can either strip our relationship of its life and vitality or help it blossom and thrive for years to come.

Speaking words that are harsh and insensitive is an unhealthy pattern many couples fall into. Spouses often bottle up all the little irritations that accumulate throughout the day. Then they arrive home, and those frustrations spill over onto the easiest target—usually the other spouse. If that sounds like your marriage, I have some good news: It doesn't have to be that way. With a little forethought and effort, you can use your words for the art of *affirming* your mate.

By *affirmation*, I'm suggesting that you make a concerted effort to look for the good in your spouse and nurture your husband or wife with your words.

Does your husband like to work on projects around the house? Commend him on his craftsmanship and attention to detail. Does your wife have a unique way of surprising the kids with special outings and fun games? Why not praise her for it? Build each other up instead of tearing each other down.

> Let no corrupting talk come out of your mouths, but only such as is good for building up, as fits the occasion, that it may give grace to those who hear.
>
> EPHESIANS 4:29

Lord, show me ways I can encourage my spouse. Help me use only words that will build up my beloved.

Regrets of Divorced Couples

One of the biggest lies about divorce is that ending your marriage will fix everything. The truth is that most couples who divorce suffer deep regret.

Terri Orbuch is a research professor at Oakland University. She identified the top five things divorced couples regret not having done more of while they were still together, things that might have saved their marriage.

One big regret people mention is not having done more to boost their ex-spouses' mood. Encouraging and affirming your spouse can accomplish a lot. One study found that husbands and wives who expressed love and affection were twice as likely to stay married. Simple gestures of kindness can have a tremendous impact. Buy some flowers, write love notes, and look for the humor in life.

Another regret divorced couples point to is not having gotten over the past. Every spouse will make poor choices at some point. Couples who can't forgive past hurts will grow bitter and resentful and perhaps walk away from their marriages. Talk it over with each other or with a trusted friend. If necessary, speak with a professional counselor.

> Live in harmony with one another. Do not be haughty, but associate with the lowly. Never be wise in your own sight.
> ROMANS 12:16

Lord, I need Your wisdom, counsel, and strength to save my marriage. Guide me in how to reconnect with my spouse and follow Your lead to begin restoring our relationship.

Ripped Apart

Some of you feel you've reached the end of your marriage and have decided divorce is the only answer. Obviously, I don't know your circumstances, but I encourage you to do everything possible to save and restore your relationship. As the head of an organization that comes alongside thousands of struggling couples every month, I can assure you divorce isn't the easy solution you may think it is.

Picture a man and a woman as two separate sheets of paper. Marriage is a bit like gluing those pieces together. Not only are the two sheets bonded, but in a very real sense, they've become one. Now imagine pulling those two pieces of paper apart. There is no way to do it cleanly. No matter how you go about it, both sheets end up torn.

That's divorce in a nutshell. As difficult as your marriage may be now, you're bonded together in practical and deeply spiritual ways. And no matter how you go about pursuing divorce, it'll have a lasting and damaging impact.

Obviously, reconciliation isn't exactly a cakewalk. But the process will not only restore your relationship; it'll strengthen each of you on a personal level as well.

> They are no longer two but one flesh. What therefore God has joined together, let not man separate.
> MATTHEW 19:6

Lord, I know what it's like to want to flee my marriage, to break my wedding vows. But my spouse and I are bonded together by You, and I ask for the patience, wisdom, and strength to hold fast to our relationship.

Is Your Marriage Worth Fighting For?

I believe your marriage *is* worth fighting for . . . for a lot of reasons.

Research shows that divorced couples aren't significantly happier once their marriage ends, and most people wish they had worked harder to save their marriage.

But what happens if you put in the work to repair and strengthen your marriage? Again, the research shows that in most cases each spouse experiences greater physical, mental, and emotional health, and their relationship is stronger and happier.

You don't have to choose between staying in an unhappy marriage or divorcing and being just as miserable. If both of you are willing to try, your marriage can be restored. It'll take work, but it *is* possible to develop the happiness and intimacy you and your spouse have been looking for all along.

God is not a God of confusion but of peace.
I CORINTHIANS 14:33

Father, remove from us confusion, chaos, and uncertainty about the future of our marriage.

Don't Quit Too Soon

What do you hope to achieve in your life? Do you have career or relationship goals? Whatever you're after—don't quit too soon.

If you know much about golf, you've probably heard of Ben Hogan. He began playing professionally in the 1930s, and many of his records still hold up today.

But before Ben became a legend, he put in a lot of hard work with no success to show for it. After ten long years on the PGA Tour, Hogan had still never won a tournament and was nearly broke. He was discouraged and almost walked away from the game forever.

Instead, he determined to hang in there. Just a few months later, in 1940, he finally won. Then he kept on winning. By the time he retired from professional golf, he had more than sixty professional victories. But Hogan wouldn't have achieved any of that success had he quit too soon.

What is it you're after? Maybe you have career goals, a marriage that's struggling, or children who have lost their way. There's a key to finding success: When things get tough, you have to lean into your problem and persevere. You just might be on the edge of turning things around.

> Let us not grow weary of doing good, for in due season we will reap, if we do not give up.
> GALATIANS 6:9

How easy it is to give up these days, Lord. But You won't let me quit on my marriage, my family, or my goals in life. Replace my weariness with the strength and hope that come from You.

Commit to the One You Love

The fastest-growing type of relationship in our culture today is a man and a woman living together outside of marriage. A lot of couples want to avoid the pain of divorce by skipping wedding promises. Some rationalize: "We don't need a ring to tell the world how much we love each other."

But research indicates these couples are playing against the odds. It's not love that makes a marriage; instead, the commitment of marriage results in *learning* to love. Whether you're married or living together, you'll encounter stretches when you just don't like each other very much. Married couples are ten times more likely to stay together through those stretches than those who cohabit. It's the promise to stick together through thick and thin that grants you the freedom to give your heart away.

If you really want a love relationship, don't settle for second best. Yes, committing yourself to someone else for a lifetime is terrifying—and love comes at a great cost. But try finding someone who's been married for fifty years who doesn't think it was worth it.

As the eighteenth-century physician and professor Joseph Barth reputedly said, "Marriage is our last, best chance to grow up." Don't miss it.

He who finds a wife finds a good thing and obtains favor from the Lord.
PROVERBS 18:22

God, a lifelong commitment in marriage is Your
original design that hasn't changed after thousands
of years. May my partner and I honor You in learning
to love as a fully committed married couple.

Sink the Ships

Commitment is critical for a successful marriage. Too many of us make excuses for not resolving conflict with our spouse. We need to sink the ships.

In 1519, the Spanish conqueror Hernán Cortés led a fleet of eleven ships to the shores of what is now Mexico. With five hundred soldiers under his command, his goal was the conquest of the Aztec Empire and its extensive reserve of gold, silver, and precious jewels.

Cortés and his men were vastly outnumbered, and many of the soldiers lost their nerve. When Cortés heard rumblings about abandoning the mission, he immediately took action to bolster his men's commitment. He told them to destroy the ships. Scuttling their ships left them with no way out but forward.

Retreating from adversity is easy when you give yourself the option. That's why successful marriages demand commitment. Committing means making a decision, and the root word for *decision* means "to cut."

When we get married, we have to cut everything out of our lives that would go against the commitment we've made. There's no room for retreat if we hope to have a relationship that will endure. Once we say "I do," we have to be all in.

I can do all things through him who strengthens me.
PHILIPPIANS 4:13

Lord, with Your strength and Your wisdom, I can be all in with my marriage. Help both my spouse and me stay committed to each other and work through tough times. May we sink any ships that seem like an easy way out.

Putting the Pieces Together

A one-thousand-piece jigsaw puzzle isn't fun if you don't know a few tricks. You sift through the pieces to find matching colors and border pieces. Then you put the border together while studying the picture on the puzzle box.

The picture is your goal. The more pieces you get in the right place, the more it will look like the box cover. Without the picture, you're creating extra headaches. The colors get mixed up, and none of the pieces seem connected. Who needs a frustrating mystery?

The first few years of marriage can be a frustrating mystery too. You barely know each other. It's like the pieces of your marriage puzzle have been dumped onto the table, and your differences are just starting to emerge. It takes patient navigation to create a happy and successful marriage. That's a daunting task when the pieces don't fit and the colors clash.

The solution? Look at the picture on the box. Get a vision for your marriage, and pursue it together. Read a marriage book, or seek out a marriage counselor. Healthy marriages are easier to piece together when couples pursue a common goal.

> In [Christ Jesus] the whole structure, being joined together, grows into a holy temple in the Lord. In him you also are being built together into a dwelling place for God by the Spirit.
> EPHESIANS 2:21-22

Jesus, thank You for knowing all the pieces of my marriage and for being the glue that fits us together in unity. Help my spouse and me pursue Your best in all areas of our lives.

Better as Teammates

I know a lot of guys with a good marriage who are unsure how to have a *great* marriage. I encourage them to consider how they can work as better teammates with their wives in order to strengthen their relationships.

Like a lot of guys, I've been involved with sports and on some great teams. One thing I know: When you create a culture of respect and hard work among teammates, you can be successful at just about anything. I once heard a two-time Super Bowl champion explain, "When teammates give their best as individuals, they make each other better."

The best teams aren't always those with the most athletic players. Winning often comes down to teammates who are willing to work hard and motivate one another toward excellence. Play as hard for the guy next to you as you do for yourself. That's key to success in sports, in business, and particularly in marriage.

Your spouse is your teammate through life. Be willing to work hard at your relationship. Excel at your role on the team. You'll only motivate your spouse to improve his or her part in your marriage if you step up and improve yours.

The soul of the sluggard craves and gets nothing, while the soul of the diligent is richly supplied.

PROVERBS 13:4

God, I commit to diligently improving my marriage by investing time and effort in my spouse, my faithful teammate. Motivate us toward excellence in our roles as husband and wife.

Obligation vs. Feelings

I cringe when I hear people say couples should only stay together because they want to. Some reason that when a relationship feels like an obligation, it's time to pack it in. In reality, a successful marriage requires not only a *want to* but also an *ought to*.

Folks will talk endlessly about passion and romance. But obligation? Who wants to trudge forward through a marriage when their heart isn't in it?

That negative characterization of obligation misses its deeper significance. Dr. Scott Stanley at the Center for Marital and Family Studies at the University of Denver says obligation—which is really just a form of commitment—is the foundation for sustaining a marriage over time.

A relationship based solely on feelings is doomed to failure. No matter how hard your spouse tries, he or she will disappoint you from time to time. That's why commitment is a positive anchor that keeps a relationship stable when other factors may change.

Yet a relationship with nothing more than a sense of obligation to keep it alive will also not remain healthy for long. So while commitment is important to a marriage, couples must strive to grow beyond it. A successful marriage is not about either commitment or passion. You need both.

If a man vows a vow to the LORD, or swears an oath to bind himself by a pledge, he shall not break his word. He shall do according to all that proceeds out of his mouth.

NUMBERS 30:2

Lord, I recognize that feelings come and go, and I do not want my marriage to be based only on emotions. Help my spouse and me hold fast to each other no matter what we face in life. Keep us striving to grow in both our commitment and our passion.

Signs of an Unhealthy Marriage

Do you know how to tell if your marriage is unhealthy? The details may be different from one relationship to another, but the results are identical: You routinely feel lied to, controlled, ignored, or degraded by your spouse.

Many people react in one of two ways when they realize that their marriage is unhealthy: Either they push back with destructive behavior or they emotionally shut down and act as though all is well when it's not. Neither choice will solve your problem.

There's another option: Form a plan of action that will move your marriage in a new, healthy direction. The details for how to do that may be different for each relationship, but every couple should keep a few things in mind.

First, if your spouse's behavior ever makes you feel in danger, then find a safe place to go. Second, stay committed to the truth. Unhealthy behavior should never be excused or allowed to continue. Third, reach out to a family member or a trusted friend who can help you cut through the emotion and make good choices. Or speak to a professional counselor who can help you chart a new course.

> He will hide me in his shelter in the day of trouble; he will conceal me under the cover of his tent; he will lift me high upon a rock.
>
> PSALM 27:5

God, You are my refuge. Cover me and guide me in this trial; strengthen my marriage and fight on my behalf.

What Are We Going to Do?

Rocky Balboa was a champion. Not only was he a tough fighter, but he also had great support in his corner.

In the original movie, Rocky was a down-and-out club fighter from the streets of Philly. The climax is when he gets a chance to fight Apollo Creed, the world heavyweight champion. Rocky trains for weeks, but the night before the big fight he confides in his wife, Adrian, and tells her his fears. "I can't beat him," he says. "I ain't even in the guy's league." Adrian looks at Rocky and says, "What are we going to do?"

Adrian didn't ask Rocky, "What are *you* going to do?" She asked, "What are *we* going to do?" Rocky may have been the one getting into the ring with Apollo Creed, but Adrian saw it as *their* fight. Whatever challenge they faced, they were going to get through it *together*.

Together is how good marriages turn into great ones and hurting marriages get rescued from the brink of divorce. You're a team. Whatever heavyweight fight your marriage is up against and you're not sure you can win, ask, "What are *we* going to do?" Then get through your battle together.

Bear one another's burdens, and so fulfill the law of Christ.
GALATIANS 6:2

You carry our burdens and invite us to do the same for one another. Give us Your strength, God.

When Things Seem Hopeless

In track and field, it was known as the four-minute barrier. Over the decades, no one had ever been timed running a mile in under four minutes. In fact, the barrier had stood for so long, many people believed breaking it was physically impossible. But that all changed on May 6, 1954, when twenty-five-year-old Roger Bannister slipped beneath the four-minute mark by six-tenths of a second.

The achievement shattered decades of preconceived ideas. In the next five years alone, more than twenty athletes broke the four-minute barrier. Today it's commonplace. The difference is what people believed was and was not possible.

Many struggling couples give up on their marriage for one reason: They're convinced there's no hope for their relationship. Yes, some conflicts are difficult to overcome, but that doesn't mean it's impossible. Unfortunately, some couples never attempt to heal their marriage because they're shackled by the idea that nothing can be done.

If your relationship seems hopeless, take one step of faith: Believe that things can improve. You might be surprised at the progress you and your spouse make once you believe change is possible.

Ah, Lord GOD! It is you who have made the heavens and the earth by your great power and by your outstretched arm! Nothing is too hard for you.

JEREMIAH 32:17

Father, how great You are! Please remind us that nothing is impossible for You—including bringing healing and rejuvenation into our marriage. You are the God of hope and miracles. Renew our trust in You.

Building Love

Writing to a young bride and groom, pastor and theologian Dietrich Bonhoeffer once advised, "It is not your love that sustains the marriage, but from now on, the marriage that sustains your love."

Many times, what sustains marriage through the difficult days we all endure is the power of the commitment made, not the feelings of love. When two people commit to each other through thick and thin, in good times and bad, love is planted. And when that same couple goes through a rough patch, love is cultivated. Yes, even the hard times can be good for your marriage.

When was the last time you signed a contract that included the stipulation "as long as I feel like it"? In contracts and in marriage, the ability to honor your commitment no matter what happens is incredibly important.

There are moments in every marriage when you might feel like your love is fading. In those times, let the commitment you've made to each other carry you through. Things will get better, and you will find—like so many couples before you—that coming through those times has truly sustained and deepened your love.

For God so loved the world, that he gave his only Son, that whoever believes in him should not perish but have eternal life.
JOHN 3:16

God, You are the ultimate example of love. Because You loved us with an unfailing love, You sent Jesus as a sacrifice for our sins. Help us emulate that love with each other by doing whatever it takes to keep our love fresh and alive.

A Marriage Saved
Is a Marriage Earned

Are you struggling to keep your marriage afloat? Do you wonder if your marriage is even worth saving?

You're not alone. At one time or another, many couples will face a crisis that threatens their relationship. Whatever you're going through, I want to assure you that your marriage *is* worth fighting for.

If you're a parent, perhaps the most important factor in your decision will be the welfare of your kids. Some claim that children simply want their parents to stop arguing and are relieved when the divorce happens. Nothing could be further from the truth! In fact, divorce is one of the top fears among American kids. And for those children whose parents did divorce, studies have shown that twenty-five years later, they still remember the loneliness and fear that the divorce caused them.

Remember, research also shows that unhappily married adults are no happier once they divorce. And for those who make the effort to repair and strengthen their marriages, over time they benefit from improved overall well-being.

Here's the good news: You do not need to remain an unhappily married couple. You also do not have to choose divorce. Your marriage *can* be healed and rejuvenated. It may not be easy at first, but working together to save your marriage—to earn your spouse back—will reap dividends of marital bliss in the years to come.

The LORD is near to all who call on him, to all who call on him in truth.
PSALM 145:18

Lord, we need You in our marriage. Help us call on You in truth, knowing that You bring marital healing and health.

Changed in a Moment

Even when a relationship seems beyond saving, one moment can change everything. That was beautifully illustrated in a social media post watched more than thirty million times in just a few days.

In the video, Caitlin, a young mother, is with her son and her soon-to-be ex-husband. There is a birthday cake on the table. Although Caitlin and her husband believe their marriage is unsalvageable, they've decided to celebrate one last birthday as a family. Then something remarkable happens. As the birthday candles illuminate the scene, Caitlin's husband looks up from their son and gazes at her. *His* eyes light up. With love for *her*.

Caitlin shares this: "I could see the love for me all over his face. I captured the exact moment I knew we could save our marriage." And they *did*. Caitlin concludes the video by explaining that she and her husband went to counseling and remain happily married.

If your marriage is in crisis, hope can be hard to find. But don't give up too soon. One moment can change everything. If you're willing to pursue reconciliation, good things can still happen even when the way forward isn't clear.

If you're considering divorce—even if you've begun the process—programs like Focus on the Family's Hope Restored can help you save your relationship. Let us show you how.

I will restore to you the years that the swarming locust has eaten,
the hopper, the destroyer, and the cutter, my great army, which
I sent among you.
JOEL 2:25

Lord, bring about moments in our relationship that open our hearts to each other and knit our souls together. In moments of darkness, give us Your light. Grant us the courage to seek reconciliation and keep hope alive.

Happiness Is No Accident

Is a happy marriage possible? I believe the answer to that question is yes. But there is a catch: Happiness isn't dependent on good things happening *to* you. It depends on you *choosing* to be happy.

One way author Kevin Thompson learned that happy marriages are no accident was by observing his grandparents, who were married for seventy years. After such a long time together, people often suggested that the couple was lucky to have so many things go their way. But Kevin's grandparents were quick to point out that they were happy *despite* their circumstances. Both of them were born into poverty, and they had married each other at an early age. They had worked long, hard hours at their jobs, and they'd struggled to raise their children on two meager salaries.

Yes, a happy marriage *is* possible, but it's not based on sheer luck or good chemistry. It's the result of commitment, sacrifice, and hard work. Anchor your relationship in your faith, and commit to sticking together through thick and thin. Happiness won't come to you by accident. You have to choose to go after it.

Whatever your hand finds to do, do it with your might.
ECCLESIASTES 9:10

Heavenly Father, help us find happiness through our commitment, sacrifice, and unwavering faith in one another. Give us the strength and determination to find joy as we remain steadfast through life's challenges.

Commitment, Not Chemistry

Many people believe the secret to a successful marriage is chemistry—some special *something* that enables couples to effortlessly agree about almost everything. When couples have chemistry, such thinking goes, they just click. But good chemistry isn't magic, and it's only part of what makes a marriage function properly.

Have you ever heard the saying *Opposites attract*? That concept isn't just a plot device in romantic comedies. Differences do play a powerful part in every relationship. Differences draw men and women together when they're dating but can also drive them apart when they're married.

The key to a thriving marriage isn't how you and your spouse handle your similarities; it's how you handle your differences. Marriage is a profound mystery on many levels, but it's rooted in a knuckles-in-the-dirt commitment to overcome your differences and come together as one. Build your relationship on a foundation of faith; then lean on those enduring principles when times get tough.

When problems erupt, dedicated couples don't give up; they get to work. Successful marriages are built on commitment, not chemistry.

Commit your way to the LORD; trust in him, and he will act.
PSALM 37:5

Father, help us work through our differences to propel our marriage forward—in tough times and joyful ones. Ground our relationship not in chemistry but in unwavering dedication to You and to each other.

SECTION 17

Healing

When It's Time to Dredge

Morehead City, North Carolina, is home to one of the deepest ports on the East Coast. It's a vital passageway for commercial and military ships. But the port developed a serious problem when Hurricane Sandy deposited sand in the channel. Several areas that had once been almost fifty feet deep were reduced to only five. Without dredging, the waterway would be inaccessible to ships, and a crucial port in the region would be shut down.

Something similar can happen in marriage. Unresolved conflict is like a never-ending storm between a husband and wife. Before long, instead of providing deep, fulfilling connection, the relationship becomes shallow and stagnant. When this happens, it's time to dredge up the past.

Obviously, by "dredging up the past," I'm not referring to its typical meaning of rehashing old conflicts to punish your spouse for his or her mistakes. I'm suggesting that a couple join together to work through the resentment that has bogged down the relationship.

It's not easy, and some marriages might need the guidance of a professional counselor to help them work through it. But with patience and the willingness to forgive, the depth of love spouses once had for each other can be restored or possibly deepened—especially for those who might never have had the depth of relationship they have always wanted.

Know this, my beloved brothers: let every person be quick to hear, slow to speak, slow to anger; for the anger of man does not produce the righteousness of God.

JAMES 1:19-20

God, You know that conflict happens in life.
Please increase our awareness of unresolved
conflict so that we can invite You into that space,
resolve our conflicts, and experience healing.

Some Wounds You Can't See

P ain has been called a messenger. Its job is to tell us something is wrong. But messages are only helpful if you understand what they mean.

It's no fun breaking your ankle. It happened to me a few years back when I tumbled off a motorcycle thanks to a winding mountain road. If there was anything positive about my injury, it was that the connection between my physical brokenness and the pain was obvious.

But emotional brokenness is often a different story. It's much harder to connect symptoms to their cause. You can't see the source of the problem, so the pain is easily mistaken for other issues. Counselors will tell you that depression, for example, is often confused with fatigue or dismissed as laziness. This applies to marriage, too. The unhealthy ways we might interact with our spouse are not always recognized as signs of emotional pain.

As a result, our struggles can go untreated and steadily grow worse. That's why we need trusted people in our lives who can help us understand what our emotional pain is really all about. Only then can we get the help we need. That insight may come from a friend, but it often requires the expertise of a professional.

> He heals the brokenhearted and binds up their wounds.
> PSALM 147:3

Lord, You know what causes me pain and what causes pain in my marriage. Show me how to be brave in opening up about my emotional brokenness and trusting You for true healing.

Surviving an Affair

An affair doesn't simply break marital trust; it shatters it.
Victims of an affair often feel an overwhelming sense of suspicion toward their spouse. Everything is interpreted through the lens of betrayal—their spouse's choice of clothing, their phone conversations, even the slightest deviation from their daily routine. The paranoia can be so intense that many spouses will attempt to monitor their partner's every move.

To someone who has been emotionally devastated, such behavior seems rational. It's an attempt to harness control over circumstances that seem wildly out of control.

But repeatedly checking on your spouse will trap you in a cycle of fear and suspicion, which will only drive you into deeper depression and higher stress. Instead, reach out for support from a counselor, family members, and friends, and slowly learn to accept that it's not healthy to habitually monitor your spouse.

If you're in this situation, releasing control of your spouse may sound terrifying. But the reality is that there's only one person you can control: you. Coming to terms with this fact will allow you to devote your energy to moving forward in life with dignity and healing—and hopefully save your marriage in the process.

Forgive us our debts, as we also have forgiven our debtors. And lead us not into temptation, but deliver us from evil. For if you forgive others their trespasses, your heavenly Father will also forgive you, but if you do not forgive others their trespasses, neither will your Father forgive your trespasses.

MATTHEW 6:12-15

Jesus, thank You for paying so dearly for my trespasses. Forgiving my spouse is deeply painful, but I want to obey You. I release my desire to control. Heal and restore as only You can.

Building a Bridge

Marriage can challenge the strongest of couples. So when serious conflict damages your relationship, do you dig a moat or build a bridge?

Digging a moat is a common reaction when your marriage is suffering. It's like an emotional trench around your heart so deep and wide that your spouse can never cross it. When you're buried in heartache, that's an understandable response. But in the long run, it'll keep you stuck in pain.

To break free, build a bridge to your spouse by finding ways to connect with each other. Rebuild what's been broken.

Your relationship won't magically fix itself overnight. Healing *can* come, but it happens one date night, one conversation, and one kiss at a time. Disconnecting from each other probably took some time, and so will reconnecting.

Prioritize your relationship. Put the kids to bed early one night so you and your spouse can have some time together. Hire a babysitter or meet for lunch. It may seem that ordinary moments like these won't get you anywhere. But they're exactly the kinds of small steps that can slowly bring your relationship back together.

If conflict has damaged your marriage, remember: Don't dig a moat. Build a bridge.

I long to see you . . . that we may be mutually encouraged by each other's faith, both yours and mine.
ROMANS 1:11-12

Lord, building bridges and not moats is such wise advice. Help my spouse and me prioritize our relationship and be consistent in everyday communication and connection. I am confident that with Your help, we'll take the small steps that will lead to big reasons to celebrate.

Repairing the Damage

When there's conflict in your marriage, how do you resolve it? Flowers? Chocolate? How about dynamite?

Fitchburg, Massachusetts, is home to a 110-ton boulder. The Rollstone Boulder was a prominent landmark for generations at the summit of Rollstone Hill. When quarrying threatened to topple the ten-foot-tall rock, townspeople were determined to save it—with dynamite! Between 1929 and 1930, they blew it up, moved all 110 tons of granite to the town common, and pieced it back together. Folks couldn't imagine this landmark not being a part of their community.

Minor marital problems can sometimes be resolved with flowers and an apology. But other times the conflict is so severe and the wounds so deep that it feels as if dynamite has blown the marriage to pieces. Unfortunately, couples in that situation often believe there's no hope of repairing the damage that's been done.

But quite often these relationships can be healed. It'll likely take the assistance and expertise of a professional counselor. And yes, it'll require a lot of hard work. But the important things in life usually do.

If your marriage seems shattered beyond repair, don't give up hope too quickly. There may still be a chance for you and your spouse to find healing and restoration.

Heal me, O LORD, and I shall be healed; save me, and I shall be saved, for you are my praise.
JEREMIAH 17:14

Lord, Your hands heal when marriages feel shattered. Restore and rebuild my relationship with my spouse before we are crushed by apathy, bitterness, and painful circumstances.

Be Delicate with an Abused Spouse

Every good marriage is built on a foundation of patience and understanding. That's never more true than for a spouse who has been a victim of sexual abuse.

By just about anyone's standards, Caitlyn was a beautiful lady, but she didn't feel that way. Lots of women say they're unhappy with their bodies, but for abuse survivors, the dissatisfaction goes much deeper than their reflection in the mirror. It's a deep soul wound.

Caitlyn was nearly in tears when it came time for her husband to see her on their wedding night. She stayed in the bathroom for almost twenty minutes and wouldn't come out until he'd turned off the lights.

Fortunately, Caitlyn's husband understood the need to be delicate with his wife's self-image. It's what you, too, will need to do if your spouse has abuse in his or her past. Sexual abuse is a deeply shaming experience, often leaving victims unable to see anything worthy in themselves. That's why even seemingly harmless remarks about physical appearance can send a spouse into despair.

So be delicate with past wounds. Offer your spouse loads of reassurance, encouragement, and affirmation. Understand your beloved's needs, and treat your mate like the priceless treasure he or she is.

Behold, you are beautiful, my love, behold, you are beautiful!
SONG OF SOLOMON 4:1

Our Creator, thank You for my precious partner.
Nothing about their past deters me from seeing
their value. Keep me mindful of treasuring and
cherishing them for their divine worth.

The Right Environment

Would you like a stronger marriage? Then pay attention to how you fall asleep.

I remember checking on my boys one night before bed. My oldest, Trent, was fast asleep. But my younger son, Troy, was restlessly tossing in bed. I poked my head into his room and whispered that it was time to get to sleep.

Troy wearily replied, "I'm trying, Dad. Honest. I have my eyes shut and everything."

Later, as I drifted off, it occurred to me that healing a marriage is like the process of falling asleep. We cannot make ourselves go to sleep. We can turn off the lights, keep warm under blankets, and shut our eyes. But once we've created the right environment, all we can do is give our bodies time to respond.

It's a good analogy to remember if your marriage needs help. You can't force your relationship to be better or to heal faster. But you can fill your home with the right conditions every day—including love, respect, healthy communication, and appropriate boundaries. Then be patient and give your marriage time to respond. Like falling asleep, changes may not happen right away, but a healthy environment gives your relationship its best chance to flourish.

Love is patient and kind.

I CORINTHIANS 13:4

Father God, show me how to fill our home each day with the conditions we need to help our marriage flourish.

Broken Heart Syndrome

Did Marjorie Hartland die of a broken heart? Her daughter thinks so. Marjorie was 97 when she died just hours after her 101-year-old husband, Clifford. That day they would have celebrated their seventy-sixth wedding anniversary. A heart attack was the official cause of Marjorie's death, but the timing convinced her daughter that Marjorie was so sad that her heart gave out.

A medical condition called "broken heart syndrome" backs up that idea. The condition describes a sudden weakening of the heart caused by extreme stress. A heart-wrenching breakup or the death of somebody close to us is a wound so deep that we can literally get heartsick.

The good news is that you can overcome your sadness. Healing comes as you grieve what you've lost and take small, positive steps each day. Even small movements are beneficial. Talk to somebody. Don't keep your emotions locked up. Open your heart and get the pain out.

Then give yourself plenty of time to heal. Heartache doesn't magically disappear. It fades . . . slowly. So be patient with yourself. Lean on your faith. And stay connected with family and friends. With their support, you can mend your broken heart and, just maybe, live happily ever after.

The LORD is near to the brokenhearted and saves the crushed
in spirit.
PSALM 34:18

Merciful God, You draw tenderly close to us when we are
heartbroken. Thank You. May I be a gentle comforter
to those I hold dear when we face loss and sorrow.

Creating a New Normal

At Focus on the Family, we hear from couples every day whose marriages have been rocked by adversity. Many have endured an affair. Others have suffered from abuse or addiction. The common thread running through them all is the challenge of reconciling when your relationship has been ripped in half.

Couples often try to recapture the feelings they had for each other before everything went wrong. It seems reasonable. In the face of conflict, people tend to gravitate backward toward something familiar and predictable.

But that can actually complicate the healing process. It's like moving back into the home where you grew up as a child. Certain things will be familiar, but it'll never feel exactly like it did when you were a kid. You're older, and you see the world through different eyes now.

In the same way, there's no going back to a time before your marriage nearly collapsed. Instead, direct your energy toward creating a "new normal." Rather than sweeping problems under a rug and pretending nothing ever happened, learn to heal the wounds and create a new life. It can be tough to face the pain, but you'll come out the other side stronger.

Create in me a clean heart, O God, and renew a right spirit within me.
PSALM 51:10

Lord, a new normal in my marriage means moving forward with a clean heart and a right spirit. Thank You for the healing and new life my spouse and I are now experiencing and will experience together in the future.

Dealing with the Pain of Miscarriage

M any couples who suffer a miscarriage are surprised by how devastating the experience can be. If you've lost a baby, here are some suggestions for beginning to walk through the pain.

Our staff counselors say the first step is learning to see your heartache as normal. You've suffered a deeply meaningful loss that can throw your emotions into turmoil. Feelings of guilt are common, as are depression, mood swings, and anger. Even jealousy toward pregnant women or new mothers can crop up, causing you to withdraw socially.

The emotional response to a miscarriage is often as intense as it is with other significant losses. To completely heal, a couple must allow the grieving process to take its course. Short-circuiting it leaves them stuck in the denial stage. From there, problems snowball, negatively impacting not only their marriage but also their spiritual, emotional, and physical health.

Just remember, the stages of grief seldom follow one another in a straight line. They usually overlap in a back-and-forth manner until the loss is resolved. But if you give yourself space to grieve, your anger and confusion should eventually give way to acceptance and peace.

> Be gracious to me, O Lord, for I am in distress; my eye is wasted from grief; my soul and my body also.
> PSALM 31:9

---

*You understand grief, Father. You watched
Your only Son die a terribly painful death. I am
grateful that You are the God of all comfort
and are present in my loss and sorrow.*

An Operation for the Soul

On a beautiful summer afternoon in 2015, Bryan Kuck and his wife, Lynn, went for a motorcycle ride. On their way home, they were run off the road by a drunk driver. Lynn was killed instantly. Bryan was critically injured with two crushed hips, a broken pelvis, and a left leg that had to be amputated.

The drunk driver was charged with homicide. At the hearing, Bryan told the court that he and his family had been given a life sentence. Bryan would live the rest of his life without his wife—and his three boys without their mother. Then Bryan turned to the drunk driver and said, "Nevertheless, I forgive you. If it weren't for God, we'd all be lost. I'm just one beggar helping another find the Bread of Life."

Bryan underwent seventeen surgeries to bring healing to his body, but only one thing could bring healing to his soul: forgiveness. Anger and bitterness feel empowering for a while, but they're an emotional cancer that will eventually destroy you. Resentment will make your days dark, will make your nights restless, and will hinder your closest relationships.

Forgiveness is like an operation for your soul, filling your heart with hope and releasing you to new life.

Jesus said, "Father, forgive them, for they know not what they do."
LUKE 23:34

God, I am unable to forgive on my own. Empower me with Your Spirit to forgive as You have forgiven.

A Man like John Wayne

One morning, my son Troy and I stumbled into a conversation about manhood and marriage. We talked about things like personal responsibility, kindness, sexual discipline, and courageous living, to name just a few.

"What does it mean to be courageous?" I asked Troy.

Without missing a beat, he said, "Courage is being scared to death but saddling up anyway."

I wondered where he had come up with that witty definition. "It's written on your coffee mug," he answered. I looked and, sure enough, there was the famous quote from John Wayne—a man's man.

It's a good definition of courage—and a facet of manhood. There are other principles to grasp too. Marriages often fail because too many men (and women) have a mixed-up sense of what true manhood is all about, perhaps because their fathers failed to model what it means to be a man. As a result, a lot of men are either too passive or too aggressive in their marriages.

True masculinity is a proper balance of strength and gentleness. Someone once told me, "Show me strength without tenderness, and I'll show you a brute. Show me tenderness with strength, and I'll show you a true man."

> Whoever pursues righteousness and kindness will find life, righteousness, and honor.
> PROVERBS 21:21

Father, whatever role my earthly father played in shaping my idea of masculine strength, show me Your vision for what a true man is meant to be.

The Greatest Virtue in Marriage

According to the Smalley Relationship Center—well-known experts in restoring troubled marriages—the greatest virtue that can help repair a marriage is *forgiveness*. With that in mind, here are three tips to make seeking forgiveness from your spouse easier and more effective.

First, take a humble approach. Be sensitive to your spouse's feelings. If you blame him or her in any way for your mistakes—even subtly—you'll likely deepen your conflict, not lessen it. Forgiveness can only flourish in the presence of honesty and humility, not avoidance and arrogance.

Second, fully acknowledge the pain you've caused. You'll likely feel tempted to minimize your behavior. Instead, own the damage you've done. Allow your spouse some space to vent their pain and to be honest about how hurt they feel.

Third, recognize that forgiveness is a journey. Reconciliation is rarely instantaneous, especially if your mistakes have been egregious. As you move forward together, don't expect resolution overnight. Allow yourself time to grow stronger, little by little.

Offering forgiveness and seeking forgiveness are rarely easy, but they are absolutely essential for a healthy, satisfying marriage that can withstand the test of time.

Confess your sins to one another and pray for one another, that you may be healed.
JAMES 5:16

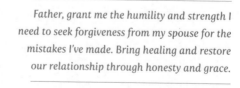

Father, grant me the humility and strength I need to seek forgiveness from my spouse for the mistakes I've made. Bring healing and restore our relationship through honesty and grace.

There Is Strength in Community

Many couples have a good marriage but little to no social life with other married couples. They work full-time jobs and spend most of their free time with their children and running errands. Their schedules don't slow down on the weekends, either—all of which leaves little time (or energy!) for a social life.

Yet other than an occasional nap, a healthy social life may be just what your marriage needs. Isolation cuts you off from good people who can influence you in positive ways. And when the only voice you hear is your own, it doesn't take long for the good in your marriage to turn bad, and for what's bad to get worse.

The ancient Roman army was seemingly invincible because the soldiers locked their shields together, uniting them as one. The giant sequoia trees of the Pacific Northwest have stood for centuries, largely because they intertwine their roots. The key to success in the face of adversity is not isolation, but the strength of community.

Like most couples, you probably feel immense pressure at times. You need all the encouragement and support you can get. So step out of isolation and connect with people who influence your relationship in positive ways and encourage you when times are tough.

> Let us consider how to stir up one another to love and good
> works, not neglecting to meet together, as is the habit of some,
> but encouraging one another, and all the more as you see the Day
> drawing near.
> HEBREWS 10:24-25

God, open our hearts to the influence and support of a
nurturing community of friends who enrich our marriage
journey through wisdom, love, and encouragement.

Routine Maintenance

You don't have to be married long to know that daily life can take a toll on a relationship. Day after day, challenges come at you from all directions—from hectic work schedules and household responsibilities to finances, friendships, and a never-ending maze of parenting decisions.

To prevent the daily grind from robbing your marriage of its spark, don't neglect to give your relationship some routine maintenance. For example:

- Communicate your expectations to each other clearly.
- Be honest about which activities you do and don't find enjoyable.
- Negotiate how often you'd like to dine out each week, go to the movies, or spend money on a round of golf.
- Talk openly about your sexual relationship. What's working? What could be improved?
- Discuss how household responsibilities should be divided.
- Find common ground about career aspirations, long-term goals, and work commitments.

Attempting to read each other's unspoken thoughts is not an effective strategy for strengthening your relationship. Instead, vocalize your expectations. Communicate. Get on the same page, moving in the same direction. That's the way to maintain a marriage that will go the distance.

We are to grow up . . . into Christ, from whom the whole body, joined and held together by every joint with which it is equipped, when each part is working properly, makes the body grow so that it builds itself up in love.
EPHESIANS 4:15-16

Lord, foster good communication in our marriage. Help us express our thoughts and feelings with clarity, kindness, and wisdom. Strengthen the bonds of our love through open dialogue that enriches our marriage.

Like a Living Organism

Trees are only as healthy as what's happening on the inside, beneath the bark. If a tree's vascular system is healthy, it will likely thrive. But if its inner tissue comes under attack via insects or rot, the tree will begin to weaken from the inside out. And you'll probably never notice—at least until a powerful wind arises. That's when a tree that once looked vibrant and strong can split right down the middle. Only after it's too late is it clear that the tree had been growing weaker and weaker from within.

And so it is with marriages that lack the essential nutrients necessary for a thriving relationship. Such marriages become susceptible to attack from without and within. Selfishness, pornography, conflict, resentment, and more can all weaken a relationship from the inside out. Everything might seem fine on the outside, but when the winds of life blow—and they *will* blow—that's when unseen weaknesses are exposed.

But you can stave off those weaknesses by tending to your marriage—growing it into a living organism as strong as a healthy oak tree. Begin by protecting your relationship from within. Infuse your marriage with all the nutrients it needs to thrive: love, grace, connection, and intimacy.

> He is like a tree planted by streams of water that yields its fruit in its season, and its leaf does not wither.
>
> PSALM 1:3

Lord, like a tree that's alive and growing, fill our marriage with nutrients that help it bear fruit and thrive.

How Do You Forgive Evil?

How does a person forgive evil?

Few people are as qualified to answer a question like that as Anthony Thompson. Anthony's wife, Myra, was leading a Bible study in Charleston, South Carolina. That day, the group welcomed an unexpected visitor. A young man named Dylann Roof wandered into their church and joined their Bible study. Three of the people present later said they noticed nothing unusual about Dylann . . . until everyone stood for the benediction and bowed their heads. That's when Dylann started shooting. Anthony's wife, Myra, was one of nine people killed.

Few people would blame Anthony if he responded with bitterness toward Dylann Roof. But at the bond hearing, Anthony got an opportunity to speak. Anthony says he actually felt his hatred disappearing as he told Dylann, "I forgive you. My family forgives you. Get yourself right with God."

Forgiveness doesn't excuse someone who has taken your spouse from you. Yet forgiveness frees you from all the nasty stuff that causes wounds to fester and never heal. Responding to evil with evil of your own won't ease your pain or help you move forward. Don't be overcome by evil; overcome evil with good . . . and forgive.

> Put on then, as God's chosen ones, holy and beloved, compassionate hearts, kindness, humility, meekness, and patience, bearing with one another and, if one has a complaint against another, forgiving each other; as the Lord has forgiven you, so you also must forgive.
> COLOSSIANS 3:12-13

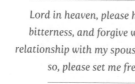

Lord in heaven, please help me be humble, let go of my bitterness, and forgive what needs to be forgiven in my relationship with my spouse or with anyone else. In doing so, please set me free from bitterness and anguish.

Healing Your Marriage after an Affair

Can a marriage overcome an affair? The answer is yes, but there's no quick fix. It takes humility, sacrifice, and commitment. Here are three steps that will give you the best opportunity to save your marriage if one or both of you have been unfaithful:

1. *Repent. Repentance* isn't a very popular word these days, but it's crucial. You must do more than simply say you're sorry. Take full responsibility for your poor choices, and resolve to make better ones.
2. *Be accountable.* Allow a pastor or a trained counselor to help you develop a plan for healing and restoration. Rely on friends and family to hold you accountable for following through.
3. *Rebuild.* Trust has been broken, and it won't return overnight. It'll take months, maybe even years, to reassure your spouse that you won't make the same mistakes again. Don't complain; just keep working hard to stack one success on top of another until healing finally comes.

Restoring a marriage after an affair isn't easy, but if a couple is willing, powerful things can happen. And don't try to navigate the journey alone. Speak to a professional with experience in this area, or consider Focus on the Family's Hope Restored program. We can not only help you restore your relationship but also help you build a marriage that thrives.

I will restore health to you, and your wounds I will heal, declares the LORD.
JEREMIAH 30:17

Lord, give us Your grace to heal the wounds in
our relationship caused by an affair. Help us find
forgiveness, understanding, and reconciliation so
that we may rebuild our shattered trust and love.

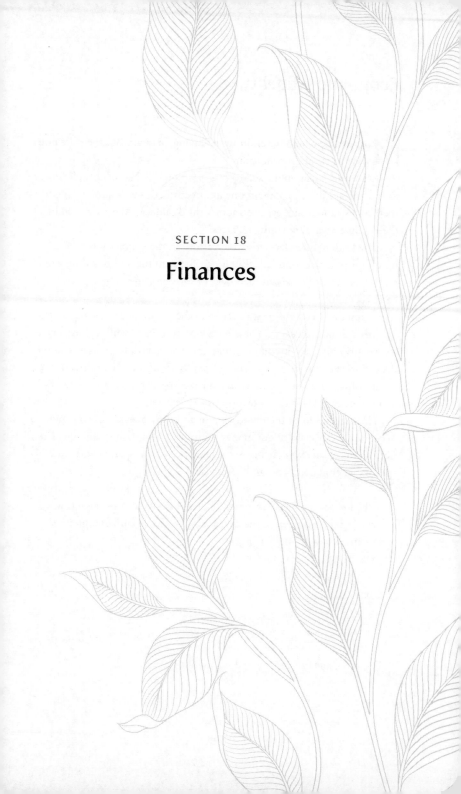

SECTION 18

Finances

Economic Infidelity

Most people would never dream of having an affair. But there are other ways to cheat on your spouse.

According to an online survey by *Forbes* and the National Endowment for Financial Education, about one in three Americans admitted lying to their spouse about money, and another third said they were deceived by their spouse regarding family finances.

The leading offenders either hid cash from their spouses or covered up minor purchases and bills. But a significant number also said they hid major purchases, lied about their debt or earnings, and even kept secret bank accounts.

In response to the survey, the chief of the National Endowment for Financial Education said, "These indiscretions cause significant damage to the relationship." No kidding! Among those surveyed, 67 percent said the deception led to an argument, and 42 percent said it caused mistrust in the relationship. And sadly, more than a quarter of the respondents said lies about money led to either a divorce or a separation.

Honesty has to be the foundation of a healthy marriage. Lying and deception—especially about money—can have devastating consequences. Let's all make sure we're being open, honest, and transparent with our spouses when it comes to family finances.

The love of money is a root of all kinds of evils. It is through this craving that some have wandered away from the faith and pierced themselves with many pangs.

1 TIMOTHY 6:10

Lord, money is important to survive in this world, but guard me from loving money more than I do my spouse. Steer me clear of lying about our family finances, and help me seek and speak truth always.

Dealing with Debt

Studies show that arguments over finances are one of the leading causes of divorce. Turmoil over a mountain of debt can be huge.

Financial experts Ron Blue and Jeremy White note that men and women respond to debt differently. Men tend to become workaholics, but longer hours are not the answer. A wife typically wants her husband home more during a financial crisis, not less. Also, a husband often won't tell his wife when he takes on more debt, because he's afraid she'll react negatively. Some men even blame their wives for their debt and refuse to accept any responsibility.

Women, on the other hand, have an innate need for security, so debt makes them anxious. Even if a husband suggests going into debt to finance a business opportunity or investment, many wives will respond negatively. Some resort to nagging their husbands about finances. This often indicates their desire for open communication on the issue. Others pretend the debt doesn't exist and spend money carelessly.

When it comes to finances, the husband's basic drive to provide may conflict with his wife's basic need for security. That is why spouses need to communicate with each other before debt is assumed.

Which of you, desiring to build a tower, does not first sit down and count the cost, whether he has enough to complete it?

LUKE 14:28

Father God, help my spouse and me wisely consider our finances before we take on debt. Teach us how to improve our communication about money so we can avoid unnecessary conflict in our relationship.

Your Relationship with Money

Millions of people feel insecure and anxious about their finances. Most of them fear they don't have enough money. But *more* isn't always the answer.

Obviously, if you're struggling to pay overdue bills, more money *would* be helpful. But that's only a short-term fix. Financial freedom is much more a function of your *attitude* about money than your amount of money.

Your *relationship* with money influences its role in your life. More money won't help you for long if you're a chronic spender. And if all you do is save, you're probably not using your money to the best benefit of you and your family.

Probably the worst relationship you can have with money is believing that *more* is always the answer for greater happiness and security. Americans have been trained to desire *more* and *better* no matter how good life already is. Ironically, the pursuit of *more* doesn't fill us with peace—it leaves us restless and anxious about losing what we have.

Money can't satisfy the deepest needs of your soul or replace the intimacy of a good marriage, the connection of a good friendship, or the love of your family.

> No one can serve two masters, for either he will hate the one and love the other, or he will be devoted to the one and despise the other. You cannot serve God and money.
> MATTHEW 6:24

Lord, my relationship with You brings ultimate contentment. Free me from anxiousness over finances, and replace that worry with peace in knowing You will always be my ever-present provider.

Money Problem or Marriage Problem?

If your marriage is struggling because of debt, you might not have a money problem . . . you might have a marriage problem. There are at least three possible causes of money-related conflict.

The first is that you believe more money will solve your financial problems. Most of the time it won't. Extra income won't compensate for overspending or poor money management. Decrease your debt and learn how to handle money well.

The second reason couples have conflict over money is poor communication. Studies show that 77 percent of couples never discuss their finances. If you're not discussing your problems, you're not discussing solutions, either.

The third reason for conflict is a difference in perspective. One spouse is a saver, and the other is a spender. One likes budgets. The other doesn't. Differences like those aren't right or wrong, but they do create conflict. Make your financial choices a matter of *we*, not just *me*.

If you and your spouse argue about money, take a deeper look at your relationship. Focusing on how, when, and where your money goes is good, but don't forget to focus on how you communicate about it. *Unity* is your greatest opportunity for improving your relationship *and* your finances.

He who loves money will not be satisfied with money, nor he who loves wealth with his income; this also is vanity.
ECCLESIASTES 5:10

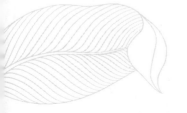

God, help me honor my spouse in our communication. Guide us to pursue each other rather than wealth.

Conflict over Finances (Part I)

Conflict over finances can be hard on a marriage. In fact, research shows that couples who argue about money are twice as likely to divorce as those who don't. So let's talk about how spouses can develop a financial team strategy.

According to counselors, an important first step is to figure out the underlying causes of your disagreements. Typically, money issues won't be resolved until you both understand what drives you. For example, some may use money to compensate for a deprived childhood or to ease depression or anxiety. So when making financial decisions, ask, "What's our motivation?" If either of you answers "To find fulfillment" or "To escape pain," reconsider how you're using your money.

Similar conversations should take place regarding your financial goals. To get on the same page, you'll need some common ground about spending and saving. In these initial stages, the details aren't as crucial as agreeing on general principles. Once you're headed the same direction, it'll be easier to find creative solutions. Above all, emphasize the health of your relationship over the minutiae of budgets and savings accounts.

> Keep your life free from love of money, and be content with what you have, for he has said, "I will never leave you nor forsake you."
> HEBREWS 13:5

Dear heavenly Father, help us be on the same team financially. Help us also be content with what we have and happy in each other's arms.

Conflict over Finances (Part 2)

When you decide to live within your means, more than likely, you'll have to take a closer look at the cost of your lifestyle. Most couples struggling with debt have no clear idea how much they spend each month on groceries, car payments, and entertainment. Without a willingness to live on what you earn, it's not a matter of *if* but *when* your finances will be sent crashing over the edge.

It's important to establish a budget. There are a number of resources available to walk you through how to do that. But for now, a plan is a crucial tool to help you live within your means and to make saving for a rainy day possible.

Why? Because budgets force you to prioritize your spending habits. It'll probably mean less of *this* and no more of *that*. You'll have to make tough decisions, which is a key reason many folks avoid budgets altogether. But remember the goal here: getting your money under control so you can reduce the conflict threatening your relationship.

Choices about finances don't have to become a straitjacket. They can liberate not only your bank account but your marriage as well.

Where your treasure is, there your heart will be also.
MATTHEW 6:21

Lord, You are our provider. Help us properly steward
the finances You have given us, but let our treasure
be found in You, Your goodness, and Your mercy.

Learning Your Spouse's Money Language

What is your money language?

In 1992, Dr. Gary Chapman wrote the *New York Times* bestselling book *The Five Love Languages*. I'd love to see him follow it up with a book on money languages. After all, when couples argue about budgets and bills, they are not just talking about dollars and cents.

Money represents something unique to each of us. Unfortunately, most people don't know their own money language, let alone their spouse's language. She may be arguing to save what he wants to spend. But they never learn to express why they approach money the way they do.

Couples who remain united in how they use their money learn to understand what money represents for each other. They become aware of the emotions that accompany their financial preferences. Perhaps a husband wants to have some money in the bank because he fears losing his job. Or maybe a wife wants some spending money because it represents freedom.

Ultimately, every couple needs to come to an agreement about setting a budget, saving for retirement, and handling debt. But those discussions will be much more meaningful if you learn to discover the *why* behind the *what*.

A good name is to be chosen rather than great riches, and favor is better than silver or gold.

PROVERBS 22:1

Father, a good reputation and favor are more important than riches. Likewise, how we approach and learn to understand each other financially is more important than the money itself. Help us discover the why behind the what, and as You do, draw us even closer as a couple.

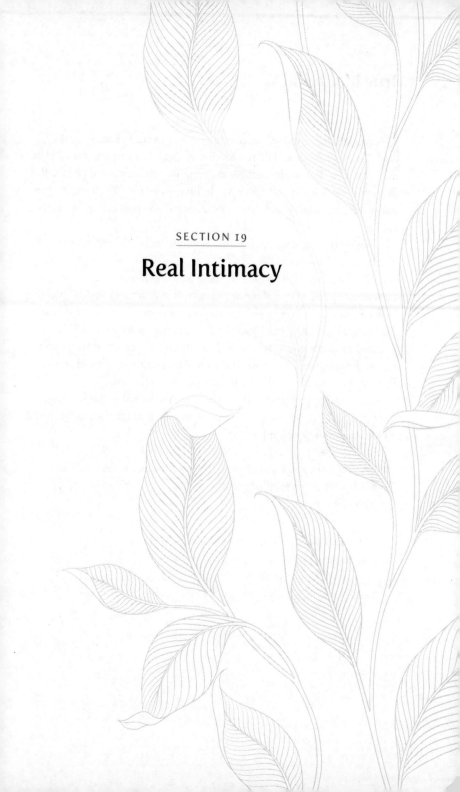

SECTION 19

Real Intimacy

True Manhood

Dana Jennings survived prostate cancer and wrote a column for the *New York Times* to tell his story. The surgeries and treatments had left him impotent. In his editorial, he observed how difficult it can be to suffer from this condition in today's world. In his own words: "I'm just trying to understand . . . what it feels like to be damaged goods in our oversexualized culture."

Despite the challenge, Mr. Jennings refused to be defined by the media's worship of sexuality.

"True manhood," he wrote, "is about love and kindness. It's about responsibility and honor, about working hard and raising your children the best way you know how, with love, respect, and discipline. . . . I feel that the life my wife, Deb, and I lead is more intimate than ever. . . . As I was buffeted by diagnosis, treatment and the aftermath, she was my advocate, my confidante, my unwavering caregiver. And everything she did was suffused by her love for me. It was an intimacy beyond words."

Sex is an important part of marriage, of course; but as the Jennings family discovered, *intimacy* is something that runs much deeper. We could all learn from their example.

Owe no one anything, except to love each other, for the one who loves another has fulfilled the law.
ROMANS 13:8

God, increase the intimacy in our relationship.
Help us reflect Your love in all that we do.

A Bottomless Well of Discovery

None of us goes into marriage knowing our spouse fully. We learn about him or her along the road of life. Day by day we understand a little better how to love our spouse in a way that is meaningful. We each have love languages that are formed by our personality and our past.

My wife knows that I became an orphan in childhood and had to make a lot of adult decisions by the time I was twelve. She knows that my experiences shaped me into an independent person and molded the way I give and receive love. And I've made the same discoveries about my wife. Jean's expressions of love are shaped by her personality and life experiences as much as mine are. We've been married for more than thirty years now, and we understand each other better now than we did on our wedding day.

What says *love* to your spouse? Words of affirmation? Quality time together? Figure out what it is. Study your spouse. Learn what makes him or her tick.

You fell in love with a stranger, but there's always room to learn something new when you treat your marriage like what it is: a bottomless well of discovery.

This is my commandment, that you love one another as I have loved you.

JOHN 15:12

Thank You for designing my spouse intricately and specifically. Reveal his or her needs and desires to me daily.

Two Halves Don't Make a Whole

Thanks in part to Hollywood, generations of young people have been taught that marriage is best when two people who are broken and lost meet, and their relationship completes them. In real life, relationships like that are doomed to years of struggle.

Genuine intimacy within a marriage can only occur between two people who are healthy and whole as individuals. People who feel incomplete inside tend to rely on others to fill them up. But this is like a bucket with a hole in the bottom—no relationship is ever enough to fill it.

And this leads to a second problem. Healthy people feel emotionally content inside, so they are able to freely give of themselves to their spouse. Someone who is wounded, however, rarely has anything to give because he or she seeks to have needs met by the spouse.

In math, two halves make a whole. But marriage isn't a math problem; it's a relationship. Two broken people cannot combine their wounds to create a successful relationship. A strong marriage consists of two healthy individuals who are content inside and able to give themselves to each other in love and sacrifice.

"A man shall leave his father and mother and hold fast to his wife, and the two shall become one flesh." So they are no longer two but one flesh.

MARK 10:7-8

Lord, my spouse and I are one flesh. Bind up any wounds we have so we can live as a healthy, confident, loving couple.

Take Off the Mask

Most women feel emotions deeply, and they're usually more motivated than men to heal their pain. Guys feel pain too, but we'll often try to mask it instead of talking to someone. That's why guys are more likely to have a dozen hobbies, to be workaholics, or to build surface-level friendships.

It's also why, sooner or later, almost every wife will say, "I really wish you would open up to me."

For men, communicating feelings can seem like trying to speak a foreign language. Most of us just don't have the vocabulary to share our hearts in the way our wives desire.

But guys, not knowing how is no excuse for never trying. The kind of intimacy your soul craves is only found in opening up—even if it's just a little at first. Tell her your hopes, your dreams. Describe some of your fears and struggles. Then listen closely when she shares hers with you. Learn to feel comfortable going to those deeper emotional places with your wife.

Turn your marriage around, guys, or make it even better. Learn the language of the heart. Show some vulnerability. Taking off your mask is a skill you can develop. It's the path to intimacy with your wife and to the marriage you want.

The heart of her husband trusts in her, and he will have no lack of gain.

PROVERBS 31:11

Jesus, I want my wife to entrust her heart to me;
I just feel clumsy about initiating that with her.
Guide me in developing an openness with my spouse
and in relating to her more deeply every day.

Expressions of Love

Maybe you've heard the story about a man who's asked how frequently he says "I love you" to his wife. The man responds, "I told her I loved her at the wedding. If I change my mind, I'll let her know." Unfortunately, such weak expressions of love are not that unusual for many couples.

Men, I want to challenge you to increase the intimacy in your marriage. Here's a simple way to do it: Be specific in the way you tell your wife you love her. Why limit yourself to the typical expression "I love you"? Compliment things that often go unnoticed, like how she cares for the children and the home. Let her know you love her smile, her laughter.

Men often forget how powerful the spoken word can be in the lives of those they love. Few things will make your wife's heart come alive like hearing her husband speak words of affirmation and encouragement in specific terms.

Someone once said romance "begins when a man whispers sweet nothings. It ends when he says nothing sweet." Speak to your wife; connect with her heart. Let her know the special ways she enriches your life. Your words have the power to make her feel truly cherished.

> Hear, for I will speak noble things, and from my lips will come what is right.
> PROVERBS 8:6

Lord, help me speak noble, empowering words to my wife. Remind me to say "I love you" for the countless ways she demonstrates her love to me. Thank You for blessing me with the incredible gift of my bride.

Marriage Gets All over You

Lucille Williams was on a weeklong honeymoon cruise with her husband, Mike. On their final night, while they were enjoying dinner with friends, Mike was suddenly hit with seasickness and began vomiting uncontrollably. The disgusting mess splashed all over Mike and all over Lucille. Later, as she scrubbed her clothes in the tiny cabin sink, she thought, *This is marriage. Your spouse's bad stuff gets all over you, and* your *bad stuff gets all over* him.

If you're a young couple who's about to get married, I'm sure you'd rather focus on your wedding plans and dreams for the future than the imagery of vomit. But there's a lot of wisdom to be found in Lucille's story—namely that if you go into marriage focused on yourself, self-centeredness is going to splash all over the place. Nothing good ever comes to a marriage through selfishness.

The converse of that concept is equally true. When you sacrifice for each other and strive for unity, you splash a lot of *good* stuff on each other too—things like love, compassion, grace, and forgiveness.

That's the intimate nature of marriage. Marriage is about *us.* The healthiest couples aren't *me*-focused; they're *we*-focused.

> Finally, all of you, have unity of mind, sympathy, brotherly love, a tender heart, and a humble mind.
> I PETER 3:8

Jesus, it's not easy to face the yucky sides of a marriage relationship, but those times are part of life's natural ebb and flow. Lead me in extending genuine love and care to my spouse through anything we encounter together.

Stranded on a Deserted Island?

Compassion and empathy aren't easy for me. I'm sure that's partly because I grew up in a dysfunctional home and developed something of a survivalist mentality. I've always appreciated my resilient spirit and my ability to "tough it out."

That's a handy skill to have . . . if I'm ever stranded on a deserted island. But it doesn't do me much good at home with my kindhearted wife. To Jean, empathy is second nature.

It's no surprise that she wants me to be vulnerable with her. My usual response is to clam up and try to handle everything myself. But that's not how intimacy is forged in marriage.

I've also learned that I can serve Jean by listening to her thoughts, insecurities, and fears—without passing judgment or presenting a quick solution. I'll share my perspective when it's appropriate or helpful, but what she craves more than anything is to be *heard* and *understood*.

Over time, I've learned how to resist my natural tendency to go it alone. When I take down my defenses and share my innermost thoughts with Jean, we're better able to overcome the challenges we face. And we deepen our emotional connection along the way.

> Two are better than one. . . . For if they fall, one will lift up his fellow. But woe to him who is alone when he falls and has not another to lift him up!
>
> ECCLESIASTES 4:9-10

Going it alone is not how You intend a marriage partnership, Lord. Teach my spouse and me to trust each other with our thoughts, insecurities, and fears. May we honor You in how we lift each other up.

Core Behaviors

Many husbands and wives today are running in opposite directions. They have so much going on that they don't have time left for each other. Dr. Harold Arnold has developed an acronym—CORE—to help couples put intimacy back in their marriage.

Commitment. Commit to a specific day and time each week when you and your spouse can spend an hour in conversation—without any distractions.

Openness. Developing marital intimacy means being honest with your spouse about your needs, desires, and fears.

Repentance. Are the supposed flaws you see in your spouse associated with *your* past behaviors? Own up to your mistakes, and be willing to forgive your spouse for theirs.

Empathy. Your spouse will only open up to you if he or she senses that you understand and love who he or she is unconditionally. Be willing to take time to listen without prejudice and to respond unselfishly.

Commitment, openness, repentance, and empathy—the CORE of marriage. If you and your spouse can put these important behaviors into practice, you'll be on the road to deeper and more fulfilling marital intimacy.

> Whoever conceals his transgressions will not prosper, but he who confesses and forsakes them will obtain mercy.
> PROVERBS 28:13

God, give me the discipline to put my marriage first.
Give me eyes to see my own faults, and help me
forgive and understand my spouse more fully.

False Intimacy

Many couples too easily settle for a cheap knockoff of marital intimacy instead of real connection.

Intimacy is the deepest relational need we have. It's a state of emotional connection with another person in which the good about us is known and celebrated and our flaws are met with love and healing.

But developing true intimacy in a marriage can be a challenge. It requires us to feel emotionally safe with another person. Without this deep sense of trust, we simply won't be vulnerable with our spouse or share the deepest parts of ourselves. True intimacy takes effort and a willingness to risk.

So what happens when our lives lack this authentic sense of connection and closeness? Quite often, we'll turn to a counterfeit, or as many counselors call it, a *false intimacy*. It's a term that describes the different ways both men and women seek a feeling of connection without the emotional vulnerability that true intimacy requires.

False intimacy usually takes the form of an affair, pornography, or even romance novels. But it's only a temporary solution to a much deeper need. It can't offer the authentic closeness, trust, and support we crave, because true intimacy can be found only in a committed relationship.

[Love] does not rejoice at wrongdoing, but rejoices with the truth.
I CORINTHIANS 13:6

God, lead me in the path of true intimacy in my marriage. Keep me from the counterfeit temptations that masquerade as authentic connection.

Love through Challenges

Most couples want a loving marriage that'll endure. So why do so
few relationships seem to actually experience that kind of genuine
intimacy?

Part of the answer lies in what we expect from relationships. The primary reason we're attracted to people is because of the way they make us
feel. But superficial emotions aren't enough of a foundation to sustain a
relationship or to create deep, fulfilling intimacy. Why? Because as soon
as the good feelings disappear, so does the person's commitment to the
relationship. It's why people abandon friendships and give up on marriages.

True love is something quite different. Love is patient and understanding. And yes, love can be hard. It sacrifices for someone else and
chooses to stay committed in spite of the other's faults. Instead of running
away, love faces challenges head-on to break through to something richer
and more meaningful. I've heard it said that love is "seeing the darkness in
another person yet resisting the impulse to jump ship."

Very few things in life are as enriching as true intimacy in marriage.
But the path to authentic, soul-fulfilling intimacy in a relationship isn't
always strewn with rose petals. Sometimes there are a few thorns along
the way.

Oh give thanks to the LORD, for he is good, for his steadfast love
endures forever!
PSALM 107:1

Loving God, You model faithful, steadfast love.
May my marriage do the same, especially when
we are both tired and facing a few thorns.

What's Written on Her Heart?

When speaker Arlene Pellicane first dated her husband, he often looked deep into her eyes. One night over dinner he asked her, "Do you know what I see in your eyes?" Arlene expected his answer to be something romantic. Instead, he told her, "I see the letters *AV* in your contact lenses." She later found the *AV* imprinted on the rims of her contacts. Arlene thought, *Here is a man who looks into my eyes so deeply that he knows what my contact lenses say.*

Do you look *at* your wife? Or do you look *into* your wife? Do you see her so deeply that you can read what's written on her heart? That is true marital intimacy.

Intimacy is about getting beneath the surface and understanding what your wife feels. It's learning her love language. What makes her feel special, loved, and valued?

To make your wife's heart come alive, treat your relationship like a flower in need of care, not like a checklist or a job description. Marriages thrive on desire, not a list of rules. Romance your wife. Sit with her. Look deeply into her eyes. Notice what's written on her heart.

Turn my eyes from looking at worthless things; and give me life in your ways.

PSALM 119:37

God, turn my eyes to see the priceless value of my wife's heart and soul. Thank You for creating her and our marriage.

Don't Settle for Counterfeits

Couples want their marriage to thrive, but instead of pursuing authentic intimacy in their relationship, many settle for a substitute.

Consider the Grand Canyon. We've all likely viewed it on TV or a postcard, but those versions can't compare to standing at the edge and looking out over the beauty of God's creation. Getting there in person is the more challenging alternative, but it'll immerse you in the grandeur of nature.

Or think of the Sistine Chapel. You've probably seen it in photographs, but there's nothing like standing inside that epic landmark to see firsthand Michelangelo's historic paintings.

Who prefers a substitute over the real thing? Unfortunately, it happens all the time in marriage.

Most people understand that being open to love means risking pain. So they protect themselves with counterfeits. Counterfeits offer connection without the emotional vulnerability that authentic intimacy requires. Men may gravitate toward pornography; women may seek fulfillment in romance novels. Individuals might feel safe hiding behind these substitutes, but in doing so, they're missing out on the real deal.

True intimacy can come only from immersing yourself in the experience of a committed relationship.

The simple believes everything, but the prudent gives thought to his steps.

PROVERBS 14:15

God, I truly long for genuine connection in my marriage. Help us both give careful thought to our steps in what we put before our eyes and let sink into our hearts and minds.

The Inner Circle

Dutch writer and theologian Henri Nouwen once described fear as the enemy of intimacy. Similarly, author Donald Miller shares an illustration that explains how fear keeps us from experiencing true intimacy. He starts by asking us to imagine three concentric circles. The innermost circle represents our true self, the person we really are at our core.

The second circle represents our shame. At some point in our lives, we suffer emotional wounds. Those wounds make us fearful of being hurt again, so we pull away from people we ought to be drawing closer to.

The outer circle represents the masks we wear. Our mask might be humor, beauty, or whatever we feel comfortable showing to the world. It keeps people away from the *real* us.

To experience true intimacy, we have to allow someone past the two outer circles into the inner circle. But that also means we have to be vulnerable and expose people to our failures, our shame, and our past hurts.

It's a dilemma we all face. We're designed to be in relationship, but we're scared of being truly known. To experience intimacy that enriches our lives, we have to be willing to take the risk.

> You did not receive the spirit of slavery to fall back into fear, but you have received the Spirit of adoption as sons, by whom we cry, "Abba! Father!"
> ROMANS 8:15

Help me rest in the truth of my adoption into Your family. Conquer my fear, and guide me into greater intimacy.

Getting to Know Your Spouse

A lot of newlyweds have the same question: "Should my spouse and I know *everything* about each other?" The answer is yes and no.

Vulnerability and transparency are important qualities in any marriage. But it can be risky to share too much too soon. If the two of you have sexual histories with other people, neither one of you may be prepared to hear the full truth about each other's past. It may be best to have those conversations in the presence of a counselor. These sessions can help you work through delicate matters without mistrust infecting your relationship.

Of course, for some of you, it's too late to handle that conversation differently. That's okay, because it's not too late to work through issues that discussions about your past may have raised. Still, the advice is the same: Get some guidance. Don't allow resentment to get a foothold in your relationship.

Be intentional about exploring your relationship, but also be careful to respect your spouse's boundaries where more personal or intimate topics are concerned.

The wisdom from above is first pure, then peaceable, gentle, open to reason, full of mercy and good fruits, impartial and sincere.
JAMES 3:17

Father, help us be wise, peace loving, gentle, reasonable, merciful, fair, and sincere as we learn how to be vulnerable with each other.

Building Intimacy

Men and women generally define *intimacy* in very different ways, so it's hard for them to get on the same page and meet each other's needs.

For a man, intimacy tends to happen with his wife when they engage in an activity together. That's why male friends play golf, go hunting, and go to ball games. For a husband, something as simple as going out for coffee or for dinner or seeing a movie is all it takes to feel connected with his wife. The fact that he and his wife do these activities together is what makes him feel close and connected.

For women, going bowling or having coffee together typically isn't enough to build intimacy if it isn't accompanied by meaningful conversation. It's all about connecting at a heart level through talking and sharing with each other.

Remember, you and your spouse probably experience intimacy differently from each other. So you have to be intentional about doing things that will allow both of you to feel like you've made an intimate connection. That usually means your time together must include both a fun activity and the opportunity for meaningful conversation.

> Above all these put on love, which binds everything together in perfect harmony.
> COLOSSIANS 3:14

God, please help us remain intimately connected with You, and intimately connected with each other, in a very purposeful way.

Sympathy or Empathy?

According to one study, 63 percent of people who say they feel lonely are currently married. Two people drive in the same car, sit at the same table, and sleep in the same bed . . . yet they feel worlds apart.

My colleague Dr. Greg Smalley discovered how lonely his wife was when he spent a few weeks cooking the family meals. Until then, he had no idea how much pressure she was under to plan dinners, buy ingredients, and worry about whether anyone appreciated her hard work. That experience made him wonder, *Does she feel alone in other areas of our marriage as well?*

What Greg discovered in that moment was the value of empathy for his wife. *Sympathy* is feeling bad *for* someone. *Empathy* is feeling bad *with* someone and helping him or her carry the burden.

Empathy combats loneliness by connecting you and your spouse at a deeper level, and by helping you understand an issue from each other's perspective. With empathy, your spouse will feel loved, understood, and valued. And when your relationship has those elements in abundance, connection and intimacy between you and your spouse will flourish.

Rejoice with those who rejoice, weep with those who weep.
ROMANS 12:15

Dear Jesus, I know that I desperately need to have empathy for my spouse just as You have empathy for me. Help me live this out, day by day.

Melding as a Couple

There's a well-known phrase in traditional marriage vows that refers to a man and a woman becoming one flesh. But becoming one flesh can be a struggle when marriage happens later in life.

Latecomers to marriage often face unique difficulties. After living on their own for years, older individuals may have built a career and purchased their own home. They likely have an established group of friends and activities that fill their social calendar. But once they marry, priorities have to shift. For some couples, learning to compromise can be more of a struggle than they expected.

If you're entering marriage later in life, you and your spouse will have to learn to be intentional about getting on the same page. Start by realizing that you have to go into this situation with your eyes open. Take some time to discuss how your careers and personal interests can blend in a way that satisfies both of you and enriches your relationship.

There's no question that marrying later in life can have its difficulties, but it can also bring a new sense of meaning and richness to your life.

I know the plans I have for you, declares the LORD, plans for welfare and not for evil, to give you a future and a hope.
JEREMIAH 29:11

Lord, please help me and my spouse know that no matter what, Your plans for our lives are good. Please help us see new opportunities for our marriage to grow deeper, even amid difficulties, because we know You have given us a hopeful future.

More Than Roommates

Is the intimacy in your marriage gone? A lot of couples say their relationship isn't growing any deeper. Instead of lovers on a journey through life together, they're married roommates.

One of the most common reasons husbands and wives don't enjoy deepening intimacy is that they connect poorly. Some couples rarely talk. And when they do, they talk about functional things, like work schedules, the children, or financial matters.

To improve your connection and become more than roommates, try a few of these simple ideas.

Spend five minutes together reading aloud from a book of your choice—then talk for five minutes about what you read. Take a walk through your neighborhood and share how you feel about something that happened that day. Cook a meal. Pray together.

Any couple can have a better relationship tomorrow than they do right now, but it takes a little work. The journey of two individuals becoming one only happens when each spouse gets beneath the surface and connects with the other's heart. That's not always easy. But if you're willing, your marriage can be more than a business arrangement. It can be a romance.

Do two walk together, unless they have agreed to meet?
AMOS 3:3

Jesus, my spouse and I do not want to be just roommates.
Instead, we want to be an intimately connected couple.
We know this means that we must agree to walk through
intimacy together. Please help us begin doing so today.

Into Me, See

You've heard the word *intimacy* before. A friend of mine suggests that if you try pronouncing it as "Into me, see," you may begin to understand what intimacy can mean to your marriage.

Too many marriages sound something like this: The husband says, "I don't understand my wife. I'm always hot; she's always cold. I want to relax in front of the TV, but she complains about it. I'm beginning to wonder if we should have gotten married at all!"

Meanwhile, the wife says, "Of course I'm cold. He keeps the thermostat so low I'm always shivering. And our family can't spend quality time together because he's a couch potato in front of the TV. Maybe there's not any hope for our relationship."

If that sounds like your marriage, remember "Into me, see." Learn how to "see into" each other's heart. After all, that's what true intimacy is really about—understanding life from your mate's perspective. Appreciate what makes your spouse tick. Think of ways to put his or her needs above your own. And don't be afraid to take the first step. Learn what makes your spouse feel loved and valued, and you'll start to rekindle the flame your marriage once had!

Let us pursue what makes for peace and for mutual upbuilding.
ROMANS 14:19

Father, it's so easy to see life only from my own perspective. Help me see into the heart of my spouse so that we can experience the peace and harmony You desire to cultivate in our marriage.

Keep Your Standards High

It's not unusual for people to look for easy solutions. Take sixteen-year-old Mark, for example. His dad, Steve, watched as Mark played basketball in the driveway one day. He was trying to dunk the ball but couldn't quite reach the hoop. Steve hoped his son would keep at it and work to improve. But after several failed attempts, Mark took another route: He lowered the rim.

Many adults try to fix their marriage the same way. Instead of striving for a better relationship, some couples lower their expectations. Rather than putting in the work to grow and develop deeper intimacy, they settle into a life of dull complacency. Before long, their relationship looks more like roommates splitting the cost of rent than a husband and wife who have committed their hearts and lives to each other.

A better idea is to grow as individuals and as a couple so you can build the relationship you've both dreamed about. It's not easy. It takes commitment, time, and dedication, but it's the only way to create a marriage that satisfies.

Do not be slothful in zeal, be fervent in spirit, serve the Lord.
ROMANS 12:11

Father, I want to be many things in my marriage and for my spouse, but slothful isn't one of them! Remove any complacency from our hearts, and give us a vision—and a desire—for the rich relationship You have created us to experience.

Learn to Read Your Spouse

There's an ancient Greek fable about a disagreement between the wind and the sun. To settle their dispute, they agreed on a challenge to see which one could get a traveler passing below to take off his coat. The wind went first, blowing cold and hard against the traveler. But the traveler pulled his coat tighter. When it was the sun's turn, it shone bright and warmed the earth. This time the traveler loosened his coat and eventually shed it completely.

According to the fable, the sun understood what the traveler would respond to. Marriage isn't all that different, really. It's about understanding what will resonate with your spouse. Building deep connection isn't about expressing love in a way *I* would prefer. So although buying flowers and doing laundry are nice gestures, if those aren't things that connect with your spouse's heart, your beloved won't feel nurtured and loved.

Instead, find out what *is* meaningful to him or her. Wives may enjoy receiving love notes or engaging in conversation. For guys, it may be eating a home-cooked meal or getting some time to relax and watch the game. It's all about finding those things that make your spouse feel loved and showering him or her with them.

> O LORD, you are our Father; we are the clay, and you are our potter; we are all the work of your hand.
> ISAIAH 64:8

Father, my spouse is the work of Your hand, and You have crafted my beloved with intention and delight. Give me wisdom as I seek to learn what resonates with my spouse and to show love in ways that feel personal and meaningful.

The Slow Burn of Romance

Ladies, how do you measure whether your marriage is romantic enough? Does your husband have to chase you to your gate at the airport? Does he have to toss pebbles at your bedroom window and serenade you? How about a long kiss on the beach while waves tumble over you?

Guys, what about you? Do you imagine yourself as the hero—a valiant knight who sweeps your wife off her feet and carries her, literally and figuratively, into the future?

Romance is tricky. Sharing beautiful moments together is important. They create lasting memories and help deepen emotional bonds. But at some point after every fairy-tale wedding, the daily grind of life takes its toll, and romance fades. What your relationship needs then is not some dream sequence sprinkled with fairy dust, but a romance that carries your relationship day by day through the ups and downs of life.

My advice to you is this: Pursue fairy-tale romance every chance you get. Take sunset walks on the beach. Eat dinner by candlelight. Kiss in the rain. Enjoy beautiful moments together that help your relationship. But cultivate love and intimacy *between* those grand moments as well. Strong marriages need more than fireworks. They need a love that endures through the tough times.

Let all that you do be done in love.

1 CORINTHIANS 16:14

Father, we bring our hearts before You, grateful for the love that binds us as a couple. Kindle the flames of our passion. Infuse our relationship with Your divine love. May our romance reflect Your enduring, selfless love every day.

Spiritual Intimacy

Every marriage has defining points: money, sex, communication. And one that often gets overlooked: spiritual intimacy. As the words suggest, spiritual intimacy involves how much a couple feels unified in their beliefs about faith and spirituality.

Couples who don't come together spiritually often run into trouble. Take Maria and John. They didn't talk much about their spiritual beliefs while they were dating. After they got married, they were unprepared when the challenges of life exposed just how different their deepest values actually were.

Your views on God and faith shape your heart and soul. Likewise, spiritual intimacy shapes the heart and soul of your relationship. Unity in this area enables you to grow ever deeper in your union together. I'm sure that's a pretty lofty goal on those days when you're busy with kids, work, and stuff that needs to get done around the house, so let me offer a couple of suggestions:

1. Find ways to connect with each other spiritually while you're on the move. Take advantage of technology—it only takes a moment to text your spouse a short prayer or word of encouragement.
2. Make time to sit with each other and have meaningful conversation— even if it's not until later in the evening. Take a few minutes, look each other in the eye, and connect.

Above all, remember that spiritual intimacy, at its core, isn't about what you *do* together. It's about who you *are* together.

I appeal to you . . . that there be no divisions among you, but that you be united in the same mind and the same judgment.
I CORINTHIANS 1:10

Father, align our hearts with Your divine purpose. May
Your presence be the foundation of our relationship.
Lead us into a profound spiritual union that
deepens our connection with You and each other.

Get Naked

For a happier marriage, get naked.

Now that I have your attention, let me clarify that by "get naked" I'm talking about emotional intimacy, not clothing removal. In Genesis 2:25, after God created Adam and Eve, we're told that they "were not ashamed" by their nakedness. That description isn't included merely to point out that Adam and Eve felt comfortable in front of one another without clothing. It also describes their union on a much deeper level.

Adam and Eve were not only physically compatible but emotionally and spiritually compatible as well.

Physical intimacy is an important part of a healthy marriage, but it's only one part. Healthy couples also bare it all emotionally and spiritually. They anchor their relationship in honesty and believe that secrets and lies are the enemies of trust and intimacy. They understand that they cannot have a thriving marriage while nurturing hidden bank accounts, secret cell phones, private internet searches, or undisclosed relationships—either in person or on social media. Healthy couples practice honesty and transparency.

Open your heart to your spouse in a way that communicates, "Here I am. Both the good and the bad. I've got nothing to hide." To deepen the intimacy in your marriage, get naked—emotionally and spiritually.

The man and his wife were both naked and were not ashamed.
GENESIS 2:25

Lord, help us embrace vulnerability in our relationship. Give us the courage to open our hearts and share our deepest fears and desires. Envelop us with Your grace such that honesty and vulnerability deepen our connection.

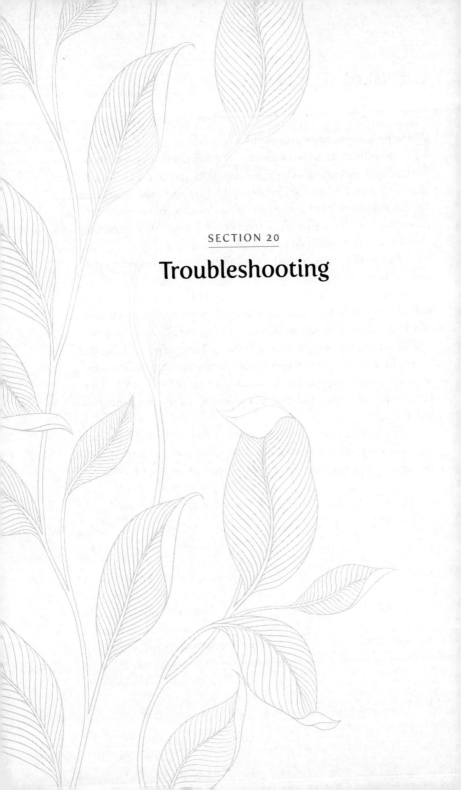

SECTION 20

Troubleshooting

Preventing a Collapse

What do you do when you see a crack developing? Ignore it? Figure out the source of the problem and fix it? Your answer could make a big difference in your marriage.

In 1995, employees at a five-story department store in Seoul, South Korea, noticed cracks developing around one of the support columns. Engineers gave an urgent warning that the building was structurally unsound—yet the store's owner refused to close the building for repairs. Just a few hours later, the entire south wing collapsed, killing more than five hundred people.

Similar catastrophes take place within marriages every day. Couples often notice the cracks in their marriage yet choose to ignore them. The problem seems so small and insignificant. What couples fail to recognize is that the cracks may be the first sign of a larger issue developing within the relationship. Ignore those problems, and the structure of the marriage could weaken over time, causing the whole marriage to crash.

If you want a healthy marriage, look beneath the cracks in your relationship and address the larger problems hiding there. Strengthen your marriage by repairing small problems before they become large ones.

> The way of a fool is right in his own eyes, but a wise man listens to advice.
> PROVERBS 12:15

Lord, I do not want to be foolish and miss the cracks creeping into my marriage. Help me be attentive to the needs of my spouse and listen to wise advice to keep our marriage strong and healthy.

Check Your Warning Lights

A few years ago, my family and I were about to hit the road for a vacation. The night before we were supposed to leave, I double-checked the roadworthiness of our van, and that's when a dashboard warning light came on. I tried to troubleshoot the issue, but there were no obvious problems. The worst part was that I had to tell my family we couldn't leave for vacation until we got the van to a mechanic.

That's usually how we respond with our cars, isn't it? An indicator light goes on, and we try to get the car to the shop as soon as possible. But for some reason, when warning lights go off in our marriage, we just keep driving. We don't ask questions or troubleshoot the issue. We just keep pushing forward and hope everything will work out.

Mechanics help us because they've seen the same engine troubles over and over, and they know how to fix them. It's the same with counselors. They've likely seen your marriage struggles in other couples, and they know how to help.

So don't go on year after year ignoring the signs of deeper problems in your marriage. Reach out for help. Figure out what that indicator light is all about, and resolve the problem.

Where there is no guidance, a people falls, but in an abundance of counselors there is safety.
PROVERBS 11:14

Reveal any indicator lights in our marriage. Point us to people who are rich with Your wisdom, and give us the humility to receive counsel from them.

Unresolved Anger

Author Ted Cunningham explains that anger is a secondary emotion. That means couples sometimes engage in conflict that's triggered by deep wounds, not the particular issue they're fighting over.

Listen to Dave and Linda's story, and I think you'll agree. Dave once came home from work thirty minutes late. It made Linda furious. But Dave couldn't understand why. He was rarely late, and this night, he'd simply gotten hung up at work. Still, Linda spent most of the evening crying angry tears.

It wasn't until later, while in counseling, that they discovered what was underneath. It turns out that when Linda was a kid, her dad often came home late . . . because he was cheating on her mom. Dave's tardiness wasn't really the problem. It simply triggered something deeper within Linda.

It's the same story for other couples whose relationships are drowning in anger. There's usually a deeper issue beneath the surface driving all that negative emotion. Author Dr. Gary Smalley said, "You never bury anger dead. You bury it alive. And sooner or later it'll resurface." So if your marriage suffers from ongoing conflict that never seems to get resolved, take a look underneath to see what may be driving it.

I will restore health to you, and your wounds I will heal, declares the LORD.
JEREMIAH 30:17

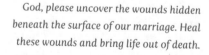

God, please uncover the wounds hidden beneath the surface of our marriage. Heal these wounds and bring life out of death.

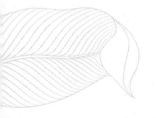

All That You Misperceive

Have you ever noticed that you believe what you *perceive* to be true—not what is *actually* true?

For example, a friend's cat once got spooked by the sound of boots on the hardwood floors and disappeared under the bed for two days. But the cat only *perceived* that she was in danger. The *actual* truth was that no one wanted to harm her.

Misperception is often why friends argue or why conflict erupts at work, on highways, or between neighbors. I even know a guy who feared eating vegetables for years after a childhood friend convinced him that they were bad for him.

Misperception makes us miss out on good things. Have you ever accused your spouse of being angry with you when she wasn't? Or gotten into an argument over something that you later discovered wasn't true? We see our marriage relationships through layers of assumptions and biases that influence how we interpret situations. We don't always see our marriages as clearly as we think we do.

That's why open and honest communication is crucial for any couple hoping to enjoy a happy marriage. Clarity dispels confusion and deepens your connection by turning the *perception* of love and intimacy into reality.

> How can you say to your brother, "Brother, let me take out the speck that is in your eye," when you yourself do not see the log that is in your own eye? You hypocrite, first take the log out of your own eye, and then you will see clearly to take out the speck that is in your brother's eye.
>
> LUKE 6:42

Lord, open the eyes of my mind and heart to see reality more clearly. Show my spouse and me how to connect more deeply through open and honest communication.

Too Many Cooks in the Kitchen

Many couples consider the kitchen to be the heart of the home. But some marriage counselors consider the kitchen the setting for all sorts of potential trouble, from power plays to resentment to passive-aggressive behavior.

The average married couple can point to each other's annoying habits, including ones that take place in the kitchen. It could be the way your husband loads the dishwasher, or perhaps it's your wife's proclivity for buying exotic spices when you think normal salt and pepper would do.

Marriage therapists report that when couples argue over dishwashers or spices, that's not the real problem. Instead, it usually means a spouse is feeling micromanaged—or even worse, disrespected, unappreciated, and criticized.

I learned early in our marriage that my wife, Jean, knew her way around the kitchen. I also discovered I'm better off as her one-man cleaning crew and cheerleader. How about you? I'd encourage you to give each other some space and show heartfelt appreciation for each other's gifts and talents.

And until you make that happen with regularity, consider making dinner reservations.

Whatever you do, in word or deed, do everything in the name of the Lord Jesus, giving thanks to God the Father through him.
COLOSSIANS 3:17

Lord, guard our kitchen from becoming a troublesome spot in our home. Help us make every word and deed honoring to You.

Want To? Or the Will To?

If your marriage is in trouble, it's possible to restore it—but only if you ask the right question.

Most people ask, "Do I want to work on my marriage?" This is the wrong question, because *wanting* something is a function of the emotions . . . and emotions come and go. A couple may leave a counselor's office feeling hopeful and by the next morning feel hopeless again. Couples need something deeper to sustain them through the recovery process.

The *right* question to ask is "Am I *willing* to work on my marriage?" Recovery is an act of the will. Couples must choose to keep moving forward even when their circumstances seem bleak. If you're willing to do what's necessary to restore your relationship, regardless of how you feel at any given time, then God can also work.

Everybody *wants* something better for their relationship, but only those who make a commitment will get it. Moving your troubled marriage out of conflict and into connection takes grit and hard work. You won't get where you hope to be without overcoming a few challenges. You can do it! But it'll take more than a *want* to—it'll take "I *will*."

It is God who works in you, both to will and to work for his good pleasure.
PHILIPPIANS 2:13

God, help my will align with the good You intend for my marriage. My emotions can be fickle at times, and I ask for the determination and commitment to help rebuild my marriage day by day.

The Chicken or the Egg?

Which came first—the chicken or the egg?

That question has been floating around forever, probably because a satisfactory answer has eluded most scientists and philosophers. But their confusion can be your marriage's gain.

Think about why the chicken and the egg is such a conundrum for secular thinkers. All chickens hatch from eggs, but all chicken eggs come from chickens. You can't get one without the other existing first. Yet somehow, they both exist. The question does nothing but spin in an endless circle of reasoning with no satisfying conclusion.

That's how conflict usually goes in marriage, too. The husband accuses the wife of starting an argument, and the wife accuses the husband of starting it. Round and round it goes in an endless loop. That's the problem: A couple will never bring their disagreements to an *end* if they argue in circles about how their disagreements *began*.

Stop the blame game. It deepens your conflict and drives a wedge even further between you and your spouse. Instead, start working together on a solution. Your goal shouldn't be simply to win an argument. Your focus is to resolve your differences while strengthening your relationship along the way. To do that, you must first drop the chicken-and-egg routine.

> Whoever is slow to anger is better than the mighty, and he who rules his spirit than he who takes a city.
>
> PROVERBS 16:32

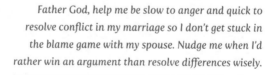

Father God, help me be slow to anger and quick to resolve conflict in my marriage so I don't get stuck in the blame game with my spouse. Nudge me when I'd rather win an argument than resolve differences wisely.

Best Friends (Part 1)

Many married couples start out saying they're best friends. But then kids come along, and careers take off. Life gets crowded with commitments and responsibilities. Before you know it, these former best friends are disconnected and distracted strangers.

There are steps you can take to keep the bonds of friendship strong between you and your spouse. Author Alyson Weasley has developed a list of twelve suggestions to deepen your bond. Here are the first six:

1. Recognize that friendship takes a lot of work—and time.
2. Establish a few hours each week to spend quality time together, and then protect it.
3. Choose to spend time together. Give each other priority in your schedules.
4. Explore your spouse's interests, whether it's baseball, theater, or gardening. Find out what she's passionate about. Then join her, even if it's not your cup of tea.
5. Find things that you and your spouse both enjoy, and engage in them. Plan fun activities together. Try something new.
6. Use conflict to sharpen and purify your friendship. It's okay to disagree. In fact, it's essential for healthy communication.

I'll share the remaining suggestions on Alyson's list tomorrow.

> Above all, keep loving one another earnestly, since love covers a multitude of sins.
> I PETER 4:8

Dear Lord, help us evidence our love for each
other with the time that You have given us.

Best Friends (Part 2)

Married couples can drift apart when children, careers, and other pressures start to dominate their lives.

Yesterday I shared the first six ideas from author Alyson Weasley's list of twelve suggestions couples can use to keep their friendship strong in the midst of real life. Today let's look at the rest of the list:

7. Nourish and care for one another. You'd put a caring arm around a childhood friend; do the same for your spouse.
8. Make accountability and mutual respect a priority. This applies to areas such as sexuality, finances, and relationships.
9. Establish daily habits with your spouse. Pray together. Take a walk. Even a few uninterrupted minutes together can work wonders.
10. Affirm each other every day. Highlight your spouse's strengths. Offer encouragement, a loving touch, and kind words.
11. Be transparent. If you're feeling angry or sad or depressed, don't be afraid to say so. Open your heart and share it.
12. Communicate, communicate, communicate. Relationship experts agree that regular communication between spouses builds a friendship that can weather life's storms.

Building and maintaining a friendship is work, but it's worth the effort, and it will help you and your spouse develop deeper intimacy and avoid potential problems down the road.

Let no corrupting talk come out of your mouths, but only such as is good for building up.
EPHESIANS 4:29

Lord God, let my words and actions continually build up my spouse. Guard our times together, and remind us to communicate honestly and openly even when life's pressures want to pull us apart.

Clearing Life's Hurdles Together

American track star Aries Merritt is an expert on clearing obstacles. As of this writing, he holds the world record for the 110-meter hurdles, clearing ten hurdles in 12.8 seconds. Aries says runners don't usually stumble on open stretches. Victory or defeat is about successfully clearing the obstacles.

It's the same for marriage. Relationships don't stumble when life rolls along smoothly. Problems develop when couples face obstacles, such as stresses with work, parenting, or major life transitions.

My wife, Jean, and I have faced our share of obstacles. We've relocated to new cities, raised two boys, and dealt with issues in extended families. Ironically, one of the biggest marriage challenges was when I became the president of Focus on the Family.

I was taking on the leadership of an organization created to help families worldwide. Would we be expected to have a perfect marriage? Perfect children? We had to think through those questions and recognize that we didn't need to have it all together. Instead, we just needed to be intentional and work together to keep our relationship strong.

Great marriages don't happen by accident. You can't coast on autopilot. Love and sacrifice are daily choices. Obstacles can cause you to stumble. Or you can work together to turn obstacles into opportunities for your marriage to thrive.

I have said these things to you, that in me you may have peace. In the world you will have tribulation. But take heart; I have overcome the world.
JOHN 16:33

Jesus, You have overcome the world, and You long for my marriage to clear the obstacles that block us from loving each other well. Keep my spouse and me grounded as we seek to be a smooth-running team.

Discerning Your Spouse's Needs

Have you ever thought, *Married life would be so much easier if I could read my spouse's mind*?

You can gain insight into what your spouse is thinking by observing his or her behavior. Your spouse may not say what he or she needs from the relationship, but your spouse's behavior toward you will often reveal it.

Ray discovered this when his wife became unusually clingy one night at bedtime. At first, he assumed her behavior was simply a sign of affection toward him. But when he didn't put down his book and return her cuddle right away, she seemed genuinely hurt. That's when Ray realized his wife wasn't snuggling to *give* him affection but to *get* affection from him.

What about your spouse? Does he or she talk a lot? Your spouse is probably trying to draw you into conversation. Does your beloved surprise you with gifts? It could be your spouse's way of saying he or she feels most loved when you gift something special.

Direct communication is usually clearest, but a spouse doesn't always speak with words. Sometimes he or she communicates with actions. If you pay careful attention—and maybe employ a little detective work—you just might discern what your spouse needs from the relationship.

It is my prayer that your love may abound more and more, with knowledge and all discernment.

PHILIPPIANS 1:9

Gracious God, help me pay careful attention to what my spouse really needs each day. I want to be discerning and wise in how I interpret my partner's behavior.

Pay Attention to the Little Things

If you want to know somebody's true character, pay attention to the little things.

A wife joined her husband for a round of golf with a potential client. Over the course of eighteen holes, the men got to know each other and talked business. After the round, the men shook hands on a tentative agreement.

But when the businessman and his wife got into their car, she said, "I don't think you should go into business with that man. He cheats. I saw him kick his ball out of the rough and onto the fairway. Several times."

Her husband said, "We were playing for fun. Every hobby golfer does that. It's called a mulligan."

His wife said, "Yes, but he looked around first to see if anyone was watching. That's called cheating."

As it turns out, the wife was correct. The other guy popped up in the news a few months later for illegal activity. He was a cheater at heart.

Obviously, you shouldn't overreact to a person's every flaw. But small flaws often point to bigger and deeper character problems. And it doesn't hurt to listen carefully to your spouse when he or she points out something that you might have missed!

Whoever walks in integrity walks securely, but he who makes his ways crooked will be found out.

PROVERBS 10:9

God, give me the ability to see past people's flaws, but also give me discernment. Keep me from the same mistakes, and remind me to live with integrity in the small things.

Make Room for a Different Perspective

Imagine you and your spouse are standing on opposite sides of a large sculpture. Neither one of you can see the whole thing. You see the art from one angle, and your spouse views it from another. Later on, if you're willing to listen to each other's unique perspective, you both can get a sense of what the whole sculpture looks like.

But what if you each believe your perspective alone is the right one? More than likely, you'd say the color was green instead of blue or the top was curved rather than straight. You might even end up arguing with each other, trying to prove how wrong the other is.

That scenario is really no different when the object you're looking at is your marriage. It can be hard to step outside your own perspective and see things from your spouse's point of view. And that can make it awfully tough for couples to find enough common ground to resolve disagreements and take their marriage to a deeper level.

So make room for each other's perspective. Husbands and wives each see pieces of the whole story. Only together can they understand the full picture of what their marriage can be.

As in one body we have many members, and the members do not all have the same function, so we, though many, are one body in Christ, and individually members one of another.

ROMANS 12:4-5

God, You are so gracious in how You've designed us. Thank You for not giving me all the answers.

Focus on Your Own Dance Steps

Karen Kain is one of the most respected ballet dancers in the world, having given more than ten thousand performances in her career. Someone asked Karen if age was the dancer's worst enemy. Karen answered, "Sometimes it's age, but sometimes it's the dancer themselves."

Karen's response gets at the heart of dance. Dance is the art of movement. It's all about moving in concert with your partner. Every step forward is at risk of becoming a mistake. Your partner could step on your toe, or you could step on his. The solution is for each dancer to recognize that the only movement she can control is her own. Each dancer has to focus on his *own* steps, not on his partner's.

That's great advice for dancers, and it's great advice for married couples, too. Marriage is the art of movement in its own way. Relationships change over time because couples change over time. Husbands and wives discover the marriage they dream about as they learn to adjust their steps and to move in concert with each other.

If possible, so far as it depends on you, live peaceably with all.
ROMANS 12:18

Father, there's so much in life I can't control—including my spouse! Help me focus, however, on the things that are within my control. Help me surrender myself and my movements to You and let You handle the rest!

Clear the Debris

There's something about mankind that makes us want a clear path. Unless we're trekking through the rugged wilderness—or jumping hurdles at a track meet—we usually want a clear, smooth road from point A to point B.

For centuries, kings and queens have relied on servants to clear their way. Someone always rode ahead of nobility to remove debris and other dangerous roadblocks from their path. The modern equivalent is the King's Guard. The president has the Secret Service. Even we commoners rely on driving apps that alert us to accidents, construction detours, and heavy traffic. Avoiding roadblocks is almost second nature to us. Entire industries have been built around ways to help us get past whatever is in our way.

But that same instinct doesn't seem so obvious to us when it comes to our personal lives. The happiest people don't sit back and hope nothing bad happens. They clear the debris from their path. If something is interfering with their marriage, their children, or their career, they uncover the problems and address them.

Treat yourself like nobility in your career, your marriage, and your family. That is, protect your priorities. Clear the debris to better envision the path to your dreams.

What you have learned and received and heard and seen in me—practice these things, and the God of peace will be with you.
PHILIPPIANS 4:9

Heavenly Father, please help us understand what You want us to learn from the debris in our way. Help us remove the debris so we can better see the path before us and have a clearer view to dream as a couple.

Finding the Middle Ground

Our childhood upbringing is probably the most significant influence on how we behave in our marriage. A person raised in a troubled home likely grew up with parents who constantly fought with each other. When that child becomes an adult, he or she may do everything possible to avoid interacting as his or her parents did . . . such as refusing to engage in conflict even if it means never expressing his or her opinion within the relationship.

But there's also a downside to growing up with a mom and dad who never allowed their conflict to be seen. Kids from these homes often feel their relationship has to be a carbon copy of their parents'. And when that first disagreement pops up in their marriage? They feel like failures and believe their marriage is doomed.

Allowing your expectations to swing to either extreme can damage your relationship. The best solution is to find healthy middle ground. Don't focus on running from the negativity of your past. But don't waste all your energy trying to recreate the good parts either. Every marriage is unique. You and your spouse need to find an identity for your relationship that best fits your personalities.

If anyone is in Christ, he is a new creation. The old has passed away; behold, the new has come.

2 CORINTHIANS 5:17

Jesus, You know how we were raised. Now, as a married couple, we are a new creation. Help us let go of the past, move into the future, and keep our identity with You at the center of it all.

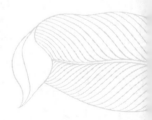

Regular Checkups

If professionals recommend that we schedule regular checkups to maintain healthy bodies, teeth, and even finances, it also makes sense to have at least a yearly checkup for our marriages.

According to recent research, only 19 percent of married couples have taken part in marriage counseling, and only a third of divorced couples ever sought counseling before ending their marriages.

Many couples have practically limped into the offices of pastors and counselors for help after years of ignoring problems. Often, this is viewed as the last resort, the final hope for their marriage, or even the seal of doom that the marriage is beyond saving.

Even the most desperate marriages can be revived with two willing people; however, it is much less painful to address problems as they arise rather than letting them pile up for years.

You might start your marriage checkup by doing something as simple as asking your spouse, "How do you think our marriage is doing?" or "Tell me one thing I can do to be a better partner to you." If the thought of those questions seems like wading into dangerous territory, that may be a sign to meet with a counselor.

Lying lips are an abomination to the LORD, but those who act faithfully are his delight.
PROVERBS 12:22

Jesus, help us be honest with ourselves and honest with each other about the state of our marriage. Only then can we be ready to act faithfully toward making our marriage right in Your sight.

Reach Your Happily Ever After

The 1950 animated Disney classic *Cinderella* ends with her marriage to Prince Charming, followed by these words: *and they lived happily ever after*. That same hope is shared by nearly every woman who stands at a wedding altar and dreams that her husband is also a Prince Charming, ready to sweep her off to a marriage fit for a fairy tale.

Unfortunately, fairy tales don't prepare women for the realities of being married to a fallible human being. Every couple hits a few speed bumps on the journey toward "happily ever after." Week in and week out, there's the monotony of working a job, paying bills, and raising children. Those speed bumps often include financial stressors, communication problems, illnesses, or unexpected life changes. When real life sets in, the dreams you once had for your ideal marriage begin to fade.

Ladies, if you've ever felt disappointed that you didn't marry Prince Charming, remember that he didn't marry a princess either. The good news is that neither one of you needs to be perfect to have a good marriage. You won't reach your happily ever after by demanding fairy-tale-like perfection from each other, but by centering your marriage on God and persevering together through the ups and downs of day-to-day life.

Do not throw away your confidence, which has a great reward.
HEBREWS 10:35

Lord, I don't want to experience disappointment in my marriage just because our relationship isn't the stuff of fairy tales. Help me have confidence in my spouse so that together we can support each other through life's difficulties.

Spring Cleaning

Sooner or later, every home needs a good spring cleaning. But have you ever thought your marriage could use one as well?

After several years of living in the South, author Kim Wier began looking forward to spring cleaning. But it wasn't the *tradition* of spring cleaning that inspired her; it was her allergic reaction to all that pollen in the air! That's when she realized that, like air heavy with allergens, marriages can also be, in her words, "plagued by irritants." To keep things fresh, Kim offers three suggestions:

1. *Declutter*. Agree on at least one thing you can cut out of your schedules to minimize stress in your marriage. Also, eliminate grudges.
2. *Polish*. As Kim says, care for yourselves "like you did when you longed to catch each other's eye." Commit to focused communication as well.
3. *Make room*. Take time for just the two of you—even if it means squeezing in a five-minute walk here and there. If you're traveling, talk by phone or FaceTime.

Every relationship could use a good spring cleaning from time to time. Taking a few moments to sweep away the dust and cobwebs can leave you breathing easier—and your marriage stronger.

The aim of our charge is love that issues from a pure heart and a good conscience and a sincere faith.
1 TIMOTHY 1:5

Lord, let it be the aim of our hearts to be pure, good, and sincere. Help us identify our marital areas that need decluttering, polishing, and making room.

Take Out the Trash

Charlie smelled something terrible when he moved into his new house. He had to dig through a mountain of boxes to discover what it was. For some reason, the movers had packed the garbage from his old house and moved it right along with the furniture into his new home. It took Charlie a couple of weeks to air out the smell.

Not many people would bring garbage from an old house into a new one. But a lot of people bring the garbage from their first marriage into their second. When a marriage does end in divorce, the best way forward is to resolve the issues that caused it. Unresolved anger, conflict, and trust issues will sabotage a new marriage. It doesn't take long for that kind of trash to stink up what you were hoping would be a fresh start.

Unfortunately, leaving emotional garbage behind isn't as easy as dragging a Hefty bag to the curb. But if you're willing to challenge yourself, you can move forward in the best way possible: by leaving your past in the past and getting your new life off to a good start.

Behold, I am doing a new thing; now it springs forth, do you not perceive it? I will make a way in the wilderness and rivers in the desert.
ISAIAH 43:19

Jesus, we invite You to do a new thing in our marriage. We ask that You show us where we have emotional garbage so that we can remove it and move on with our lives.

Is Your Reflection in the Mirror?

One of the most well-known characters in classic literature is Dracula, the ghoulish vampire created by Bram Stoker in 1897 and famously portrayed on film by Bela Lugosi in 1931. Since then, vampires have become synonymous with black capes and fangs. But there's another characteristic often featured in these dark tales: A vampire's reflection is never seen in the mirror.

On the surface, it might not seem as if this obscure quality would have any application to our relationships. But let me ask you: On an emotional level, do you see your reflection in the mirror? Sometimes conflict is difficult to resolve because one spouse refuses to see himself or herself as part of the problem. She doesn't recognize her own bad attitude; he's unaware when he speaks harshly to others. Even when someone points it out, the spouse denies that it's true.

What about you? Is it hard for you to consider the part you play in problems facing your relationship? If so, you may have trouble seeing a true reflection of yourself. Let me encourage you to work through this issue with a counselor, pastor, or trusted friend. Marriage problems are created by both partners, but so are the solutions.

How can you say to your brother, "Let me take the speck out of your eye," when there is the log in your own eye? You hypocrite, first take the log out of your own eye, and then you will see clearly to take the speck out of your brother's eye.
MATTHEW 7:4-5

Father, the temptation to overlook our own faults and focus on the faults of others is a common problem. Reveal to me the things I've refused to see about my part in our struggles, and give me the compassion and grace to make different choices.

What Your Spouse
Really Needs

Just Listen

On any given weekend, you'll find a lot of guys in their favorite hangout: their garage. Some even have a workshop—or at least a workbench. Wherever they are, they're probably surrounded by an impressive assortment of power equipment and tools.

But even if a husband doesn't own so much as a socket wrench, he'll often try to fix other things—like his wife. And that's usually when the trouble starts. She'll start to share her feelings, and her husband will offer the perfect solution before she's stopped talking. That's when she'll cross her arms and look right through him . . . and he'll realize he's made a big mistake.

This issue gets to the core of who we really are as men and women. Guys often try to take the mystery out of things, especially relationships. They want to solve what's wrong. Women want to be heard and connected with, not "solved."

So, guys, remember this the next time your wife opens up: She's probably not asking you to crack a code or solve her problem. She just wants you to listen and offer your love, understanding, and support.

If I speak in the tongues of men and of angels, but have not love,
I am a noisy gong or a clanging cymbal.
I CORINTHIANS 13:1

Lord, I am desperate for Your wisdom. Teach me
how to better love and listen to my wife.

Do Her Eyes Sparkle?

The book of 1 Peter encourages men to cherish their wives as they would a priceless treasure. The ancient Greek text uses rich and meaningful language for wives that evokes images of delicate strength. The same language could be used to describe valuable artwork or elegant pottery. Is *that* the image you have of your wife?

In the early days of marriage, most guys do a good job of cherishing. They show their wives affection and engage in meaningful conversation. But somewhere along the way, they give up the pursuit. Their primary focus shifts to work, hobbies, or friends, and the sparkle in their wives' eyes fades.

The key to making your wife's heart come alive is not treating your relationship like a checklist. Marriages thrive on desire more than duty. Romance her. Take her to dinner. Sit on the couch and spend a few minutes talking with her and looking her in the eyes. Deeper intimacy is a skill that every husband can learn.

Are your wife's eyes alive and vibrant? The more you cherish your wife, the more she'll come to life. You'll see it in her eyes . . . because she'll see it in yours.

> Husbands, live with your wives in an understanding way, showing honor to the woman as the weaker vessel, since they are heirs with you of the grace of life, so that your prayers may not be hindered.
>
> 1 PETER 3:7

God, You designed my wife with such profound beauty and delicate strength. Rekindle the romance in our marriage, and amaze me with new aspects of her design every day.

Respect Your Husband

The old adage proclaims that the way to a husband's heart is through his stomach. But even more than a good meal, a man is hungry for his wife's respect.

Respect—properly understood—can transform a good marriage into a great one. Respect is the relational mechanism that creates the love wives are looking for in their marriages.

For guys, respect is like air—they *need* it. It's what inspires soldiers to serve and die for each other. It's what motivates athletes to battle alongside one another in a big game. It's what enables husbands to fight for their marriages and to love their wives more deeply.

Showing your husband respect can be as simple as making eye contact with him and listening to him. Publicly affirm him on social media or when you're together with friends. Compliment him to his face. Tell him exactly what you love about him.

Healthy, proper respect for a husband is never degrading to a wife. It'll elevate you in your husband's eyes and connect the two of you at a heart level in deeper, more intimate, and more meaningful ways. Respect is what your husband is hungry for, and it's an important key to unlocking his heart to you.

> Wives, be subject to your own husbands, so that even if some
> do not obey the word, they may be won without a word by the
> conduct of their wives, when they see your respectful and pure
> conduct.
>
> I PETER 3:1-2

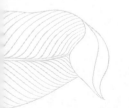

*Lord, may I show respect to my husband in the everyday
little things such as listening and complimenting.
Keep us active in the battle to safeguard our marriage
with deeper love and meaningful intimacy.*

That's What Real Men Are Made Of

M any men believe the ultimate sign of manhood is physical ability or brute strength. It's how much weight you can bench press or how well you use your fists. But there's a deeper strength that defines true masculinity.

Most guys are drawn to the bravado typically associated with manhood. Even guys who don't think of themselves as tough would lay down their lives if their families were threatened. But as noble and heroic as that idea may be, it's a sacrifice few of us will ever make.

What we really need from men is the inner strength to lay down their lives every single day. It's the little sacrifices that enrich family life. Like when a dad plays catch in the front yard even though he feels too tired after a long day at work. Or when he talks his daughter through her boy crushes even though he'd rather she not grow up at all. Sometimes it's as simple as a husband running an errand for his wife.

That's real masculinity. Inner strength is what a man needs to serve his wife and kids through daily personal sacrifices. It's how he'll become their hero, not just once, but day after day after day.

I am the good shepherd. The good shepherd lays down his life for the sheep.
JOHN 10:11

Jesus, thank You that You laid down Your life for us. Your inner strength and ultimate sacrifice model the importance of serving and loving others even in the little things.

Three Roles of a Spouse

Successful couples strive every day to make their marriage better. They accomplish that by excelling in three key areas of their relationship: They treat their spouse as a friend, a partner, and a lover.

As friends, these spouses play and laugh together. Among the happiest and healthiest couples are those who laugh together. That's because laughter is only partially about humor. It's mostly about connecting with another person.

As partners, these spouses communicate well and have healthy conflict. They respect each other like teammates. Their marriage is connected and intimate because they use their differences *in service of* their relationship.

As lovers, these spouses have a relationship that sizzles. The journey of two people becoming one only happens when those individuals get beneath the surface and connect at a heart level. Romance isn't just good for a marriage; it's crucial.

Successful marriages thrive not because of good fortune or luck, but because each partner sacrifices his or her own interests for the sake of the other. Both spouses invest daily in their relationship and take joy in each other's happiness.

Successful couples endeavor to be the best friends, partners, and lovers that they can be.

Walk in love, as Christ loved us and gave himself up for us,
a fragrant offering and sacrifice to God.
EPHESIANS 5:2

I am forever grateful, Lord, for my spouse. Draw
us closer as we pursue our commitment to being
each other's friend, partner, and lover.

Give It to Him Straight

My wife, Jean, and I have two boys, Trent and Troy. For Christmas the year after Trent was born, Jean put his hospital baby cap in a box, wrapped it up, and placed it under the tree for me.

I took the cap out of the box and asked, "Is this for Trent?"

Jean looked back at me like *Are you really that dense?*

"Did you miswrap this? What does this mean?"

Jean shook her head at me, and then she said, "Dear, I'm pregnant."

Looking back, I suppose her message to me should have been clear. But ladies, allow me to offer you a bit of advice about your husband: Don't ask him to read your mind. Things like what my wife did with the baby cap at Christmas are good fun, but if you want your husband to "get it" about romance, sex, money—anything, really—be *clear*. Little clues around the house might not register for him. Sorry. Be straight with him, and tell him exactly what you need.

You're probably thinking, *That doesn't sound very romantic.* Well, give it a try. You may change your mind when you see how your husband appreciates being in the know—instead of in the dark!

A word fitly spoken is like apples of gold in a setting of silver.
PROVERBS 25:11

*Father, communication between us can be
challenging at times, and yet it doesn't have to be
that way. Give my spouse and me wisdom and grace
with each other as we learn how to communicate
in ways that honor each other and You.*

Listen to Her Heart

Things are rarely black and white in a marriage. Even when a guy thinks he knows exactly what to do, he can't be so sure. Believe it or not, that can become a strength.

Before my lovely wife, Jean, went into labor with our oldest son, Trent, she told me she wanted to give birth naturally. She said, "I don't want any drugs when I go into labor. Even if I'm screaming for medication, do not give it to me."

A few weeks later, she went into labor, and it was a lot harder than she'd anticipated. She struggled with Trent for twenty-seven hours. Somewhere in the middle of all that, she looked right at me and said, "Get the doctor. I want the epidural. Now!"

I tried to talk her out of it. I said, "But honey, you told me not to let you do that." What can I say? I was a new husband. I had a lot to learn. Finding better ways to serve your wife is part of what will make you a good husband. Listen to your wife's words *and* her heart.

A man shall leave his father and mother and hold fast to his wife, and the two shall become one flesh.
EPHESIANS 5:31

God, I ask that You remind me of the best path forward in the moment. I yearn to live in a place where I am constantly reminded that I should hold fast to my wife and consistently make decisions in her best interest.

Are You Paying Attention?

Heartfelt condolences to Dorothy Naylor, whose day trip was spoiled when her husband, Oliver, left her at a service station . . . and drove seventeen miles before noticing his wife was not in the car.

The couple stopped to change a tire. Mr. Naylor drove off and didn't notice his wife's absence until he asked her a question. When she didn't answer, he turned to discover that he had left her behind.

You may have never forgotten your spouse at a service station, but do you give your husband or wife your full attention? Do you notice when he or she has had a stressful day or needs some extra encouragement? Do you take the time to really listen when he or she is talking?

In today's busy world, it's easy to slip into doing the work of marriage by multitasking. You know what I mean—you try to answer a few emails while talking to your husband on the phone or watch the news while listening to your wife share about a concern.

Take at least ten minutes every day to focus completely on each other with no other distractions.

Let your eyes look directly forward, and your gaze be straight before you.

PROVERBS 4:25

In the midst of a busy world, it's so important to pay attention to my spouse. God, please help me devote the time that is needed to properly focus on my marriage.

Showcase Your Wife

I doubt ballet will ever rank up there with football, baseball, or golf as must-see viewing for guys. But ballet can teach us how we ought to treat our wives in a way even we weekend warriors can understand.

Famous ballet choreographer George Balanchine once said, "Ballet is a woman." What he meant is that the beauty of the dance is primarily captured by a woman's grace, her strength, and her expression of beauty through the language of movement.

The male ballet dancer's primary role is to showcase his female partner. When he lifts her and twirls her, she should glow in the spotlight and wow the audience. Then, while the audience celebrates and adores her with a thunderous standing ovation, the male dancer steps back into the shadows.

What if husbands adopted that same attitude toward their wives? What if men asked themselves, *How can I showcase my wife and honor her?*

I've never seen the ballet, but I understand what Balanchine meant when he said, "My job is to make the beautiful more beautiful."

I think that's the job of every husband as well.

An excellent wife is the crown of her husband, but she who brings shame is like rottenness in his bones.
PROVERBS 12:4

Lord, thank You for my excellent, beautiful wife.
Help me treat her like a crown jewel, lifting her
above me and my desires and showcasing her for
the wonderful and valuable bride that she is.

What's Important to Your Spouse?

I once took my family to Glacier National Park in Montana for a summer vacation. We all hiked toward a place called Hidden Lake, but we were stopped several hundred yards away. From where we were, we could see bears splashing through the water, hunting for fish. My boys and I could see them. My wife, Jean, is nearsighted, and we didn't have our binoculars.

That was a huge disappointment for Jean. She loves animals. In fact, she wanted to go back the next day. The problem was, we had already scheduled a fishing trip. But I knew it was important to her, so I encouraged her to go back on her own to observe from a safe distance.

The next morning, Jean hiked back to the lake—this time with binoculars—and spent the whole day watching the bears. When she got back later that night, she was exhausted, but she said it was one of the best days of her life.

Encourage your spouse to get out there and do something that's important to him or her. It's a simple way to communicate how valuable your spouse is to you.

A new commandment I give to you, that you love one another:
just as I have loved you, you also are to love one another.
JOHN 13:34

Lord, help me always remember to show my love in a way that makes my spouse feel encouraged and important.

Intentional Acts of Kindness

Guys, you've heard the phrase *random acts of kindness*, right? Well, for a strong marriage, forget the word *random* and think *intentional*.

I'm not against spontaneity. But if your marriage is like most marriages, day-to-day life will hijack your schedule. You'll wake up one morning hoping to do something special for your wife that day. Then you'll remember that project at work. Plus the kids need a ride to soccer practice. And the lawn needs to be mowed. At day's end, you'll fall into bed exhausted, and your wife will have been shoved once again to tomorrow's schedule.

With so many plates to keep spinning, it's easy to lose sight of your marriage. That's where *intentional* acts of kindness become important. No need for elaborate plans—little things make a big difference. Like setting the timer on the coffee maker so your wife has hot coffee waiting for her in the morning. Or taking care of that sink full of dishes. Or placing a love note where she'll find it. Or texting her to say you're thinking of her.

Successful marriages don't happen by accident. They're built, in part, by making intentional acts of kindness a part of your daily routine.

Do not neglect to show hospitality to strangers, for thereby some have entertained angels unawares.
HEBREWS 13:2

Father, if it pleases You when I show kindness to strangers, how much more is Your heart delighted when I show kindness and hospitality to the bride You have given me to cherish! Help me find acts today that, though small, will communicate the big message of my love for my wife.

Make Your Wife Feel Special

To Western sensibilities, marriage traditions in other cultures seem strange—almost offensive. Not only are many relationships arranged, but young women can also be bartered for cattle.

Out of that tradition comes the story of one South Pacific man nicknamed Johnny Lingo, whose heart was set on a young woman named Sarita. None of the villagers considered Sarita to be worth more than four cows. But Johnny surprised everyone when he offered eight, an unprecedented number.

Sometime later, the villagers stood amazed at the sparkle that had developed in Sarita's eyes in the months since her marriage. Johnny said, "Sarita believed she was worth nothing. Now she knows she is worth more than any other woman on the islands."

Men, does your wife carry that sparkle in her eye because she knows how valuable she is to you? If not, get to work. Treat her as the most precious person in your life, and make it your mission every day to make her heart come alive.

> There is no fear in love, but perfect love casts out fear. For fear has to do with punishment, and whoever fears has not been perfected in love.
> I JOHN 4:18

Father, the power of Your love is transformative. Because You love us, fear is banished, identity is established, and our hearts are transformed. Help me love my spouse in a transformative way. I can't do it on my own—but by letting You love my spouse through me, I can make a difference.

SECTION 22

Creating Life Balance

Marriage Is a Team Sport

The secret to winning in a team sport isn't a secret at all: Teammates share a common goal, and they work together to achieve it.

That commitment to unity is what makes a marriage work too. But working together as a team isn't always easy. Just ask experienced counselors and marriage partners Dr. Joshua and Christi Straub. Even *they* occasionally overlook the importance of teamwork.

Like the day Joshua came home and told Christi about his exciting work projects. But Christi began to cry. "Why don't you ever ask about *me*?" she said. Right then, Joshua knew he had been too distracted by his own pursuits. He wasn't working as part of a team, and their marriage suffered.

Fortunately, Joshua and Christi tried the same practical ideas that helped so many of their clients reconnect. Like this one: Every day, Joshua and Christi set aside ten to fifteen minutes to focus on each other. Not work. Not the kids. Not all the house projects.

That simple idea won't change your marriage overnight, but if you'll devote just ten minutes a day to your marriage, you can get your relationship back on track.

> Two are better than one, because they have a good reward for their toil.
> ECCLESIASTES 4:9

Lord, help me always be mindful of my teammate in marriage. I know my spouse needs and deserves my full attention.

Out of Balance

Life can get out of balance. When we push harder and faster, we often miss out on the very things that make life worth living.

A few years back, a pastor conducted a businessman's funeral. The man had built a large, successful company and had amassed cars, houses, and exotic vacation destinations.

But all that work came at a price. The man had put in long, hard hours—sometimes seven days a week. His stress levels soared, his health suffered, and he died at a young age.

Fast-forward a couple of years, and that same pastor performed the wedding of the businessman's widow, who was restarting her life with a new husband.

Do you see the irony? The first husband had no balance, and it cut his life short. The new husband got to enjoy everything the first one had worked to achieve.

Hard work is valuable, but if you're always determined to push harder and faster, you're out of balance. The things we earn are meaningless unless we share them with our loved ones. So make room for the important people in your life. You may own less, but you'll enjoy life far more.

I considered all that my hands had done and the toil I had expended in doing it, and behold, all was vanity and a striving after wind, and there was nothing to be gained under the sun.

ECCLESIASTES 2:11

Loving God, thank You that You want us to live balanced lives. Show us how to make room for what really matters as we juggle everyday life together.

Firmly Flexible

My wife, Jean, had a four-year plan for pursuing marriage. She wanted to date for two years, be engaged for two more, and then experience a fairy-tale wedding years in the making.

Then *I* came along. I proposed to Jean after we'd been dating only four months. I'd been offered a job that would require me to travel for a year, and I wanted Jean with me. So I asked her, "How would you like to get married in six weeks?"

My wife could have chosen to make her *plans* her top priority. Instead, she kept her approach to life flexible by taking advantage of good opportunities when they unexpectedly came along. We've been married now for more than thirty years, and we have faced many surprising, joyful moments throughout our journey together.

The willingness to be flexible with life but firmly committed to each other is one of the secrets to a happy marriage. Set goals. Make plans. Work hard every day. And when life is beyond your control—whether for good or bad—dig in and support each other.

The heart of man plans his way, but the LORD establishes his steps.
PROVERBS 16:9

Father, Your plans are for my good. You established
my steps to join up with my spouse's steps.
May we stay flexible yet firmly committed
to each other, no matter what we face.

Saying No to Saying Yes

You're booked solid with work, family, and obligations to your church and community. So how do you fit margin—unscheduled time in your day—into your busy life?

For starters, think of your schedule as a buffet line of activities. Each of the options may look appetizing, but you can only fit so much on your plate. Once your schedule is full, you can't add anything else to it—including margin—without first removing something else. If you overpack your schedule, your plate will get overloaded, and things will slide off—your children, your marriage, even your physical and spiritual well-being.

Moments of rest are as crucial to a healthy life as times of activity. You need more than just a blank spot on your calendar. You need room to clear your mind and decompress. Not just once a year on vacation, but monthly, weekly, even daily.

No one hands you margin. You have to take it. Which means telling people no—with wisdom and grace. You always want to handle opportunities and other people well. But it's okay to have boundaries that say, "Enough is enough."

With good margins, you can say no to things that don't matter . . . and yes to things that do.

Come to me, all who labor and are heavy laden, and I will give you rest.
MATTHEW 11:28

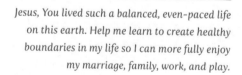

Jesus, You lived such a balanced, even-paced life on this earth. Help me learn to create healthy boundaries in my life so I can more fully enjoy my marriage, family, work, and play.

More, More, More

What does success look like to you? That's not always an easy question to answer. Many people are financially rich yet live in relational poverty.

Author Chuck Bentley tells about a time early in his marriage that taught him how relationally broke a person could be. It happened one night when he took his wife out for dinner. The evening was pleasant . . . until one of Chuck's clients walked into the restaurant. Chuck excused himself from the table and chatted with his client for nearly fifteen minutes. Just as Chuck was saying how much he hoped that they could finish a deal soon, he glanced at his wife. She was sitting alone, crying. That evening wasn't just any dinner. It was their wedding anniversary.

Making money is important to a good life, but so is a strong marriage. Like Chuck, many guys believe that money can solve any problem. The more successful they become, the happier their wives will be. But sooner or later, every guy learns that's not true.

When working harder and earning more money isn't making your marriage as happy as you'd hoped, you can chart a new course by redefining *prosperity*. A wealthy life isn't just about having a lot of money in the bank. It's about the riches of a thriving marriage as well.

> [Jesus] said to them, "Take care, and be on your guard against all covetousness, for one's life does not consist in the abundance of his possessions."
>
> LUKE 12:15

Dear God, please help us always steer clear of covetousness. An abundance of possessions will not create an abundance of closeness in marriage. Help us give our time where we will see the greatest return: to each other.

Are You Too Connected?

Today's technology allows spouses to be easily available to each other—maybe too much.

Mark and Sara's marriage was in trouble, but it took a while to pinpoint exactly where things were breaking down. There was no substance abuse or financial problems, and neither one was having an affair. So what was the problem? Technology. Texting, email, and smartphones had given them too much access to each other.

The idea of spouses being *too available* to each other probably sounds strange to some, but it's a real problem in more and more relationships. It's not just convenient to communicate all the time—it's almost *expected*.

But that mindset can distort a relationship's boundaries. Whether he was in an important meeting or just hanging out with friends, Mark felt obligated to answer Sara's messages, no matter how trivial. If he didn't, Sara felt unloved and believed Mark cared about others more than her. And with no sense of personal space, Mark felt smothered.

Relationships are at their healthiest when there's a good balance between togetherness and separateness. True intimacy allows couples to feel connected even when a husband and wife are in different places, enjoying individual space.

A just balance and scales are the LORD's; all the weights in the bag are his work.
PROVERBS 16:11

Lord, help our marriage have good balance in honoring each other's individual space. Help us use technology appropriately so that it is a positive force, not a negative factor, in our marriage.

A Cure for the Yawns

I've often said that every marriage has a case of the yawns now and then. I also believe that boredom, left unchecked, can easily take over a relationship, which can lead to trouble. This includes things like living separate lives and potentially looking outside the marriage for relational enjoyment.

A cure for the yawns? Purposefully engage one another. Sounds simple, right? The key is to find out what makes your spouse tick. There is no shame in rediscovering and rekindling the things that make each spouse special. Without doing this, a husband and wife can end up neglecting each other. This puts the marital bond of love and peace at high risk.

It doesn't have to be that way—if you'll be deliberate about your marriage.

Here's an idea: Take some time to write down a few simple things you can enjoy together, away from any distractions. Make room for those items on the calendar. Make them a priority. Be persistent. You'll be glad you did.

> [Bear] with one another in love, eager to maintain the unity of the Spirit in the bond of peace.
> EPHESIANS 4:2-3

Lord, please help me be deliberate about my marriage. Guide us to maintain the bonds of peace and love by purposely engaging each other.

Never Stop Dating

When you were dating, the role of romance seemed clear. It was intentional and purposeful, moving the relationship from "I'm interested" to "Let's get married." But after the wedding, romance often becomes secondary. Instead of seeing your relationship as special, it becomes commonplace.

Over time, couples can fall into routines—or more specifically, *ruts.* They get busy and distracted, and they take each other for granted. Their priorities begin to shift until romantic gestures fade away and they stop engaging in shared activities that once brought them joy. Left unchecked, a couple's intimacy can reach a point where the marriage feels more like a business arrangement than a passionate and life-giving romance.

To help nurture your relationship back to life, make time for each other. Be creative. Carve out a few hours to cook a meal together, eat your dinner by candlelight, and share meaningful conversation. Hearken back to your dating years and infuse your relationship with renewed energy and thoughtfulness.

Lift your marriage above the mundane by treating each other as a unique gift from God with whom you get to share life. That's marital wisdom!

Look carefully then how you walk, not as unwise but as wise, making the best use of the time, because the days are evil.
EPHESIANS 5:15-16

Jesus, help me remember all the things that make my spouse so special. Help me focus on those traits, keep the dating mindset alive, and apply marital wisdom so our marriage remains exclusive and special.

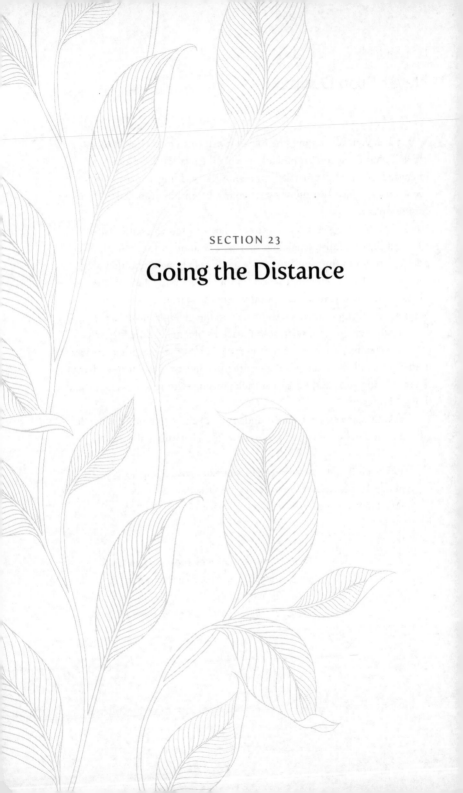

Going the Distance

Marry for Keeps

B efore his death at age eighty-eight, Glynn "Scotty" Wolfe held the Guinness World Record for the most marriages—twenty-nine to be exact.

Over the years, he was referred to jokingly as a "mass marrier" and a "spouse-iopath." After marrying Helen, his first wife, around 1930, he said, "I realized . . . being married was the greatest thing in the world."

Yet months later he divorced Helen and married Marjorie. Then came Margie and later her friend Mildred. Several of his marriages lasted just a few months. His final marriage to Linda Essex was reportedly a publicity stunt, earning Linda the female world record for the most marriages at twenty-three.

In the end, Wolfe, who claimed nineteen children and forty grand-children, died penniless and alone in a nursing home. Nobody claimed his body. None of his twenty-nine ex-wives attended his funeral.

As Wolfe prepared for his twenty-sixth marriage, he reportedly declared, "I marry 'em for keeps."

Most people don't go into marriage anticipating it will fail. Like Wolfe, we marry "for keeps." But good intentions aren't enough. Successful relationships aren't built only on the good times, but by sticking together when the going gets tough.

[Christ] is before all things, and in him all things hold together.
COLOSSIANS 1:17

Father God, You hold all things together, including marriage. Help me always regard marriage as a sacred commitment to You and to my spouse, not some fickle relationship roulette.

The Final Frontier

What is it about human nature? Our ability to appreciate the majestic is only rivaled by one thing: our ability to grow bored with it.

In 1961, President John F. Kennedy challenged the United States to put a man on the moon. Throughout that decade, the American public had an insatiable appetite for space flight. The euphoria culminated in 1969 when the Apollo 11 crew landed on the moon, an event witnessed by an estimated half billion people.

But amazingly, less than a year later, public interest in moon landings had all but evaporated. A feat as incredible as humans walking on the surface of the moon had become little more than a footnote on the nightly news.

It's human nature to lose interest in things that ought to inspire us. Like marriage. When a man and a woman wed, it seems impossible that their passion could ever fade. Yet fast-forward, and for many couples, their life together has deteriorated toward the mundane.

It's natural, but couples must fight this tendency. Make time in your day to connect with each other. Get a babysitter and do something special. Be proactive about reviving the fire that drew you to your spouse in the first place.

> Love one another with brotherly affection. Outdo one another in showing honor.
> ROMANS 12:10

Lord, rekindle my interest and passion in connecting deeper with my spouse. Thank You for modeling how to love so I can be intentional when life is mundane.

More Fun Than Marriage Counseling

Why does love often fade over the years of a marriage? One reason is that daily pressures slowly push laughter and fun to the wayside. Worse yet, a vital piece of the couple's marriage usually disappears with the fun.

According to an old proverb, "You can learn more about a man in an hour of play than in a year of conversation." Fun and laughter can reveal things about a person that you won't notice in routine situations. You'll see more deeply into your spouse and learn what opens him or her up to life's joys and happiness.

But you have to make room for these beautiful times of discovery. Jean and I usually have fun on dates, but we've had amazing times together camping. We've seen wildlife and enjoyed the wilderness beauty. We've hiked, gotten caught in the rain, and laughed at being covered with mud.

If you need to get your marriage out of a rut, find something fun to do *together*. That could be enjoying a fancy restaurant dinner, taking a painting class, or camping under the stars. Smiles and laughter can do your marriage a world of good.

Be glad in the LORD, and rejoice, O righteous, and shout for joy, all you upright in heart!
PSALM 32:11

Laughter is such good medicine, Lord. May our marriage overflow with fun, laughter, and love as we reflect Your joy to our often-grumpy world.

What's Your "Affection Span"?

I'm sure you know what it's like to be around people with short attention spans. They can only focus on something for a little while before a distraction swoops in and leads them off to the next thing. With their interests so scattered, it can be hard to know what's really important to them.

A lot of husbands and wives suffer from a similar problem. Their "affection spans" are too short. They allow too many distractions that keep them from connecting with their spouse. It could be a husband cutting short a phone conversation with his wife when a buddy calls. Or maybe dinner conversation is repeatedly interrupted by a wife checking her social media from her smartphone.

Whatever the case, husbands and wives need to learn to slow life down and give their full attention and affection to each other, without distraction. Relationships, by definition, require two people to *relate* to each other. That takes time and commitment. There's no way to develop a meaningful connection in a hurry.

So talk with your partner about how the two of you can make your "affection spans" longer. It'll improve your marriage by helping both of you feel like you really matter to each other.

Catch the foxes for us, the little foxes that spoil the vineyards,
for our vineyards are in blossom.
SONG OF SOLOMON 2:15

Help me focus on my marriage and weed out the distractions. Build our affection for each other.

An Epic Love

In the blockbuster movie *Titanic*, audiences were infatuated with Jack and Rose. It was an epic romance that could only exist in the movies, right? Well . . . not so fast.

Isidor and Ida Straus were aboard the *Titanic* when it sank in the Atlantic Ocean on April 15, 1912. As that ill-fated journey unfolded, the couple knew that after forty years of marriage, they were about to spend their last moments together. "Women and children first" meant Ida would have to leave behind her beloved husband. But she refused, saying, "As we have lived, so we will die—together." Numerous accounts of that night indicate the couple then settled into deck chairs and held hands, waiting for the inevitable.

The phrase *till death do us part* lies at the heart of traditional marriage vows. Unfortunately, its meaning has become more of a romantic novelty than a sacred commitment. That's why few couples experience in real life the marriage they've so often dreamed about. The amazing love illustrated in the lives of Isidor and Ida Straus doesn't magically arise in a moment of crisis. It's the result of a husband and wife living out their love each and every day.

A wife is bound to her husband as long as he lives.
I CORINTHIANS 7:39

God, romances written by Hollywood are heartwarming at times, but I desire for my marriage to model authentic, lifelong commitment. Keep my spouse and me flourishing in our love each new day You give us together.

Drive-Through Marriage or Lifelong Commitment?

A bizarre Hollywood tale involves a wannabe actress, her writer boyfriend, and a trip to Las Vegas. The duo hailed a cab and, on a whim, asked the driver to stop at a drive-through wedding chapel. Without even leaving the car, they had a mock ceremony, leaned out the window for pictures, and were back on the road in less than ten minutes. It was all in good fun.

At least, it was supposed to be.

Fast-forward two decades, and that dating couple had since called it quits. But one lawyer discovered paperwork buried in a file drawer that indicated the now-successful actress and writer had gotten married for real that night! They'd been legally married for almost twenty years . . . and neither one of them knew it.

I've known a few couples who seemed to have married in a drive-through chapel. They rushed into the relationship and married for the wrong reasons. Or they invested more time and money in the wedding ceremony than they ever will in the marriage.

Weddings can be big or small. They can be elaborate or simple. But happy, successful marriages all require the same thing: a husband and wife who understand that a lifelong relationship demands a lifelong commitment.

Let marriage be held in honor among all.
HEBREWS 13:4

God, You take marriage vows seriously. Thank You that our desire for a happy, successful marriage for a lifetime starts with our lifelong commitment. Keep us intentional about honoring our vows as we are directed by Your counsel.

The Long Haul

Author Karen O'Connor has identified four suggestions for staying happily married—for life.

First, be available. It can take a lifetime to get to know another person. If you're not available, it won't happen. Set aside a regular date night to talk and reconnect with your spouse. Don't let the demands of life rob you of this precious time with your mate.

Next, be attentive. Look your spouse in the eye. For heaven's sake, put away your smartphone and turn off the TV and computer. Really *listen* to what your spouse is saying.

Also, be aware. Pay attention to those nonverbal cues your spouse might give when something is bothering him or her. Learn to understand the things that your spouse enjoys, the things that cause stress, and so on.

Finally, be appreciative. Gratitude is not optional. If you take your spouse for granted, you're inviting trouble. The more you express genuine appreciation for your mate, the more you'll both avoid resentment, judgment, and other negative emotions that can derail a marriage.

Be available, be attentive, be aware, and be appreciative. That's a good recipe for a marriage that will stand the test of time!

Whoever conceals his transgressions will not prosper, but he who confesses and forsakes them will obtain mercy.
PROVERBS 28:13

God, I invite You into the time I spend with my spouse. Give me awareness and gratitude for things that I don't normally see on my own.

Two Ingredients
of Successful Marriages

Years ago, Dr. Lilian Wahome and I were exploring ways my organization, Focus on the Family, could come alongside families in Africa. I wondered if the needs of American couples differed from those of couples elsewhere in the world.

So I asked Dr. Wahome, "Do you think Focus on the Family's understanding about what makes marriage work will be relevant in Africa?" She said that couples around the world all need essentially the same things from their marriages.

Dr. Wahome's comments to me almost twenty-five years ago were confirmed in a recent University of Washington study. Researchers there concluded that nearly all successful marriages exhibit two essential ingredients: *love* and *respect*. When those are present, a marriage can thrive, even if things like money and jobs are in short supply.

Most wives want to feel deeply loved by their husbands. As one author put it, a wife "needs love just as she needs air to breathe." And husbands have an equally important need from their wives: respect.

Despite differences in culture, language, and socioeconomic status, all marriages are constructed very similarly. From around the world to *your* home, the two ingredients for your marriage to thrive are love and respect.

Beloved, let us love one another, for love is from God, and whoever loves has been born of God and knows God.

I JOHN 4:7

God, stir up love and respect in me and my
spouse. Remind us of the importance of
honoring each other in these ways.

Strike *Divorce* from Your Vocabulary

Have you ever noticed the power of the words we speak? They can build up and heal our relationships, or they can tear them down and destroy them. Careless words are like runaway horses. Once they're out in the open, they'll lead you down trails you never intended to travel. That's why it's important to put up strong fences early on in your relationship that'll guide you in what you should and shouldn't say to each other.

One of the most effective boundaries for protecting a relationship is removing talk of divorce from your conversations at all costs. It's not wise for spouses to threaten an end to their marriage as a tactic for getting their way. Remember, if you allow yourself, in the heat of an argument, to raise the possibility of divorce, it suddenly becomes a real option. Instead, make up your minds in advance that, come what may, divorce is off-limits. It'll motivate you to find other ways to settle your differences.

So the next time trouble comes to your relationship, take *divorce* out of your vocabulary and get to work finding other options to resolve the issues you face.

> There is one whose rash words are like sword thrusts, but the tongue of the wise brings healing.
>
> PROVERBS 12:18

God, You gave us power in our words. Give me strength to use mine to build up my spouse and never to harm.

Marry the Wrong Person? (Part I)

It's common for spouses to fear they've married the wrong person. The problem is that, at any given moment, we've all married the wrong person.

Not long into her marriage, Denise had a terrible feeling that she and her husband weren't right for each other. As with a lot of people, Denise believed marrying the "right" person meant a mostly effortless relationship. But hers felt like a mismatch. They had different interests, and they didn't see eye to eye on almost anything. That nagging feeling of incompatibility frequently led to conflict.

But the truth is that every couple seems compatible on their wedding day. And spouses find out in the years that follow all the ways they don't match up. It's the natural process of growing together with another person. At some point, we all can feel that we've married the wrong person.

What makes a marriage right isn't mysterious twists of fate that bring two perfectly matched people together. A happy marriage takes two people being giving and thoughtful to each other. It means kindness, consideration, and sacrifice. It's two people willing to *be* the right person instead of counting on the luck of the draw in *finding* the right person.

> The fruit of the Spirit is love, joy, peace, patience, kindness, goodness, faithfulness, gentleness, self-control; against such things there is no law.
> GALATIANS 5:22-23

Holy Spirit, shower my marriage with Your abundant fruit of love, joy, peace, patience, kindness, goodness, faithfulness, gentleness, and self-control. Help me daily express these character qualities to my spouse so that we draw even closer to You and each other.

Marry the Wrong Person? (Part 2)

Let's talk about how to *be* the right person in your marriage.

The first step is to learn to be content with yourself. If you've been married long, you probably already know that your spouse can't make you happy all the time. That's because marriage usually amplifies who you were when you were single. If you were unfulfilled before marriage, you'll probably have the same struggle afterward. On the other hand, people who felt complete as individuals often feel even more satisfied as a couple.

Second, learn to appreciate your spouse for who he or she is instead of trying to change your beloved into who you want him or her to be. When dating, people tend to gloss over their loved one's flaws. It's why a woman may fear she married the wrong person if he doesn't listen to her feelings as much after the wedding as he did before. In reality, he probably wasn't as wonderful as she thought he was, and he's not as bad as she now perceives him to be.

Third, remember the true meaning of *love*. Author Erich Fromm says, "To love somebody is not just a strong feeling—it is a decision, it is a judgment, it is a promise." In other words, true love is a choice.

> I will betroth you to me forever. I will betroth you to me in righteousness and in justice, in steadfast love and in mercy. I will betroth you to me in faithfulness. And you shall know the LORD.
> HOSEA 2:19-20

God, despite my flaws, You remain faithful.
Help me love and choose my spouse in the same
way that You have loved and chosen us.

Hidden Potential

A friend of mine owns the ugliest dog I think I've ever seen. He's a two-and-a-half-pound Yorkie-poo—a mix between a poodle and a Yorkshire terrier. He's lost most of his fur and teeth, and he walks around on three legs because the fourth is arthritic.

But don't give the poor thing too hard of a time. Tidbit is almost sixteen years old, so he's earned the right to look a little tired.

Why am I telling you about an ugly little dog? Because Tidbit can teach a lot of couples something important about marriage. Even though Tidbit looks near death, the vet says the dog is a lot healthier than he appears.

Your *marriage* may not look so hot on the outside either, but I hope you won't underestimate its hidden potential. You can rediscover the parts of your relationship that made you want to be together in the first place. But to find them, you can't give up on each other just because your relationship looks like it could breathe its last at any moment. Looks can be deceiving. Your marriage probably has a lot more life flowing through it than you realize.

They who wait for the LORD shall renew their strength; they shall mount up with wings like eagles; they shall run and not be weary; they shall walk and not faint.

ISAIAH 40:31

Lord, breathe new life into my marriage. I admit sometimes it can feel hopeless when things seem stuck and weary, but You have the power to create change. Revive us, O Lord.

Don't Get Too Comfortable

Is it possible to become so familiar with our spouse that we start paying less attention to him or her?

Daniel Oppenheimer writes that people better remember information they've read "when it's printed in smaller, less legible type." Turns out, when readers "encounter . . . something hard to decipher, they become less confident in their ability to understand, and that nervousness makes them concentrate harder and process the material more deeply." In short, making people "slow down and read more carefully improves their recall."

This offers some great insight into building and maintaining a strong marriage.

Throughout courtship and early marriage, husbands and wives intently learn about each other. The as-yet-unknowns create a desire to understand who the other person is—likes and dislikes, quirks and comfort zones, and more. So couples naturally concentrate harder on each other.

But as time passes, spouses might think they have each other figured out. In losing the focus that defined their early years together, they also risk losing that deeper intimacy.

Our spouse will always be a complex individual worthy of our study and pursuit. If we take the time to slow down and read each other more carefully, our marriage can only get stronger.

Pay careful attention to yourselves.
ACTS 20:28

God, You advise us to pay attention and notice what is happening in the lives of those we love. I know it's easy to drift apart in marriage when we already know so much about each other. So, Lord, help my spouse and me rekindle our study and pursuit of each other.

Reminiscing

Couples spend a lot of time thinking about their future. But it's a good idea to reflect on your past, too.

Reminiscing from time to time is a valuable activity for couples. There's a bond that forms between two people who have shared experiences together. Your past is more than a collection of random memories. The journey you and your spouse have taken together infuses your relationship with richness and meaning.

Reminiscing is especially helpful if you've been married many years. It's healthy to remember the good times and the difficulties you've overcome together. Reminiscing can encourage you to hope for good times ahead and remind you of the troubles you can get through if you stick together.

Reminiscing is for new couples as well. If you're newlyweds, you probably have good memories together from the months or years before you got engaged. Reflect on those times, even if they weren't that long ago.

Intimacy doesn't develop in the newness of a relationship but over the miles you travel together. Fun memories about when you first met, your first date, or other heartwarming moments from your relationship are crucial building blocks that will carry you into the future.

Remember the days of old; consider the years of many generations.
DEUTERONOMY 32:7

I love reminiscing with my spouse about our tough times and our triumphs. Keep me mindful of the incredible good times You've blessed us with, Lord.

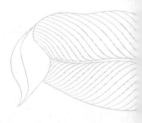

Renew the Pursuit

Once upon a time you and your spouse did almost everything together. But what changed?

Maybe you can relate to Chuck and Renee. When they were dating, they loved spending time together. She didn't care for sports, but she'd run off to his softball games anyway. And he could often be found roaming a mall with her even though he'd tell you it wasn't "his thing." But now, years into their marriage, they rarely enjoy shared activities.

This same problem is found in a lot of marriages, and yet few couples understand what happened. How did they lose their once-deep connection? In many ways, it boils down to the thrill of the chase. When a couple is dating, they're striving to win each other's heart. But once they say their "I dos," the pursuit is over. That's where they go wrong. They don't realize that giving up the chase snuffs out the flames of romance.

So if the fires that once burned in your relationship are now smoldering embers, take heart! You can ignite those flames once again. Let your wedding day mark the time when your pursuit of each other was just getting started—not when it ended.

Keep loving one another earnestly, since love covers a multitude of sins.

1 PETER 4:8

I praise You, Lord, for pursuing me with Your steady love. Help me stay fervent in my love for and pursuit of my beloved spouse.

Fall Back in Love

When Jean and I started dating, we lived an hour and a half apart—depending on jam-packed Southern California traffic. I braved the freeways to be with her as much as I could. But after we married, I started to wane in my extra efforts to woo her.

We do that, don't we? Once we're married, we stop pursuing our spouse like we did when we were dating. Many couples fall "out of love" because they stop listening to each other and serving one another.

It's as if we think saying "I love you" one time should last forever. The truth is that love has a shelf life. It has to be actively renewed every single day—not once a month or once a year. We can't bank on that big vacation we took last year or that romantic gesture we made last month to sustain our feelings of togetherness.

So if your marriage isn't what it used to be, fall back in love by treating your spouse with the same dedication you did when you were first dating. Give your mate your attention. Listen to him or her. Make your beloved a priority again. Restore the passion you once had when your relationship was new, and your feelings of love will grow.

> If there is any encouragement in Christ, any comfort from love, any participation in the Spirit, any affection and sympathy, complete my joy by being of the same mind, having the same love, being in full accord and of one mind.
>
> PHILIPPIANS 2:1-2

Lord, keep me eager to restore the passion I once had for my spouse. Guard us from complacency and falling out of love. Thank You that Your Spirit gifts us with the ability to express enduring love and unity to each other every day.

In Search of Spring Thaw

Sometimes marriage feels as cold as winter. Conflict causes the relationship to feel icy and distant. Instead of connecting, spouses hunker down and avoid talking to each other. And if they do speak, they're arguing. It's not a season of marriage where you want to spend much time.

What everybody wants, of course, is a marriage that feels like spring. Spring is the season of growth and new beginnings. You're communicating, resolving conflicts, and deepening your intimacy. You're discussing life and growing together spiritually. There are also new beginnings, like when you forgive each other's past failures. It means you look for the positive and offer each other grace and support.

The trouble is that some couples have been at odds for so long, they wonder if the ice between them will ever thaw out.

I believe that no matter how deep into winter your marriage may feel, you can bring springtime back. Fortunately, the seasons of marriage aren't like the weather. You don't have to wait for the months to slowly go by. You can move your marriage out of winter and into spring anytime you're willing to make positive changes and do some work.

Whoever covers an offense seeks love, but he who repeats a matter separates close friends.
PROVERBS 17:9

You are the God of life. Heal the brokenness of my marriage, and bring it into Your abundant life.

Commitment Is the Foundation

Travel through our country's small towns, and you'll likely come across an array of honorable folks who still seal their agreements with a handshake and who consider their word an unbreakable bond.

In the business world, contracts are much more formal, of course, crafted with highly detailed legal jargon that reads like a foreign language. Whatever form these commitments take, the purpose has always been the same—to offer protection, not when everything is running smoothly, but when things become difficult.

Commitment is perhaps never more important than when it comes to marriage. It provides strength and stability when a relationship encounters challenges. Unfortunately, many couples take an opposite approach when things turn sour—they run, rather than digging in their heels when commitment requires it the most.

As the president of an organization dedicated, in part, to strengthening marriages, trust me—I understand that relationships can encounter serious difficulties that are not easily resolved. But with nearly 50 percent of all marriages breaking apart, it's evident that our society rushes too quickly toward divorce instead of diligently working to restore a relationship to health.

Remember, commitment is the foundation for surviving conflict.

Let what you say be simply "Yes" or "No"; anything more than this comes from evil.
MATTHEW 5:37

Dear God, please help us experience strength and stability in our marriage by remaining committed in both word and deed.

What Makes Your Spouse Tick?

What does it mean to know your spouse?

Gilbert Hill liked to tell people that his wife, Sadie, could wake up, get dressed, and put the coffee on in just twelve minutes. Sound like a strange thing for a husband to brag about? Maybe not, when you realize that Gilbert and Sadie were both over one hundred years old—and that they celebrated eighty-one years of marriage before Sadie passed away.

After her death, Gilbert reflected that Sadie was the "biggest half" of him. The fact that Gilbert knew exactly how long it took Sadie to get ready in the morning speaks volumes about the depth of their bond.

Marriages that go the distance don't just happen. They're nurtured. That means taking time to build on common ground and resolve conflicts. It also means being authentic and allowing our spouse to know us, even as we make every effort to know him or her. So whether you're newlyweds or have been married for decades, value every opportunity to learn what makes your husband or wife tick—even how long it takes your beloved to get ready in the morning.

> Wives, submit to your husbands, as is fitting in the Lord.
> Husbands, love your wives, and do not be harsh with them.
> COLOSSIANS 3:18-19

Great King of kings, help my spouse and me
never forget the importance of intimately
understanding each other. Help us honor and
value each other as we honor and value You.

Stop Searching for Perfection

What is the most profound change in young adults over the last twenty years?

The late Chuck Colson asked that question while interviewing candidates for a college presidency. The candidates overwhelmingly responded that the biggest change was that people today are less willing to commit to anything.

Whether you're talking about career, marriage, or faith, studies back up their observation. Many young people today are avoiding life's obligations and commitments, choosing instead to keep their options open. I can understand why. Today's young adults have more opportunities than any previous generation. They can travel the globe, try different jobs and relationships, and engage in a dozen causes at the same time.

Life is filled with trade-offs, and the choice to avoid commitment is no exception. Many young adults find that their adventurous lives lack the direction, connection, and fulfillment that come through commitment. As Colson wrote, "By abandoning commitment, our narcissistic culture has lost the one thing it desperately seeks: happiness. Without commitment, our individual lives will be barren and sterile."

Instead of searching the world for the perfect spouse, job, or cause, consider committing to one right in front of you.

Commit your way to the LORD; trust in him, and he will act.
PSALM 37:5

I do not want to go through my life without any sense of connection. I understand that a key to happiness and fulfillment is commitment. Please help my spouse and me remain devoted to You, Lord, and to each other.

It Takes a Covenant

E ven if you've never heard the term *covenant relationship*, you know what it means, especially if you're a parent. You pour your heart and soul into your kids every day, don't you? Why? Because they offer the same measure of love and respect back to you? No, loving your children is simply the right thing to do. Every day, you give them what they need, not what they want or deserve.

When your love is grounded in a covenant, your choices aren't based on how you *feel*. A covenant is about how you act and what you do. It's about action.

Now apply that train of thought to your marriage. Maybe your relationship is in crisis, and you don't *feel* love for your spouse. What now?

If your relationship is about convenience, you'll do whatever gets the good feelings back. Which means you'll give in when you ought to stand firm. Or you'll stand firm when you ought to give a little.

If your relationship is about covenant, you'll act toward your spouse according to what's best for him or her and for your relationship.

A relationship as intimate and profound as marriage can't be built on convenience. It takes a covenant.

> Let not steadfast love and faithfulness forsake you; bind them around your neck; write them on the tablet of your heart.
> PROVERBS 3:3

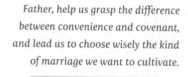

Father, help us grasp the difference between convenience and covenant, and lead us to choose wisely the kind of marriage we want to cultivate.

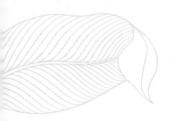

MARRIAGE Getaways
BY **FOCUS ON THE FAMILY**

Make Your Marriage Feel Brand-New

Longing for deeper connection in your marriage? Refresh your relationship at a Marriage Getaway.

Enjoy restful time together as you learn new communication tools from our certified Christian counselors. Growing closer together starts here.

LEARN MORE:
FocusOnTheFamily.com/**Getaway**

MARRIAGE *Assessment*
BY FOCUS ON THE FAMILY

Keep Growing Your Marriage.

Find your strengths – and opportunities for growth – with the Focus on the Family Marriage Assessment! You and your spouse will get a detailed report on ways to make your marriage even stronger. You'll also get resources that will help you deepen your bond.

Take the Assessment at
FocusOnTheFamily.com/MarriageAssessment